Y0-BSY-111

Encyclopedia of Canadian Country Music

by

Rick Jackson

Other Quarry Press Music Books

Some Day Soon: Essays on Canadian Songwriters
Douglas Fetherling

Neil Young: Don't Be Denied
John Einarson

Magic Carpet Ride: The Autobiography of John Kay and Steppenwolf
John Kay and John Einarson

The Encyclopedia of Canadian Rock, Pop & Folk Music
Rick Jackson

Superman's Song: The Story of Crash Test Dummies
Stephen Ostick

American Woman: The Story of The Guess Who
John Einarson

Oh What A Feeling: A Vital History of Canadian Music
Martin Melhuish

STOMPIN' TOM CONNORS

SHANIA TWAIN

WILF CARTER

MICHELLE WRIGHT

Encyclopedia of Canadian Country Music

PATRICIA CONROY

TOMMY HUNTER

by
Rick Jackson

Quarry Press

GEORGE FOX

CARROLL BAKER

HANK SNOW

ANNE MURRAY

This book is dedicated to everyone in it.

Copyright © Rick Jackson, 1996.
All rights reserved.

The publisher gratefully acknowledges the assistance of The Canada Council, the Department of Canadian Heritage, and the Ontario Arts Council.

Canadian Cataloguing in Publishing Data

Jackson, Rick
Encyclopedia of Canadian country Music

Includes bibliographical references and discographies.
ISBN 1-55082-151-2

1. Country musicians--Canada--Biography.
2. Country music--Canada--Discography. I. Title

ML102.C7J33 1995 781.642'092'271 C95-900874-8

Design by Susan Hannah.
Printed in Canada by Best Book Manufacturers, Toronto, Ontario.

Published by Quarry Press, Inc.,
P.O. Box 1061, Kingston, Ontario K7L 4Y5.

Contents

8 Preface by Rick Jackson
11 Chef Adams
11 Alibi
12 Gerry Allard
12 Ross Allen
13 Ward Allen
14 Lucky Ambo
14 Sharon Anderson
14 Abbie Andrews
15 Ruth Ann
15 Applejack
16 Con Archer
17 Lee Bach
17 Jack Bailey
17 Mary Bailey
18 Carroll Baker
20 Kidd Baker
21 Smiley Bates
21 Mac Beattie
22 Debbie Bechamp
23 Curtis Blayne
23 The Blue Valley Boys
23 Dieter Boehme
24 Maurice Bolyer
24 Bootleg
25 Marie Bottrell
26 Cori Brewster
26 Lisa Brokop
26 Heather Brooks
26 George Brothers
27 Linda Brown
28 Hal Bruce
28 Gary Buck
29 Johnny Burke
30 Burton & Honeyman
30 Colin Butler
32 C-Weed Band
32 Cindi Cain and the Cheeters
33 The Canadian Sweethearts
34 Canadian Zephyr
35 Terry Carisse
36 Ralph Carlson
37 Glory-Anne Carriere
37 K.C. Carter
38 Wilf Carter
42 Cedar Creek
42 Charlie Chamberlain
42 Cathy Chambers
43 Billy Charne
43 Al Cherny
44 Peter Chipman
44 Terry Christenson
45 Cindy Church
45 The City Slickers
46 Terri Clark
46 Sam Crosby and The Cavalry
46 Stew Clayton
47 Don Cochrane
47 Tex Cochrane
48 Coda The West
48 Wade Colt
49 Johnny Comfort
49 Tommy Common
50 Stompin' Tom Connors
52 Patricia Conroy
52 Country Hearts
53 Ted Daigle
53 Dick Damron
55 Stu Davis
56 The Debenham Brothers
57 Andy Dejarlis
57 Jack Diamond
58 The Dixie Flyers
58 Freddy Dixon
59 Donna & Leroy
60 Double Eagle Band

61 Debbie Drummond
62 Eagle Feather
62 Eddie Eastman
63 Gerry Edge
63 June Eikhard
63 Carl Elliott
64 Ellis Family Band
65 Allen Erwin
66 Family Brown
67 Farmer's Daughter
68 Joel Feeney
69 Shirley Field
69 Joe Firth
70 Gary Fjellgaard
72 Foster Martin Band
72 George Fox
74 Rena Gaile
74 King Ganam
75 Bourbon Gauthier
75 Suzanne Gitzi
75 Gilles Godard
76 Bruce Golden
77 The Good Brothers
78 Michael Dee Graham
79 Susan Graham
80 Curtis Grambo
80 Great Western Orchestra
80 Ray Griff
82 J.K. Gulley
83 Larry Gustafson
84 Albert Hall
84 Dyanne Halliday
85 Dallas Harms
86 Ken Harnden
86 Kelita Haverland
86 Harvey Henry
87 Len Henry
87 Bill Hersh
88 Kenny Hess
88 Earl Heywood
90 Dixie Bill Hilton
90 Gary Hooper
91 D.J. Hopson
91 Tommy Hunter
93 Ron Hynes
94 P.J. Jackson
94 Jimmy James
94 Elaine Jarvis
95 Jerry & Jo'anne
95 Johner Brothers
96 Lynn Jones
96 Lori Jordan
98 Ronnie Kartman
98 Carl Kess & the Golden Fiddle Music Co.
99 Terry Kelly
99 Evan Kemp
100 Joan Kennedy
101 Bob King
103 Scott Kyle King
103 Jack Kingston
104 Chris Krienke
105 Mark LaForme
105 Bobby Lalonde
106 Ned Landry
106 k.d. lang
107 Willie Lamothe
109 Iris Larratt
110 Mel Lavigne
110 Claudette Lefebvre & the Country Jewels
111 Diane Leigh
112 Vic Levac
112 The John Lindsay Band
113 Bill Long
113 Anne Lord
114 Myrna Lorrie
115 Sharon Lowness
115 Julie Lynn
116 Harold Macintyre
116 Brent McAthey
117 Jason McCoy
117 Fred McKenna
118 Ron McLeod
118 Ron McMunn
119 Larry Magee
119 Charlie Major
120 Bev Marie
120 Shelley-Lou Marie
121 Jim Matt
121 The Mercey Brothers
123 Larry Mercey
123 Don Messer
125 Midnite Rodeo Band
126 The Mighty Mohawks
126 Vic Mullen
127 Anne Murray
131 Don Neilson
131 Dick Nolan
133 One Horse Blue
133 Marg Osburne

134 Al Oster
136 Jerry Palmer
136 Rae Palmer
137 The Panio Brothers
137 Terry Parker
138 George Pasher
138 Greg Paul
138 Roy Payne
139 Anita Perras & Tim Taylor
141 Colleen Peterson
142 Stu Phillips
142 Prairie Oyster
144 Irwin Prescott
144 Orval Prophet
145 Ronnie Prophet
146 Tony Prophet
147 Quartette
148 Diana Rae
148 Diane Raeside
148 The Rainvilles
149 Keray Regan
150 Buddy Reynolds
151 Donn Reynolds
151 Rhodes & Marshall
152 The Rhythm Pals
153 Hank Rivers
154 Bud Roberts
154 The Romaniuk Family
155 Wayne Rostad
155 Bob Rowan
156 Terilynn Ryan
157 Ron Scott
157 Joyce Seamone
158 Terry Sheridan
158 Shotgun
159 Vic Siebert & the Sons of the Saddle
159 Kevin Simpson
160 The Singing Post Family
160 Ray St. Germain
161 Alberta Slim
162 Smilin' Johnnie & Eleanor Dahl
163 Hank Smith
163 R. Harlan Smith
164 Reg Smith
164 Hank Snow
169 Mary Lou Sonmor
169 South Mountain
170 Lucille Starr
170 Stevedore Steve
170 The Stoker Brothers
171 The Stoltz Brothers
172 Stoneridge
172 Straight, Clean & Simple
173 Terry Sumsion
174 Julien Tailly
174 Gordie Tapp
174 David Thompson
175 Tim Thorney
175 Graham Townsend
177 Dougie Trineer
177 Shania Twain
178 Ian Tyson
179 Sylvia Tyson
181 Cassandra Vasik
181 Laura Vinson
183 George Wade & his Cornhuskers
183 Michael T. Wall
184 Jerry Warren
184 Dan Washburn
184 Sneezy Waters
185 Paul Weber
185 The Western Sweethearts
186 Billy Whelan
187 Whiskey Jack
187 Chris Whitely & Caitlin Hanford
188 Darlene Wiebe
188 Brent Williams
188 A. Frank Willis
189 Tom Wilson & his Western All-Stars
190 Jim Witter
190 Michelle Wright
191 The York County Boys

193 Appendix A: *Noteworthy Artists*
197 Appendix B: Canadian *Country Music Association Awards 1982–1995*
203 Appendix C: *Country Juno Awards 1964–1994*
206 Bibliography

Preface

The *Encyclopedia of Canadian Country Music* is not meant to be a critical look at country music in Canada but an authoritative listing of artists and groups from the 1930s to the present. In essence, this is a reference book for the country aficionado, disc jockey, or 'student' of popular culture, who may be looking for the facts about a particular Canadian country artist or group, including a listing of their singles and albums.

When I finished my *Encyclopedia of Canadian Rock, Pop & Folk Music,* I decided to concentrate on country since this part of the Canadian music industry has been neglected far too long. Due to the dearth of material available on Canadian country music, I had to depend largely on country collectors who have the articles, the albums, and the knowledge. Without them, our musical heritage would be lost forever. Since no charts existed before *RPM Weekly* came along in 1964, I researched record company catalogues and press releases in order to date the albums and singles by each artist and group. *RPM Weekly* and the country charts from CFNB, Fredericton, New Brunswick were used for the albums and singles released in the last thirty years. For some albums prior to 1969 I was unable to find a date since there were none on the album jacket or on the record itself. An "n.d." in some entries of the book means no date was available. I invite the reader to write to me in care of the publisher should you know any dates, or have any pertinent information that would be useful in future editions. In the case of the albums by Stompin' Tom Connors, I have listed the original release dates since so many of them have been reissued more than once. With the demise of vinyl in Canada, certain older artists (like Stew Clayton) have released new recordings on cassette. These are listed wherever possible.

Included in this book are some artists who have been charted as country in *RPM* and *The Record*, Canada's two weekly trade papers, and have been played on country stations. They include Anne Murray, Colleen Peterson, and Gary Fjellgaard. k.d. lang is here, too, since her songs switch back and forth between pop and country. One Horse Blue belongs as well. Although they started out playing rock, they have switched to country. Not included are Rita MacNeil, The Rankin Family, Susan Aglukark, and Blue Rodeo who range from rock to light folk/pop.

Canada's broadcast and recorded country music heritage goes back to George Wade and his Cornhuskers who first broadcast over the CRBC, the forerunner of the CBC, in 1928. Don Messer next appeared on radio in 1929. Both Wilf Carter and Wade first recorded in 1933. Hank Snow came along in 1937. Others such as Tex Cochrane and Allen Erwin (The Calgary Kid) also made recordings during the Depression. During the 1940s the Rhythm Pals began to make an impact on the west coast, along with Stu Davis, Alberta Slim, Evan Kemp, Buddy Reynolds, Keray Regan, Smilin' Johnnie, and Vic Siebert and The Sons of the Saddle. And in the 1950s the likes of King Ganam, Tommy Hunter, and Tommy Common exposed Canadians to country music through the medium of television. The Western Sweethearts became Canada's first all-female group in 1953. By the end of the decade, Gary Buck became one of Canada's promising new stars; in 1963 he was Canada's first country artist to have a number one hit in *CASHBOX*, a U.S. trade weekly, with the song *Happy To Be Unhappy*. Canada's first bluegrass single was recorded in the 1950s by Ron Scott, *When The Bees Are In Their Hive.* The York County Boys had our first bluegrass album, BLUE GRASS JAMBOREE, on Arc Records in 1960. The Mercey Brothers, who formed in 1957, had their first hit, *Just The Snap Of Your Fingers,* in late 1961. Their popularity continued until their breakup in 1989.

In the 1970s Carroll Baker, Family Brown, Prairie Oyster, Stompin' Tom Connors, and Anne Murray arrived on the scene. Dick Damron, Ray Griff, Ronnie Prophet, and many others kept country music alive through the 1980s. Michelle Wright, Charlie Major, Patricia Conroy, and other more recent acts such as Farmer's Daughter, Jim Witter, and Shania Twain have given us "new country" in the 1990s. The tradition of Canadian country music is very much alive today.

In compiling information for this book, a number of people helped me along the way. Larry Delaney, editor and publisher of *Country Music News,* provided me with many back issues; articles, charts, and other information contained in each issue were a valuable guide.

Don Foster, a collector of early Canadian Country offered me copies of his interview transcripts as well as pictures of many artists. Other collectors who steered me in the right direction were Keith Titterington, David Whatmough, Fred Isenor, Ed Garland, Gord Grills and Ken Pinkham.

A special thank you to the following artists who took the time to talk to me about their careers, and to help set the record straight: Chef Adams, Bert Bambauch (The Dixie Flyers), Dieter Boehme, Gary Buck, Johnny Burke, Ralph Carlson, Stew Clayton, Don Cochrane, Dick Damron, Jerry Day (Applejack), Freddy Dixon, Farmer's Daughter, Wendell Ferguson (Coda The West), Shirley Field, Myrtle Gifford (The Western Sweethearts), Joe Firth, Keith Glass and Russell deCarle (Prairie Oyster), J.K. Gulley, Ken and Janet Harnden, John Hayman (Canadian Zephyr), Earl Heywood, Jack Jensen (The Rhythm Pals), Carl Kees, Terry Kelly, Evan Kemp, Joan Kennedy, Jack Kingston, L.T. and Slim Jim (The City Slickers), Ned Landry, Harold MacIntyre, John and Jackie McManaman (The York County Boys), Ron McMunn, Larry Magee, Ray Martin (The Foster Martin Band), Marcel Meilleur, Larry Mercey (The Mercey Brothers), Vic Mullen, One Horse Blue, John Panio (The Panio Brothers), George Pasher, Steve & Laurie Pittico and Dan Washburn (South Mountain), Norman Post (The Singing Post Family), Diane Raeside, Donn Reynolds, Ron Scott, Joyce Seamone, Vic Siebert (Vic Siebert & The Sons of the Saddle), Kevin Simpson, Smilin' Johnnie, Hank Smith, Johnny Stoltz (The Stoltz Brothers), Dougie Trineer, Sylvia Tyson, Tom Wilson (Tom Wilson & His Western All-Stars), Jim Witter, Patricia Conroy, Gary Hooper, and Shania Twain.

I would also like to thank Richard Green at the National Film Library for his help in tracking down album dates, Ed Lasko for his discography of Aragon Records, and the staff of CFMK, Kingston's local country station: Lorne Matthews for allowing me to go through their country singles, and Guy Brooks and Ray Bergstrom for making it possible for me to meet some of the artists in this book.

Others who contributed are John Irvine; Clair Dezan of the International Wilf Carter Fan Club; Bruce Wylie at radio station CFJR in Brockville, Ontario; Diana Kelly of International Talent Services Inc. in Vancouver; Sean Eyre at Rockland Promotions in Peterborough; Jones & Co.; Tim Rathert at Morningstar in Nashville; Charlie James at Bear Family Records in Pierrefonds, Quebec; Frank Fara at Comstock Records in Arizona; Dale Curd and Shelley Snell at BMG Music Canada; Joanna Dine at Warner Music; Gerry Vogel at Mercury/ Polydor; Paul Wiggins at Tomcat Records; Phil Anderson, Ben Weatherby and the late John Porteous of Arc Records; Patty Lou Andrews at Mary Bailey Management; Donna Martens and Sheila Hamilton (CCMA); and Don Grashey, Gerry Leiske, Brian Ferriman, Pierre Tailly, Bernie Dobbin, Lynn Russwurm, Jack Boswell, and Sadie Ambeault.

Compiling this first edition of the *Enyclopedia of Canadian Country Music* has been a labor of love.

A

Chef Adams

Chef Adams was born Adam Edward Semeniuk on a farm near Sturgis, Saskatchewan in 1929. In his late teens, he left home and worked at various jobs around his hometown. He played at weddings, dances, and jamborees until 1952 when he moved to Toronto. While working at a local restaurant, he earned the nickname "Chef."

In 1953 he organized The Country Rhythm Kings. He later signed a contract with Quality Records, who released his first single, *Now That You're Gone Marilyn Bell,* in 1957. When the label wanted him to sing rock rather than country, he left.

He teamed up with Yvonne Terry in 1963-64 to form a duo. By the early 1970s he was recording for Marathon Records under the name Chef Adams and The Adams Boys. He continued to record until the late 1970s. By 1990 he was living in semi-retirement and only playing occasionally.

Singles

Now That You're Gone Marilyn Bell 1956
We Asked For A Heartbreak 1964
Destroy Me 1968/69
If She Could See Me Now/ Wheel Chair 1969
My First Complete Memory Free Day 1975
It's All Gone 1979

Albums

SONGS FOR COUNTRY LOVERS (TOWN &COUNTRY) 1959
SONGS FOR COUNTRY LOVERS (CANATEL) 1961
SHOW STOPPERS 1964
CHEF ADAMS AND THE ADAMS BOYS AND JENNIE REEVES 1968
SINGER/SONGWRITER 1971
ROSE GARDEN (with ALICE PETRIE) 1972
I NEVER KNEW HER NAME 1973
DOES THE SUNSHINE STILL REMEMBER? 1975
CHEF & JAMIE 1977
SUCCESS SUCCESS (with JAMIE) 1978

Alberta Slim

(see under "S")

Alibi

REID BARTON (*vocals, bass*)
DAVE CLOW (*lead vocals, lead guitar*)
JOHN REDEKOP (*lead vocals, rhythm guitar*)
SHAWN SOUCY (*vocals, drums*)
STEVE SOUCY (*vocals, keyboards*): *Replaced by* JOE VORHES
ROBBIE STEININGER (*vocals, lead & slide guitar*)

Vancouver based Alibi began as a five member band in 1983 after the dissolution of Northern Express, a traditional country band. Steve

Soucy left in 1987 and was replaced by Joe Vorhes, the only American in the group. With the addition of Robbie Steininger, the group became a sextet.

Singles *Love The Night Away* 1985/86
Till The Fire's Burned Out 1986
It Only Hurts When I Cry 1987
Taste Of Romance 1987
Roller Coaster 1987
Do You Have Any Doubts 1988
To Be With You 1989
To Be Lovers 1990

Album NO DOUBTS 1988

Gerry Allard

From Ottawa, Ontario, Gerry Allard had been writing songs for over ten years when he recorded his first single, *Hey Bartender,* in 1981 on Snocan Records. In the early 1970s, he played with a country/rock band called Country Revival. It was during this time that he began writing songs. Two of them, *I Can Count On You* and *It's Going To Be A Beautiful Day*, were recorded by Colin Butler on his 1973 Marathon album, BIDIN' MY TIME.

Gerry and his own Moonshine band became well known in the Ottawa Valley. By 1983 he had a new backup band called The Barn Cats.

Singles *Hey Bartender* 1981
Gonna Meet A Senorita 1982
I Still Love You 1983
It's Not Right 1984

Album I STILL LOVE YOU 1983

Ross Allen

Toronto-born Ross Allen has been part of the Canadian country music scene since 1960, when he recorded the Arc album, MEMORIES OF HANK WILLIAMS. On it his name is misspelled as "Allan," which makes it a collector's item. He later recorded another album, RAMBLING ROSS ALLAN, on London Records.

In the 1970s and 1980s he ran his own record label called Jennie Records, and his own publishing company. *Sure Ain't Nashville* in 1981 was the first of several singles he recorded on his own label.

Singles *Sure Ain't Nashville* 1981
Hard Time Comin' Down Again 1981
Goodbye Sunshine 1982
Saturday Night 1982
Got No Way With My Woman 1982

I'll Be Seeing You Someday 1983
The Mess I'm In 1984
In The Morning Light 1984
It Just Ain't Right 1985

Album MEMORIES OF HANK WILLIAMS (as Ramblin' Ross Allan) 1960

Ward Allen

Ward Allen, whose real name was Warden Ambrose, grew up in a family of fiddle players. At four years of age, he played piano in the family home. By the time he was twelve, he and his brother played fiddle as a duo at barn dances.

In his hometown of Kirkton, Ontario he won many contests, and in 1953 became Canada's Old-Time Fiddling Champion. That same year, he was chosen to represent Canada in the International Fiddling Contest at the Louisville State Fair in Louisville, Kentucky.

During the 1950s and 1960s he recorded for Sparton Records. His best known song was *Maple Sugar* in 1957, which also became popular in the United States.

He died on August 3, 1965.

Singles

Frisco Waltz/Mary Anne Reel 1955
The Grizzly Bear/Orange Blossom Special 1957
Maple Sugar/Back Up And Push 1957
Pappy The Coon/The Iroquois Gathering 1958
B.C. Centennial/John's Polka 1958
Happy Wanderer 1959
Lord Alexander's Reel/Ward Allen Breakdown n.d.
Frank Ryan's Hornpipe/Two Step Polka n.d.
Squid Jiggin' Ground (with The Hillbilly Jewels)/You're A Little Doll n.d.
Back To The Sugar Camp/The Marsh Hen n.d.
C.N.E. Breakdown/Maple Leaf Two Step n.d.
Bread n' Butter/Pappy Daily's Breakdown n.d.
Molly Hagan/Cirassian Circle n.d.
The Road To Boston/Mountain Girl n.d.
Blue Pacific Hornpipe/Fiddler's Dream n.d.
Dancing Slippers/Uncle Jim n.d.
Frenchie's Reel/Mengie of McBride's Reel n.d.
Mitten's Breakdown/The Old Rose Waltz n.d.

Albums

CANADIAN FIDDLE TUNES 1958
BEST OF WARD ALLEN 1965
MAPLE LEAF HOEDOWN — VOLUME I n.d.
MAPLE LEAF HOEDOWN — VOLUME II n.d.
MAPLE LEAF HOEDOWN — VOLUME III n.d.

Lucky Ambo

Born in Bathurst, New Brunswick, Clifford Ambeault was one of Canada's top fiddlers. He played with the Calgary Range Riders and The Sons Of The Saddle during a distinguished career. To his many fans and colleagues he was known simply as "Lucky Ambo." On stage he was also a talented comedian.

He started out in radio at CKNB in Campbelltown, New Brunswick, and took part in various fiddling competitions. In 1955 he won the Dominion Old Time Fiddling Championships at the Frontier Celebrations in Wingham, Ontario.

In 1953 he recorded the *Orange Blossom Special* on Aragon Records. Three years later, he signed with Rodeo Records where he had success with such hits as *Lucky's Breakdown* and *Rocky Mountain Breakdown.*

He died April 3, 1984.

Singles *Orange Blossom Special* 1953; *Lucky's Breakdown* n.d.; *Down East Reel* n.d.; *Bridgeport Reel* n.d.; *Rocky Mountain Breakdown* n.d.

Album OLD TIME FIDDLIN' n.d.

Sharon Anderson

A native of Calahoo, Alberta, Sharon Anderson grew up with music all around her. Her mother Fiete was a well known singer in the area, and through her mother's guidance Sharon honed her talent as a singer. She worked with a number of Alberta bands, notably One Horse Blue.

It was her songwriting ability that led her on the road to success. She went to Nashville in the late 1980s where she joined singers Tom Grant and Alan Estes to form the trio Trinity Lane.

During the summer of 1991, her debut album, THE BOTTOM LINE, was released on Capitol Records. The first single, *Unbelievable Love,* was an immediate hit.

Singles *Unbelievable Love* 1991; *Pony* 1991; *The Wheel Of Love* 1992; *I Take It Back* 1995

Albums *The Bottom Line* 1991; *Bringing It Home* 1995

Abbie Andrews

Born on October 23, 1920 in St. Catharines, Ontario, Abbie Andrews first picked up the fiddle when he met Alec House, an old-time fiddler, while delivering papers as a young boy. At 14 he occasionally played on the local radio station, CKTB, and later formed his own group, Abbie Andrews and his Canadian Ranch Boys. By 1952 they had become well known on the Canadian country music scene, and Andrews had started to make some recordings with both the Biltmore and Maple Leaf labels.

In 1955, he was seriously injured in a car accident which left him paralyzed in his right arm. It ended his performing career, although he continued to write music. He died on August 10, 1991.

Singles *Red Heads, Blondes and Brunettes/ Orange Blossom Special* n.d.
Lord Alexander's Reel/ Uncle Jim n.d.
Candy Coated Apples/Don't Roll Your Eyes At Me Baby n.d.
The Golden Jubilee Schottishe n.d.
Abbie's Favorite Jig n.d.
The Subway Special n.d.

Ruth Ann

While growing up in Simcoe, Ontario, Ruth Ann was exposed to music at an early age by her mother, who was an accomplished musician. Ruth went on to study music at university, and after she graduated she joined a show band. She aspired to be a solo performer and it led to work at various supper clubs throughout the United States.

In November 1981 she released her first single, *Married or Single,* on Track Records. Two years later, she signed a contract with MCA Records in Nashville, Tennessee. Her debut album, HELLO IT'S ME, was released in the fall of 1984.

Singles *Married Or Single* 1981/82
Another Motel Memory 1982
Hello Its Me 1984

Album HELLO ITS ME 1984

Applejack

BOB BLOW: *Replaced by* JEFF HARRISON (1994)
JERRY DAY
GRANT MITCHELL

This Calgary-based trio started in 1982 with Jerry Day and Grant Mitchell. They had been playing together for eight years in various bands when they decided to form their own group. Bob Blow, formerly with the Vancouver rock group Stonebolt, rounded out the group.

Their big break came a year later when they were asked to join Ronnie Prophet and Glory-Ann Carriere on the western leg of their tour. Applejack's debut single release was *Red Neck City* in 1989.

Singles *Red Neck City* 1989/90
Can't Teach A Fool 1990
The Moon Is Rising Tonight 1991
Tables Have Turned 1991/92
Savannah 1992

Cassette GET IN LINE . . . IT'S PARTY TIME 1989

Con Archer Singer/songwriter Con Archer was one of the major recording acts of the 1960s and 1970s. On stage he sang a mixture of country and gospel. He was also dedicated to the music of Elvis Presley, to whom he paid tribute to in 1978 with the album ELVIS IS GONE BUT NOT FORGOTTON on his own Archer label. The title tune was written by Archer.

On January 9, 1988 he died of a heart attack at his home in Cannington, Ontario.

Singles

If I Can Help Somebody 1971
Don't Leave Me Now 1971
One More Valley 1971
Memories 1971
Robbin' The Cradle 1972
I Wonder Where You Are Tonight 1972
Sandy 1973
Talkin' To The Lord 1974
Happy Anniversary 1974
If I Had You n.d.

Album

MANY MOODS OF CON ARCHER 1971
ONE MORE VALLEY 1972
ROBBIN' THE CRADLE 1972
SANDY 1973
SINCERELY 1974
ELVIS IS GONE BUT NOT FORGOTTEN 1978

B

Lee Bach

Lee Bach's prominence in Canadian country music is his talent as a songwriter. Born in Peace River, Alberta, he learned to play the organ and piano by the time he was ten years old. While working at the CBC in Toronto in 1975, he began to write songs. He later moved to Elmira, Ontario to work at MBS, The Mercey Brothers recording studio, where he wrote many hits for the label's stable of artists.

In 1978 Bach began recording his own songs. The first was *Way Back Then*. When The Mercey Brothers closed their studio in 1980, he moved to Nashville, where he continued to write new material and collaborate with other writers. In 1990 he resumed his recording career with *Hung Up On You.*

Singles

Way Back Then 1978
Driftin' Through My Memories 1978
She Won't Let Go 1979
I'm Never Leaving Texas Again 1979
Hung Up On You 1990
She's Just Using Him To Get To Me 1990

Jack Bailey

Ever since growing up in Orillia, Ontario, Jack Bailey always had time for a song. His songs had a relaxed country feel about them. In the 1970s he moved to Peterborough, Ontario where he lived in an old converted schoolhouse.

Not until he signed to GRT Records in the early 1970s did he finally get the recognition he deserved. On his albums he always included a couple of gospel songs. He died in 1987.

Singles

(The Whole World's) Down On You 1971
On Your Way Out 1971
Darlin' 1972
Here's To Lovin' You 1972
I Can't Look Sunday In The Eye 1972
Aaron Brown 1973
Last Night I Loved His Baby 1974
Out Of Tune With The Times 1983/84
I Remembered You Baby 1985

Albums

JACK BAILEY 1972
HERE'S TO LOVIN' YOU 1973
KEEP ME 1973
TEARS OF A MAN n.d.

Mary Bailey

She was born Eveline Bailey in Toronto on December 24, 1946. Her singing career began at age five, and she made appearances throughout Southern and Northern Ontario. Mary left the stage at twelve years of age to resume her life as an adolescent.

While working for Sarah Coventry Fine Fashion Jewellery Co. (Canada) Ltd., she began writing and recording again. This led to her return to the music industry. Signed to RCA in 1976, her first hit was *Easy Feeling* (*Loving You*). It was followed by several more hits and two albums.

Singles

Easy Feeling (*Loving You*) 1976
Pitter Patter 1977
Mystery Lady 1977
One Night Lady 1979
Too Much, Too Little, Too Late 1981
I Have No Right To Love You 1982
Talk To Me Loneliness 1982
Pretend 1983
Sincerely 1984
Somebody Else 1984
If Not For Love (with ALBERT HALL) 1984/85
Once More 1988

Albums

MYSTERY LADY 1979
THINK OF ME 1981

Carroll Baker

Born in 1949 in Port Medway, Nova Scotia, Carroll Baker preferred rock and roll to country music while growing up. It was not until she heard the country hit *Almost Persuaded* on her honeymoon in the mid-1960s that she began to appreciate country music, and wanted to carve out a career as a country singer. At 19, she made her professional debut in Oakville. Her manager was Don Grashey, who also looked after Myrna Lorrie.

Gaiety Records released her first single, *Mem'ries of Home,* in 1970, which was also the title of her debut album. Like most country performers, she performed in fairs and exhibitions and became known as Canada's Queen Of Country Music.

In a career that has spanned more than twenty-five years, she has received almost every major country music award in Canada, sold more than a million albums, and had several number one hits, including *I've Never Been This Far Before*, which was a number one hit for Conway Twitty.

Singles

Mem'ries Of Home 1970/71
Love Now And Pay Later 1971
A Hit In Any Language 1971
It's Late (*And I Have To Go*) 1971
That's How My Heart Beats For You 1972
The World I Know Is Now 1972/73
Wichita 1973
All Them Irons In The Fire 1973
Ten Little Fingers 1973/74
Little Boy Blue 1974
I'd Go Through It All Again 1974
I've Never Been This Far Before 1975
The Hungry Fire Of Love 1975

One Night Of Cheatin' 1975/76
Tonight With Love 1976
Why I Had To Pass This Way 1976
It's My Party 1977
It's Late I Have To Go 1977
Cryin' Places (U.S. only) 1977
The Morning After Baby Let Me Down 1977
I Can't Get Enough 1977
I Might As Well Believe (I'll Live) 1977/78
Portrait In The Window 1978
Hooked On A Feeling 1978
I'm Getting High Remembering 1979
Build My Life Around You 1979
My Turn 1979
Hollywood Love 1980
Still Falling In Love 1980
Breaking And Entering 1981
Mama What Does Cheatin' Mean 1981
Brand New Tears 1981/82
The Second Time Around 1982
Love Hangover 1982/83
Right Or Wrong 1983
Too Hot To Sleep Tonight (with EDDIE EASTMAN) 1983
A Step In The Right Direction 1983/84
Heart On The Run 1984
You Are My Everything 1984
I'm An Old Rock And Roller (Dancin' To A Different Beat) 1985
If You Can't Stand The Heat 1985
It Always Hurts Like The First Time 1985
How Close Am I To Losing You (with EDDIE EASTMAN) 1985
A Star In Mama's Eyes 1986
I'm Taking Care Of Myself 1986
Arms That Love (Hearts That Don't) 1986/87
Death And Taxes And Me Loving You 1987
Cheater's Moon 1987/88
You've Lost That Lovin' Feeling 1988
The Best Of Love (*with* JACK SCOTT) 1988
I'd Fall For That Feeling 1988/89
As Long As We Both Shall Love 1989
One Night With You (with ROGER WHITTAKER) 1989
Dreamin' Ain't Cheating 1990
It's Only Make Believe 1990
A Carpenter, A Mother And A King 1990
I Should Have Put A Hold On Love 1991
It's How You Make Love Good 1991
I'll Be Home For Christmas 1991
Burning Bridges (with JACK SCOTT) 1992

Albums
MEM'RIES OF HOME 1970
CARROLL BAKER (COLUMBIA) 1971
I'D GO THROUGH IT ALL AGAIN (GAIETY) 1974
I'D GO THROUGH IT ALL AGAIN (RCA) 1975
CARROLL BAKER (RCA) 1977
SWEET SENSATION 1977
TO IF IT WASN'T FOR YOU 1978
TWENTY COUNTRY CLASSICS 1978
CARROLL BAKER (RCA) 1979

ALL FOR THE LOVE OF A SONG 1980
CARROLL BAKER 1981
GREATEST HITS (RCA) 1981
GREATEST HITS (K-TEL) 1983
HYMNS OF GOLD 1983
A STEP IN THE RIGHT DIRECTION 1984
HEARTBREAK TO HAPPINESS 1985
HOLLYWOOD LOVE 1979
CARROLL BAKER CLASSICS 1985
THE EARLY YEARS (1970–1973) 1986
AT HOME IN THE COUNTRY 1987
CHRISTMAS CARROLL 1989
HER FINEST COLLECTION 1990

Kidd Baker

Ransford Baker of North Tilley, New Brunswick was fifteen years old when he entered an amateur yodelling talent contest in Milinocket, Maine and won first prize. That day he also earned the nickname "Kidd," and later formed his first group, Yodellin' Kidd Baker and his Texas Cowgirls.

His fiddling career started in 1937 when he hosted his own weekly radio show on CFNB in Fredericton, New Brunswick. He met Lake Drake of The Lake Drake Show, an early country band from the Bristol area. When they broke up in 1940, Kidd organized The Maritime Ranch Boys, who disbanded after World War II. Kidd then decided to form a family show which became appropriately known as The Kidd Baker Show.

In 1952 he had signed to Gavotte Records and, two years later, he had his own TV show on CHSJ in Saint John, New Brunswick.

With his wife Ada, whom he married in 1939, Kidd recorded some duets on Quality Records. Kidd gave up performing when she was diagnosed with cancer. When she died, he remarried and started an upholstery business in Kitchener, Ontario. He then moved to Arthurette, New Brunswick where he died on May 9, 1992.

Singles / 78s

With What I've Got I'll Manage 1952
Whippoorwill's Refrain 1952
Blue-Eyed Sue 1952
Wheeling Back To Wheeling, West Virginia 1953
Baby He's A Wolf 1954
I Found The End Of My Rainbow 1954
The Mission Bells Of San Antoine 1954
Did I Hurt You Darlin' 1954
Why Can't We Renew Our Old Romance 1955
Go Away And Let Me Sleep 1955
I'm Using My Bible For A Road Map 1956
Big Rock Candy Mountain 1956
Gypsy Love 1957
Can't You See (with ADA BAKER) 1957

Albums

COUNTRY MUSIC LEGEND OF NEW BRUNSWICK 1986
WHEELING BACK TO WHEELING 1986
PLAYS OLD TIME FIDDLE FAVORITES n.d.

Smiley Bates

Born on October 16, 1937 in Kirkland Lake, Ontario, Smiley Bates was one of our most successful country fiddlers. He grew up in a musical family in which country music was a major part of his life.

He bought his first guitar from Eaton's mail order. At eleven he performed on stage for the first time, and at fourteen he formed his first band. He also had two shows on the radio, one on CJKL Kirkland Lake and CKGB Timmins. It was his unique flat-top picking and down home country songs that contributed to his overall appeal.

Albums

GOLDEN GUITAR 1968
SONGS OF THE HEART 1969
FIDDLER'S DREAM 1969
FLATTOP GUITAR INSTRUMENTALS 1969
SONGS OF LIFE 1970
HEY, MR. BANJO (with EDDIE POIRIER) 1970
MY MOTHER 1971
PATH OF MEMORIES (with EDDIE POIRIER) 1972
BEST OF BLUEGRASS (with EDDIE & ROSE POIRIER) 1972
HOUSE OF SHAME 1972
IN THE MOOD FOR PICKIN' 1973
DUELING BANJOS 1973
TRUE STORIES FROM LIFE'S OTHER SIDE 1974
HISTORY OF SADNESS 1975
INSTRUMENTALLY YOURS 1976
A MILLION MILES OF COUNTRY 1978
BANJO (with EDDIE POIRIER) n.d.
BEST OF n.d.
LULLABYES & LEGENDS n.d.
SMILEY BATES/AN ALL NEW RECORDING n.d.
A PROUD CANADIAN n.d.
SMILEY'S COUNTRY n.d.
20 GREAT COUNTRY HITS n.d.
COUNTRY FROM THE HEART n.d.
SMILEY SINGS HANK SNOW n.d.
STRICTLY COUNTRY n.d.
PICKIN' IN THE PINES n.d.
ALL MY BEST n.d.
TWENTY GREAT COUNTRY HITS n.d.
COUNTRY TEARS n.d.
FIVE STRING GUITAR BLUEGRASS n.d.
ET SON BANJO (as HENRY ROI) n.d.
REVES DE VIOLONEUX (as HENRY ROI) n.d.

Mac Beattie

He was born John McNab Beattie (Mac) on December 21, 1916 in Ottawa, Ontario. He played hockey in winter and sang with a few friends on street corners or on storefronts during the summer. He founded The Ottawa Valley Melodiers with Harold Mosley, Gaetan Fairfield, and Garnie Scheel. They performed at dances around the Ottawa area from the mid-1930s to 1941 when Mac enlisted in the Canadian Army. After the war he spent three years on the west coast.

In October 1948 he and the Ottawa Valley Melodiers were back playing again. This time they were comprised of Beattie, Scheel, Horace Blanchette on fiddle, Karen Shaw on accordion, and Maurice. They had their own radio show on CHOV Pembroke, and their theme song was *Squirrels In The Chimney.* Two years later they broke up.

During the summer of 1951 Mac started forming the second group of Melodiers after Frank Ryan, a disc jockey at CFRA, wanted them to represent the station in the Ottawa Valley. The new lineup consisted of Shaw, Blanchette, Fairfield, Scheel, and Maisy Billings as the female star vocalist. Blanchette was later replaced by Reg Hill on fiddle. Other Melodiers included Billy Shepherd on piano, Rene Desormeaux on sax, Jimmy Mayhew on piano, Allan Utronki on steel and Spanish guitar, Merv Wilson on flat top guitar, Peter Clements on drums, Gordon Summers on lead guitar, Johnny Price on lead guitar and vocals, and Bob Whitney on banjo and vocals.

Mac and The Melodiers recorded their first album on Rodeo Records in 1961, A VISIT TO THE OTTAWA VALLEY. They continued to play until 1981. Mac Beattie died on June 16, 1982.

Singles *Squaws Along The Yukon* 1969
Northern Ontario Blues 1969

Albums
A VISIT TO THE OTTAWA VALLEY 1961
CANADIAN FOLK & COUNTRY SONGS 1964
THIS OTTAWA VALLEY OF MINE 1965
SING A SONG WITH . . . 1965
INSTRUMENTAL FAVORITES 1966
THROUGH THE YEARS 1967
25TH ANNIVERSARY 1968
BY REQUEST 1969
MR. OTTAWA VALLEY 1970
OTTAWA VALLEY MEMORIES 1971
DAD & DAUGHTER (with BONNIE BEATTIE) 1973

Debbie Bechamp

A native of Chapeau, Quebec, Debbie Bechamp (pronounced Bay-Shaw) started her career at age fifteen. She played disco and rock before she settled on country. Her first record on the Big Peach label was *I Wanna Hear The Angels Singing.* When disc jockeys found her last name difficult to pronounce, she changed it to Bayshaw.

As Debbie Bechamp:

Singles
I Wanna Hear The Angels Singing 1982
Take My Hand 1983
I'm Gonna Love You More 1984
All I Ever Need Is You 1987

As Debbie Bayshaw:

Singles *Time To Move Along* 1988
Hey, Bus Driver 1991
The Bottom of the Top 1995

Curtis Blayne

Singer/songwriter/actor Curtis Blayne hails from Irma, Alberta. After graduating from high school he played in a rock and roll band in Edmonton. He then moved to Vancouver, where he attended the Institute Of Communication Arts which led to parts in several movie and television productions. His debut CD, BETWEEN YOUR HEART AND MINE, came out in the spring of 1994.

Singles *She's Dangerous* 1994
Denim Blue 1994
Georgia Rain 1995
Midnight Angel 1995

CD BETWEEN YOUR HEART AND MINE 1994

The Blue Valley Boys

JOHNNY BURKE (*bass, vocals*)
ROY PENNEY (*lead guitar, vocals*)
DICK NOLAN (*rhythm guitar, vocals*)
BUNTIE PETRIE (*fiddle, drums, vocals*)

Based in Toronto, Ontario, The Blue Valley Boys started in 1960. The original lineup featured Johnny Burke, Dick Nolan, Johnny Bourque, and Graham Townsend. For the next four years at the Horseshoe Tavern they played back up for such artists as Lefty Frizzell, Tex Ritter, Carl Smith, Loretta Lynn, Red Foley, Charley Pride, and Conway Twitty.

From 1964-67 they were the host band on Carl Smith's *Country Music Hall* on CTV. In December 1967 Johnny Burke and Buntie Petrie left. By the end of 1968, The Blue Valley Boys had split up.

Album ON STAGE AT THE DRAKE 1964

Dieter Boehme

Born in West Germany in 1952, Dieter Boehme (pronounced Deeter Boehme) moved to Kingston, Ontario when he was two years old. After playing in various bands, he decided to form his own group, The Country Rebels, in the mid-1970s. They released an album entitled FIRST TIME AROUND in 1980. Between 1985 and 1990 he had a string of successful singles on his own, and one album called SIGNATURE.

Singles *Who Is The One* 1984
This Love Affair Is Drivin' Me Insane 1984
I Do 1985
Midnight Liar 1985
Weekend Country Music Legend 1985

Somebody Else On My Mind 1986
It's Not Cheatin' Yet (with ANNE BANKS) 1986
Do It Now 1986/87
Wandering Eyes 1987
Blue Jean Queen 1987/88
Honey I Love You 1988
It Ain't No Cure 1988
Falling Again 1989
Factory Grind 1990
You Put Out The Flame 1990/91
Shoppin' In The USA 1991
Singin' A Love Song 1992
Please Come Home 1993

Albums FIRST TIME AROUND (THE COUNTRY REBELS) 1980
SIGNATURE 1990

Maurice Bolyer

Born Maurice Beaulieu in Edmunston, New Brunswick, Canada's King of the Banjo began playing the piano, his first musical instrument, when he was three years old. By the time he was eighteen, he had learned the violin, guitar, bass, accordion, mandolin, and harmonica. Maurice took up the banjo only when a musician friend persuaded him.

His big break came in 1951 when he won a CBC radio contest in Montreal. In the 1960s he recorded for Arc Records. He was also a regular on *The Tommy Hunter Show* for ten years.

Bolyer died on August 18, 1978.

Albums STRUMMIN' WITH THE BANJO 1960
HONKY TONK PIANO MAN 1960
KING OF THE BANJO 1961
TELEVISION FAVORITES 1961
AROUND THE HONKY TONK 1962
COUNTRY BANJO 1969

Bootleg

RON IRVING (*guitar, vocals*) GERRY KING (*guitar, vocals*)
BRYAN NELSON (*guitar, keyboards*): *Replaced by* PETER MORRIS (1986)
DAN PROULX (*drums*)

This Vancouver-based quartet had a Top 20 hit in 1986 with *In My Arms Tonight*. The original lineup of the group was comprised of Gerry King, Dan Proulx, Ron Irving, and Bryan Nelson, who was replaced by Peter Morris in 1986. They recorded for Rana Records, an independent label in Vancouver.

Singles *Weekend Country* 1985
In My Arms Tonight 1986
Ordinary People Pass Me By 1986
Mama (You'll Be So Proud Of Me) 1987
Taste Of Romance 1987
Keep It Up 1988
The Cowboy Thing To Do 1989
You've Got Me Hurtin' 1989/90
Bluebird Lullabye 1990
Champagne And Roses 1990

Marie Bottrell

Marie Bottrell, who was born in London, Ontario, was one of Canada's top female recording artists of the late 1970s and 1980s.

She started writing songs at seven years of age, and at age eleven she was in the Whitestone Country Band with her brother Glen, sister Sandy, and Glen's wife Darlene. By her late teens, Marie had written over 200 songs. She later signed to MBS, The Mercey Brothers label in Elmira, Ontario. Her first single was *Just Reach Out and Touch Me* in March 1978. During the summer of 1978 her debut album of the same name was released.

She went on to record for RCA in 1982. *The Other Side Of Love* was her first single on the new label. By the end of the decade her popularity had waned, but she continues to record into the 1990s.

Singles

Just Reach Out And Touch Me 1978
Always Having Your Love 1978
This Feeling Called Love 1979
Oh Morning Sun Shine Bright 1979
The Star 1979/80
Flames Of Evil Desire 1980
Ballad Of Lucy Jordan 1980
Wonderin' If Willy 1981
The Other Side Of Love 1982
Lay Your Heart On The Line 1982
Does Your Heart Still Belong To Me 1983
Only The Names Have Been Changed 1983
Everybody Wants To Be Single 1983
Lovers Moon 1984
Until Forever 1984
The Man Behind The Woman 1985
Premeditated Love 1985
Girls Get Lonely Too 1986
Hopeless Romantic 1986
Lover's Game (with DAN ROGERS) 1989
Lasso Your Love 1991
Like There's No Tomorrow 1992
I Don't Give Up So Easy 1992

Albums

JUST REACH OUT AND TOUCH ME 1978
STAR 1980
A NIGHT LIKE THIS 1983
EVERYBODY WANTS TO BE SINGLE 1983
LOVERS MOON 1984
GIRLS GET LONELY TOO 1985

Cori Brewster

This Banff, Alberta born singer was a physical education teacher before she was attracted to the stage. Her debut single on Roto-Noto Records was *Swinging On The Gate* in March 1989.

Singles

Swinging On The Gate 1989
Up To Me 1989/90
I'm On My Way To Texas 1990
Even Though 1990/91
Country Station Rescue Me 1991
Take Me As I Am 1994
Climb Up When You're Down 1995
Good As Gone 1995

Lisa Brokop

At twelve years of age, this young girl from Surrey, British Columbia won several talent competitions and wowed audiences at various outdoor festivals and jamborees. She received her vocal training from acclaimed coach Trudy Buckler-Blake. Her powerful voice and professional demeanor contributed to her mature sound which went beyond her teenage years. In 1989 her big break came when she appeared on *The Tommy Hunter Show.* A year later, she recorded her first single, *Daddy Sing To Me.* It was the beginning of a promising career that came to fruition in the 1990s. She has appeared as a backup singer in the film *Harmony Cats*, and recorded two albums.

Singles

Daddy Sing To Me 1990
A Link In The Chain 1990
Christmas Is Not The Same (Without You) 1990
Old Mister Moon 1991
Time To Come Back Home 1991/92
My Love 1992
I'm Leaving You For Me 1992
All Heaven Broke Loose (with DANNY LEGGETT) 1992
Country Girl 1993
Stand By Your Man 1994
Give Me A Ring Sometime 1994
Take That 1994
One Of Those Nights 1995
Who Needs You 1995
She Can't Save Him 1995/96

CDs

MY LOVE 1992
EVERY LITTLE GIRL'S DREAM 1994
LISA BROKOP 1996

Heather Brooks

Raised in the small town of Vulcan, Alberta, Heather Brooks became interested in singing at an early age and sang in local church choirs. Her musical influences were Patsy Cline and Paulette Carlson. Her debut single was *Rocky Mountain Night* in 1989.

Singles

Rocky Mountain Night 1989/90
Every Second Someone Breaks A Heart 1990
Under The Harvest Moon 1991
No Walkin' Easy 1991
The Next Heartache Could Be You 1992

CD

EVERY SECOND SOMEONE BREAKS A HEART 1990

George Brothers

From Halifax, Nova Scotia, George Brothers started playing the banjo in his father's band when he was six years old. Although he could play all types of music, country was George's favorite. His professional music career began in such country bands as Johnny Gold's group, The Gold Tones, and Ralph Carlson and The Country Mile.

By the late 1970s George had formed his own band, Ol' Blue, and in 1978 they had their first hit, *Fat City Blues.* After the success of their second single, *Downhill Journey*, in 1979, the group split up. George continued on his own as a singer/songwriter/performer.

As George Brothers & Ol' Blue:

Singles *Fat City Blues* 1978
Downhill Journey 1979

As George Brothers:

Singles *Cure For A Heartache* 1984
Little By Little 1988
Natural Fact 1987/88

Linda Brown

A native of Kingston, Ontario, Linda Brown had several hits in the 1970s on A&M Records. Her debut single, *Empty Closets*, in 1973 was followed by *Sing-A-Long With Me*, which was her biggest hit.

After a brief hiatus, she signed to Earth Star Records. Her first single on the new label was *Love Don't Grow In A One Man Show.*

Singles *Empty Closets* 1973
Sing-A-Long With Me 1974
Roll It On Homeward 1974/75
More And More 1975
Love Don't Grow In A One Man Show 1980
Don't You Know I've Been Cryin' 1981

Album SING-A-LONG WITH ME 1974

Hal Bruce

Born in Halifax and raised in Peggy's Cove, Nova Scotia, Hal Bruce first picked up the guitar when he was ten years old. As a teenager he was influenced by Lennon and McCartney's songwriting.

Hal began recording his own music in 1983 with the singles *I'm Leaving*, *Bambino*, and *The Sandman.* A year later he started his first group, Hal Bruce and The Drifters Band. He has since formed another backup group called The Hired Hand Band.

His first two albums, THE FIRST TIME and GOIN' HOME, were recorded in Nashville and produced by Gilles Godard.

Singles *I'm Leaving* 1983
Bambino 1983
The Sandman 1983
Don't Say You're Not Staying 1988/89
I'm Goin' Home 1991
Wake Me In Virginia 1991
I'll Cry Instead 1991/92
Gonna Make You All Mine 1993
The Legend Of My Love 1993

Goodnight 1990
Impossible Love 1990
Seems Like Only Yesterday 1994

Albums THE FIRST TIME 1988
GOIN' HOME 1992

Gary Buck

Singer/songwriter/producer Gary Buck was born on March 21, 1940 in Thessalon, Ontario, a small Northern Ontario town. Raised and educated in Sault Ste. Marie, he first picked up the guitar when he was a bass player in a high school band. In 1959 he recorded his debut album, SINGS COUNTRY GOODIES, on the Canatal label. From it came his first single, *Where Did You Go.* Four years later, he went to Nashville and recorded for Petal Records. His debut single was *Happy To Be Unhappy* in 1963, which became the first country hit by a Canadian artist to become number one in *CASHBOX*, a U.S. trade weekly.

In the mid-1960s Buck moved to Kitchener, Ontario, where he had his own TV show on CKCO from 1967-69. He established his own publishing and recording company, Broadland Music, in 1971. In addition to his own recordings, he has made a mark as a producer. He has worked with such acts as The Mercey Brothers, Dallas Harms, Dick Damron, Family Brown, Al Cherny, The Rhythm Pals, and the late Orval Prophet.

Buck is President of the Canadian Country Music Hall of Fame, which he founded in Kitchener in 1989. It moved to Swift Current, Saskatchewan in 1992.

Singles
Where Did You Go 1959
Happy To Be Unhappy 1963
As Close As We'll Ever Be 1964
The Wheel Song 1964
Nighthawk 1965
Back Streets Of Life 1965
Break The News To Liza 1965
That's All You've Given 1965
Elrod 1966
The Weatherman 1967
Love's Gonna Come Back 1967
Calgary, Alberta 1968
Mr. Brown 1968/69
Wayward Women Of The World 1969/70
Don't Hate — Communicate 1970
It Takes Time 1971
Saunders Ferry Lane 1971/72
When The Final Change Is Made 1972
If I'm A Fool For Leaving 1972/73
National Pastime 1973
Sandy's Gonna Stay 1973/74
Knowing That She's Leaving 1974
What'll I Do 1974/75
Pokarekare Ana (with EDDIE LOW) 1975
Bright Morning Light 1978

When I Want A Lady 1979
Wish That You Could Learn To Love Me 1981
E.T. Still Means Ernest Tubb To Me (with DAVID HOUSTON) 1984
Midnight Magic 1987
Blossom 1987
Champagne And Roses 1989
Adam And The Slogans Of Life 1990
One Step Of A Two-Step 1990
What's New With You 1991
Through My Eyes 1993

Albums
SINGS COUNTRY GOODIES 1959
GARY BUCK SINGS FOR EVERYBODY (PETAL) 1964
GARY BUCK'S COUNTRY SCENE (U.S. only) 1965
STEPPING INTO THE PICTURE 1966
TOMORROW TODAY 1967
WAYWARD WOMEN OF THE WORLD 1969
GARY BUCK SINGS 1970
COLD WIND ON THE MOUNTAIN 1973
GREATEST HITS 1975

Johnny Burke

Johnny Burke was born Jean Paul Bourque in the French Acadian community of Rosaireville, New Brunswick. Growing up he often listened intently to his father playing old fiddle tunes like *St. Anne's Reel* on the pump organ, and participated in family singalongs.

In the early 1960s, Johnny moved to Toronto, where he played in a country/rock group called Johnny and The Bees, then with The Blue Valley Boys, and The Maple River Boys on *Carl Smith's Country Music Hall* in the mid-1960s. He recorded his first single, *Loving You Again*, for Columbia Records in 1966. A year later he formed the Caribou Showband, and from 1968 to 1975, he and the band hosted the CTV show *At The Caribou*. In 1972 the Caribou Showband changed its name to Eastwind.

Johnny Burke and Eastwind backed up other artists and were regulars on the syndicated TV program, *The Opry North Show*. By 1984 he decided to concentrate more on his solo career, and his next album, GOLD IN HIS MIND, came out a year later on Acclaim Records. From it were released some singles, most notably *Still Feels Good.* A collection of his recent hits was released on an independent cassette called JUDGE MY SOUL AGAIN in 1994. (SEE THE BLUE VALLEY BOYS.)

Singles
Loving You Again 1966
Loving Day 1967
I Can't Even Do Wrong Right 1967
Listen 1970
Kingdom Of My Mind 1970
Hey Good Lookin' (EASTWIND) 1972
Wild Honey 1977
The Love I Want To Waste 1978
Love Don't Grow On Trees 1979
Your Love (Is Like Sugar To Me) 1979
Whiskey Dreams & Nursery Rhymes 1980

Everybody's Goin' Crazy (But You And Me) 1984
Baby You're All Mine Tonight 1984
Bad Times And Good Old Days 1985
Troubles On My Mind 1985
Still Feels Good 1985
Gold In His Mind 1986
A Picture Of You 1987
I'm Just Me (with HAROLD MACINTYRE) 1992
Judge My Soul Again 1992

Albums SINGS BUCK OWENS' BIG HITS 1965

Cassettes JOHNNY BURKE AND EASTWIND (CYNDA) 1972
STRAIGHT AHEAD COUNTRY 1974
WILD HONEY 1978
JOHNNY BURKE AND EASTWIND (GRAND SLAM) 1980
JOHNNY BURKE AND EASTWIND (CARIBOU)
JOHNNY BURKE AND EASTWIND (RODEO)
GOLD IN HIS MIND 1985
JUDGE MY SOUL AGAIN 1994

Burton & Honeyman

Dave Burton and Gord Honeyman first met in their early teens. When they discovered they had similar tastes in music, they became a duo. In the late 1960s they were part of Toronto's Yorkville scene. Signed to Condor Records, their debut album, TWO OF A KIND, was released in late 1976. In 1977 they had a number one hit with *Christopher Mary.*

Singles *Two Of A Kind* 1976
On The Road Again 1977
Christopher Mary 1977
Early Morning Dawn 1977/78
Goin' Home Goin' Home 1978
Lady Of The Night 1978
Girl's First Love 1978

Albums TWO OF A KIND 1976
BURTON & HONEYMAN 1978

Colin Butler

Born in 1960 in Sudbury, Ontario, Colin Butler was three years old when he was handed his first guitar. At five he was a frequent guest a local club events and concerts. By the time he was twelve he had appeared on *The Tommy Hunter Show*, *Family Brown Country*, and other regional and national TV shows. In 1971 his debut album, CANADA'S YOUNGEST SINGING SENSATION, was released on Marathon Records.

By the late 1970s the rigors of the Canadian music industry had begun to take their toll on the teenaged Butler, and he took a brief hiatus. To keep his hand in, he toured with Area Code 705 who backed up

Harold MacIntyre. In 1986 he marked his return with the song *Gypsy Wind.* A year later it would be included on the Burco cassette release of the same name.

Singles

Let Me In 1972
California Dream 1975/76
San Francisco Summer 1977
How Many More Miracles 1984
Gypsy Wind 1986
When She Needed Love 1987
Dandy Lyin' 1987
How'd We Let It Get This Far 1987/88

Albums

CANADA'S YOUNG SINGING SENSATION 1971
A MILLION DOLLAR CHRISTMAS 1972
JUST BIDIN' MY TIME 1973
MILLION DOLLAR CHRISTMAS 1973
COLIN BUTLER 1977

C-Weed Band

CLINT DUTIAUME (*lead guitar, fiddle*)
ERROL RANVILLE (*rhythm guitar, vocals*)
DONN RANVILLE (*drums*)
WALLY RANVILLE (*bass*)

Led by Errol Ranville, alias C-Weed, the rest of the group was comprised of brothers Donn and Wally and Clint Dutiaume. From 1980-1987 they had several big hits. In 1987 they broke up. Errol Ranville went on to have a solo career.

As C-Weed Band:

Singles
Evangeline 1980
High And Dry 1981
Hard Hearted Woman 1981
I Heard The Owl Call My Name 1982
A Little Bit Of Lovin' Tonight 1983
Bringing Home The Good Times 1984
Magic In The Music 1985
Loving You 1986
Pick Up Truck Cowboy 1986
Old Rodeo Cowboys 1987/88

Albums
THE FINEST YOU CAN BUY 1980
HIGH AND DRY 1981
GOING THE DISTANCE 1983
LIVE AT MA'S CORRAL 1985

As Errol Ranville:

Singles
Janine 1989
I Want To Fly 1990
Still The One 1990

Album
I WANT TO FLY 1990

Cindi Cain and the Cheeters

This Winnipeg born and raised star wanted to be a country singer when she was seven years old. At thirteen Cindi Curko was a special guest act on a week long tour with the legendary Ferlin Husky. In 1983 while working as a lounge act at Winnipeg's Polo Park Inn, she won a local talent search contest. Two years later, she had formed her own band under the name of Cindi Churko and The Cheeters. By June 1986 they had recorded their first single, *(I Could Make You A) Rich Man,* which became a Top 20 hit.

Canadian country music veteran Don Grashey, who had managed Myrna Lorrie and Carroll Baker, agreed to become Cindi's manager in 1988. He changed her name to Cindi Cain and she went to have several national hits, such as *Fiddle Texas Style* in late 1988 and early 1989.

As Cindi Churko & The Cheeters:

Singles
(I Could Make You A) Rich Man 1986
Two More on the Dance Floor 1987

HANK SNOW

SHANIA TWAIN

GEORGE FOX

LISA BROKOP

MICHELLE WRIGHT

WILF CARTER
CHEF ADAMS

K.D. LANG

PATRICIA CONROY

GARY BUCK

DALLAS HARMS

QUARTETTE

As Cindi Cain & The Cheeters:

Singles
You Were Listening To The Singer 1988
The Music Still In Me 1988
Fiddle Texas Style 1988/89
I Think That I'll Be Needing You This Time 1989
Just A Place Where Mem'ries Live 1989
Once The Magic's Gone 1990
Field Of Dreams 1991
You Called Her Name Again 1991
Two More On The Dance Floor 1991
(You Made A) Rock of Gibraltar 1992
You Called Her Name Again 1992
Somewhere In-Between 1993

Album A PLACE WHERE MEM'RIES LIVE 1989

The Canadian Sweethearts

BOB REGAN
LUCILLE STARR

In the 1950s and early 1960s, The Canadian Sweethearts were one of Canada's most popular country acts. Regan, who was born Bob Frederickson in Rolla, British Columbia, met Lucille Starr (nee Savoie) in the early 1950s and quickly established themselves as a duo. They moved to Los Angeles in the early 1960s, where the late Dorsey Burnett introduced Lucille to Herb Alpert, who signed her to A&M Records. Her debut single was *The French Song* in 1963. The Canadian Sweethearts also recorded for the label. Two of their hits were *Hootenanny Express and Freight Train.*

By the early 1970s they had broken up. Regan moved to Germany, where he found success as a solo act. He died of cancer on March 5, 1990. Starr continued to enjoy a solo career until she was diagnosed with polyps on her vocal chords and temporarily lost her voice. After more than a decade away from the studio, she went to Nashville in 1981 to record the album THE SUN SHINES AGAIN. It marked another beginning in the career of Lucille Starr.

As The Canadian Sweethearts:

Singles
Freight Train 1963
Hootenanny Express 1964
Looking Back To Sea 1965
Don't Knock On My Door 1966
Let's Wait A Little Longer 1968

Albums CANADIAN SWEETHEARTS 1964
SIDE BY SIDE 1967

As Lucille Starr:

Singles
The French Song 1964
Too Far Gone 1967
Is It Love? 1968
Say You Love Me 1968
Cajun Love 1969
Dream Baby (with BOB REGAN) 1970

The French Song (Reissue) 1970/71
Sock It To Satin 1971
The Sun Shines Again 1981
Power In Your Love 1981/82
The First Time I've Ever Been In Love 1987/88
Back To You 1988
Rock Steady Love 1989
Just The Way We Were 1989/90
Ecstasy 1990
Crazy Arms 1990
Hello Sadness 1991
Heartless One 1992

Albums
THE SUN SHINES AGAIN 1981
THE HITMAN 1982
BACK TO YOU 1988
SWEET MEMORIES 1990
CHANSONS D'AMOUR 1991

Canadian Zephyr

GARTH BOURNE (*lead vocals, bass*)
JOHN HAYMAN (*vocals, acoustic & lead guitar*)
JOHN HOWARD (*vocals, keyboards*)
BILL MEENS (*bass, drums*)

The history of Canadian Zephyr goes back to 1969 when John Hayman, Bill Meens, Marty Steiger, and Chris Pluis called themselves The Four Jacks. Based in Richmond Hill, Ontario, they changed their name to Canadian Zephyr two years later. In 1972 they recorded their first single on Cynda Records, *Cheap Lowdown Wine*. Shortly after its release, Stager and Pluis left. Garth Bourne, who worked as a solo act at the Robin Hood Inn in Pickering, was invited to join Hayman and Meens to make a trio.

Late in 1972 they signed a recording contract with Bronco Records. Their first album, BRINGIN' THE HOUSE DOWN, came out the following year. Meens left in 1973. He was replaced by Gord Logan on drums. John Howard on piano joined in 1975. Bourne left in 1981 and was replaced by Dario Cingilani on drums and Carl Toth on bass and vocals. Ron Musselwhite, Joe Linge, and Tom Graham also played drums.

After many successful singles and albums, Canadian Zephyr broke up in 1986.

Singles
Cheap Lowdown Wine 1972
World Of Make Believe 1973
My Sweet Caroline 1973
Lovin' My Lady 1973
Me And The Devil 1974
She Loves Away The Blues 1975
Someone Special 1975
Breaking Up With Brenda 1976
No Love At All 1976
For All I Care 1977
Stop Right There 1977
Here's Your Watch John 1978
Country Mile Better 1978
You Made My Day Tonight 1979

Love When It Leaves Here 1979
Don't Ask The Question 1979/80
I Guess I Went Crazy 1980
Lawanda 1980
Watching It Die 1981
The Time It Takes To Leave 1981
Took You Back Again 1982
Blonde And Down (From A Rodeo Town) 1983
California Blankets 1983/84
Shake This Rock 1985

Albums

BRINGIN' THE HOUSE DOWN 1973
IN THE ZEPHYR STYLE 1974
IT JUST SO HAPPENS 1976
A COUNTRY MILE BETTER 1977
BEST OF CANADIAN ZEPHYR 1979
ZEPHYR 1980
THE SONGWRITERS 1983

Terry Carisse

Long before his commercial success as a singer, Terry Carisse was a successful songwriter with longtime partner Bruce Rawlins, who died of cancer on January 22, 1987. Together they wrote several hits for The Mercey Brothers.

Carisse grew up in Ottawa. While in his teens he began writing songs. In the 1960s, he was in several bands that played both rock and country. He formed his own group, Tenderfoot, in the 1970s, but they went their separate ways in 1979. Tracks, a four-man band, backed up Carisse through the 1980s.

His first hit, *Been Thinking,* came out in 1976, but it was not until the late 1970s and 1980s that he would finally taste success, with such hits as *Sparkle In Her Eyes* and *We Could Make Beautiful Music Together.*

Singles

Been Thinking 1976
Lonely Highway Blues 1978
The Story Of The Year 1978/79
Time To Go 1979
Sparkle In Her Eyes 1979/80
All Her Letters 1980
We Could Make Beautiful Music Together 1980
Windship 1981
Ode To An Outlaw's Lady 1981
Coming Undone Again 1982
Nevada 1982
Loveblind 1983
The Closest Thing To You 1984
Two Broken Hearts 1985
Counting The I Love Yous 1985
I Wish I Had You Here Again 1985
Sweet Blue 1985/86
Love Sweet Love 1986
It Must Be October 1986/87
Old Photographs 1987
None Of The Feeling Is Gone (& MICHELLE WRIGHT) 1987
Starting Forever Again 1987
Give In 1987
I Thought Leaving Would Be Easy 1988
Loveproof Heart 1989
What About Her 1989/90
Start Of Something New (& TRACEY BROWN) 1990
Is Your Heart Taken 1990/91
That Was A Long Time Ago 1991
My Old Man 1992
Daddy's Girl 1994

Albums

STORY OF THE YEAR 1979
TRANSCRIPTION 1979
A GOSPEL GATHERING 1983
THE CLOSEST THING TO YOU 1984
LOVE SWEET LOVE 1986
NONE OF THE FEELING IS GONE 1987
THAT WAS A LONG TIME AGO 1989

Ralph Carlson

Ralph Carlson's first experience with a band came in the 1950s when he formed The Jive Rockets while in high school in Ottawa, Ontario. Born in Montreal in 1940, he moved to Ottawa from Shediac Cape, New Brunswick in 1953.

After graduating from high school, he played guitar and sang in the group Ron McMunn and His Country Cousins from 1962-65. They had a live weekly radio show on CJET in Smith Falls, Ontario. During this time he began recording his own songs. His debut album, THE GAME WAS LOVE, was released in 1965. A year later, he had a national hit with *The Phone Call*. In the late 1960s, he formed his own band, The Countrymen.

In 1970, he organized his second group, the Country Mile Band. After many personnel changes they remained as his backup band. In 1975 Carlson dropped his day job and concentrated full-time on his music. His last album was the cassette, LEGENDS & RHYMES . . . PEOPLE & TIMES.

Singles

The Game Was Love 1965
The Phone Call 1965
Three Plays For A Quarter 1966
The Johnson Family 1967
Transport Blues 1967
The Homecoming 1967
Okay Heart 1969
I'm Almost Home 1970
Don's Barber Shop 1977
Silas McVie 1978
Lights Of Denver 1979
Thanks For The Dance 1980
Somebody's Woman 1980
Out Of The Snow 1981
Ain't Got Time For The Good Life 1981
Tryin' To Get To You 1982
Honey Don't 1982
All The Love Songs Are For You 1983
A Cage Is Not For Eagles 1983
You Are The Best Thing That I've Ever Seen 1984
Bargain With The Devil 1985

Albums

THE GAME WAS LOVE WITH RALPH CARLSON 1965
RALPH CARLSON SINGS 1966
RALPH CARLSON SINGS (Golden Stereo Series) 1968
GRASS'N STUFF 1977
DON'S BARBER SHOP 1978
THANKS FOR THE DANCE 1980
THANKS FOR THE DANCE (Westwood in U.K.) 1981
BACK TO THE REAL THING 1982
RALPH CARLSON AND BYTOWN BLUEGRASS 1985
LEGENDS & RHYMES . . . PEOPLE & TIMES 1987 (cassette only)

Glory-Anne Carriere

Glory-Anne Carriere was born in Gravelbourg, Saskatchewan, a small community near the Montana border. When she was a young girl, she moved with her family to Lampman, Saskatchewan, where she began singing in high-school bands. In 1975 she won the Saskatchewan Talent Hunt Contest and it helped launch her recording career the following year, when Royalty Records released her debut album, I'D LIKE TO TAKE THE CHANCE.

By the early 1980s she was in demand for guest shots on such television shows as *The Tommy Hunter Show* and *Family Brown Country.* While touring with Ronnie Prophet in early 1981, Glory-Anne's career took a significant turn. They became singing partners and made several recordings together. Their first album was called STORYBOOK CHILDREN (1982). Both she and Prophet continued to record separately and together. They were married in 1986.

Singles

I'd Like To Take The Chance 1976
I'd Like To Tell You 1977
Rocky Road 1977
Woman Alone 1977
Pretty Little Love Song 1978
Kelly Green 1979
In My Dreams 1979/80
Sugartime 1981/82
Serious Love (with RONNIE PROPHET) 1983
You're A Fool 1983
Silver Tongue Devil 1985
Changes 1986
Small Talk 1987
Light As A Feather (with RAY GRIFF) 1987/88
The Key To My Diary 1988
Two Timin' Man 1988
I Feel A Little Down Tonight 1989/90
Do You See What I'm Sayin' 1993

Albums

I'D LIKE TO TAKE THE CHANCE 1976
KEEPER OF THE HEART 1978

K.C. Carter

K.C. Carter was born Ken Carl Wilgosh in Toronto on July 22, 1964. Growing up in Lindsay and Omeemee, Ontario, he listened to all types of music but country was special. As a teenager, he played drums in various school band competitions in Edmonton, Prince Edward Island, and Florida. In 1987 he played in a band called Ted Moore and The Border. After winning a talent contest at the Lindsay Exhibition he went on to win the Bud Country Talent Contest sponsored by radio station CFGM in Richmond Hill, Ontario. It led to his first hit single, *Lefty's Gone,* which was distributed by MCA. It was CFGM's Ted Tompkins who suggested him to change his name to K.C. Carter. The K.C. came from his own given name, and Carter from the Carter Family and Wilf Carter.

Singles

Lefty's Gone 1990
Ride With Me 1991

Wastin' Away 1990
Wildwood Dream 1990
Rolling On 1991/92
When You Left Me 1993

Wilf Carter Born on December 18, 1904 in Port Hilford, Nova Scotia, Wilf Carter was the son of a Baptist minister. At age ten he saw a Chataugua of Uncle Tom's Cabin and was inspired by the singing and yodeling of a performer known as "The Yodelling Fool." In 1923 he moved west to Calgary, Alberta, where he sang in bunkhouses, camps, house parties and dances.

In 1930 Wilf conducted his first radio broadcast on CFCN, Calgary. Two years later, he sang as a trail rider for the Canadian Pacific Railway treks in the Canadian Rockies. The CPR was so impressed by his performances he was invited to perform on the maiden voyage of the *S.S. Empress of Britain* in 1933.

While on his way to the *Empress of Britain*, he stopped at a small studio in Montreal, Quebec to record *My Swiss Moonlight Lullaby* and *The Capture of Albert Johnson.* By the time he returned from the voyage, the two sides were pressed and released by RCA Victor as Wilf Carter's first recording. It was a best seller in 1934. That same year, Wilf was given the moniker "Montana Slim" by a pretty New Yorker who typed out a couple of songs for him.

With his daughters Sheila and Carol as back-up singers and dancers, Wilf went on the road as "The Family Show With The Folks You Know" in 1953. He performed at the Calgary Stampede for the very first time in 1964. That same year, he was honored with a trophy from the officers and directors of the Calgary Exhibition and Stampede which had the following inscription: "Balladeer of the Golden West, a sincere appreciation of 33 wonderful years."

Other honors bestowed on him during his sixty years in the music industry included a place in the Songwriter's Hall Of Fame in Nashville in 1972, a plaque from RCA Records for accumulated sales of over 40 years in 1975, and the Martin Guitar Entertainer of the Year Award in 1981 for being the Canadian artist who has contributed the most to country music in Canada over the past year.

By the 1990s he had retired from recording and performing.

Singles
My Swiss Moonlight Lullaby / The Capture Of Albert Johnson 1933
The Hobo's Blues 1934
Twilight On The Prairie 1934
The Roundup In The Fall 1934
He Rode The Old Strawberry Roan 1934
My Little Grey Haired Mother In The West 1934
A Cowboy's Blues 1934
Lover's Lullaby Yodel 1934
I Miss My Swiss 1934
The Life And Death Of John Dillinger 1934
The Yodeling Trail Rider 1934

The Hobo's Dream Of Heaven 1934
Down The Old Cattle Trail 1934
The Calgary Roundup 1934
Cowboy's High-Toned Dance 1934
Trail To Home Sweet Home 1934
My Blues Have Turned To Sunshine 1934
Cowboy's Mother 1934
I'm Gonna Ride To Heaven On A Streamlined Train 1935
Sundown Blues 1935
Lonesome For Baby Tonight 1935
Prairie Sunset 1935
Roaming My Whole Life Away 1936
I Long For Old Wyoming 1936
The Rescue From Moose River Gold Mine 1936
Yodeling Hillbilly 1936
Old Barn Dance 1936
Dreamy Prairie Moon 1936
The Fate Of The Sunset Trail 1936
Roll Along Moonlight Yodel 1936
The Hobo's Yodel 1936
Rose Of My Heart 1936
Put My Little Shoes Away 1936
My Little Yoho Lady 1936
Where Is My Wondering Boy Tonight 1936
The Hindenburg Disaster 1936
Covered Wagon Headin' West 1936
Pete Knight's Last Ride 1936
Old Alberta Plains 1936
My Faithful Pinto Pal 1936
The Preacher And The Cowboy 1936
Everybody's Been Some Mother's Darling 1936
I Wish I Had Never Seen Sunshine 1936
When The Bright Prairie Moon Is Rolling By 1936
By The Grave Of Nobody's Darling 1936
Longing For My Mississippi Home 1936
Ridin' A Maverick 1936
Ridin' A Maverick 1936
My Old Montana Home 1936
There's A Love Knot In My Lariat 1937
La Verne My Brown Eyed Rose 1938
My Last Old Yodel Song 1938
By The Grave Of Nobody's Darling 1938
Answer To "It Makes No Difference Now" 1939
Down The Yodeling Trail At Twilight 1938
Little Red Patch On The Seat Of My Trousers 1939
It Makes No Difference Now 1939
I'm Only A Dude In Cowboy Clothes 1939
I'm Hittin' The Trail 1939
Golden Lariat 1939
What Difference Does It Make? 1939
The Cowboy's Airplane Ride 1939
When I Say Hello To The Rockies 1939
Memories Of My Little Old Log Shack 1939
Wilf Carter Blues 1939
Headin' For That Land Of Gold 1939

You Left Your Brand On My Heart 1939
My Yodeling Sweetheart 1939
My Lulu 1939
Wilf Carter Blues 1939
Back Ridin' Old Trails Again 1940
Why Did We Ever Part 1940
My Texas Sweetheart 1942
My True And Earnest Prayer 1942
West Of Rainbow Trail 1942
I'm Thinking Tonight Of My Blue Eyes 1942
I'll Always Keep Smiling For You 1942
Yodeling My Babies To Sleep 1942
That First Love Of Mine 1943
The Prisoner's Song 1943
I'll Never Die Of A Broken Heart 1944
My Yodeling Days Are Through 1944
Our Canadian Flag 1945
Dreaming Of My Blue Eyes 1945
Put Me In Your Pocket 1945
Smiling Through Tears 1945
Old Shep 1945
Smiling Through Tears 1945
Plant Some Flowers By My Graveside 1946
I've Hung Up My Spurs And Saddle 1946
I Ain't Gonna Be A Hobo No More 1946
My Blue Skies 1946
I've Hung Up My Spurs And Saddle 1946
Don't Wait Till Judgement Day 1947
It's Later Than You Think 1947
Dream Lullaby Yodel 1947
I'm Gonna Tear Down The Mailbox 1947
There's A Love Knot In My Lariat 1947
Hang The Key On The Bunkhouse Door 1948
The Midnight Train 1948
One Golden Curl 1949
Just An Old Forgotten Letter 1949
She Lost Her Cowboy Pal 1949
All I Need Is Some More Lovin' 1949
When The Iceworm Nests Again 1949
Unfaithful One 1950
The Little Shirt My Mother Made For Me 1950
Rudolph The Red Nosed Reindeer 1950
Apple, Cherry, Mince & Choc'late Cream 1950
The K.P. Blues 1950
The Blue Canadian Rockies 1950
Just A Woman's Smile 1951
Dear Evelina 1951
Sick, Sober & Sorry 1951
Let's Go Back To The Bible 1951
Punkinhead 1951
Tears Don't Always Mean A Broken Heart 1951
I Wish There Were Only Three Days In A Year 1951
Good-Bye Maria (I'm Off To Korea) 1952
Alabama Saturday Night 1952
Huggin', Squeezin', Kissin', Teasin' 1952
Sleep, Little One, Sleep 1952
Hot Foot Boogie 1952
Dream Lullaby Yodel 1953
What Cigarette Is Best 1953
Dear Evelina 1953
Guilty Conscience 1953
Maple Leaf Waltz 1955

Shoo Shoo Sh' La La 1955
Dynamite Trail 1955
There's A Tree On Every Road 1955
There's A Padlock On Your Heart 1956
My Little Lady 1956
The Yodelin' Song 1956
Let A Little Sunshine In Your Heart 1957
There's A Bluebird On Your Windowsill 1957
My French Canadian Girl 1958
Have A Nice Day 1976
My 50 Golden Years 1983
What Ever Happened 1988

Albums

REMINISCIN' WITH WILF CARTER 1963
MONTANA SLIM — WILF CARTER 1963
BY REQUEST 1964
32 WONDERFUL YEARS 1964
NUGGETS OF THE GOLDEN WEST 1964
YODELING MEMORIES 1965
CHRISTMAS IN CANADA 1965
GOLDEN MEMORIES 1966
BALLADEER OF THE GOLDEN WEST 1966
CALGARY HORSEMAN'S HALL OF FAME 1966
SINGS JIMMIE RODGERS 1969
GOD BLESS OUR CANADA 1967
IF IT WASN'T FOR THE FARMER WHAT WOULD CITY SLICKERS DO? 1967
WAITING FOR THE MAPLE LEAVES TO FALL 1967
"NO LETTER TODAY" AND OTHER COUNTRY AND WESTERN SONGS 1967
OLD PRAIRIE MELODIES 1967
SONGS OF THE RAIL AND RANGE 1968
HOW MY YODELING DAYS BEGAN 1968
HITTIN' THE TRACK 1969
SONGS OF AUSTRALIA 1970
AWAY OUT THERE 1970
THE YODELING SWISS 1971
WALLS OF MEMORIES 1971
BRIDLE HANGING ON THE
I'M HAPPY TODAY 1979
WALL 1972
A MESSAGE FROM HOME SWEET HOME 1972
MY HEARTACHE'S YOUR HAPPINESS 1973
40TH ANNIVERSARY SPECIAL 1974
MY OLD CANADIAN HOME 1974
MONTANA SLIM'S GREATEST HITS 1974
THERE GOES MY EVERYTHING 1975
THE GOLDEN YEARS (K-TEL) 1976
SONGS I LOVE TO SING 1977
HITS OF/COUNTRY CLUB 1977
STREETS OF CALGARY 1978
CHINOOK WINDS 1981
ALL TIME FAVORITES 1982
50 GOLDEN YEARS 1983
THE CANADIAN YODELING COWBOY (Australian) 1986
WHATEVER HAPPENED TO ALL THOSE YEARS 1988

Cedar Creek

GARLAND CRAFT (*keyboards*)
DON EDMUNDS (*vocals*)
CHRIS GOLDEN (*drums*)
KEN HARNDEN (*vocals*)
DAVE HOLCROFT (*vocals*)
TONY PERKINS (*bass*):
Replaced by JIM HILL (1983)
RON SPEARMAN (*vocals*)
SAM STRICKLIN (*lead guitar*)

Formed in 1980 in Belleville, Ontario, Cedar Creek began as a quartet, but in 1982, they became an eight-man band. That same year, they were invited to appear and perform at a Grammy Post Awards show in Los Angeles at the famous Palamino Club in North Hollywood, and went on a tour of the United States. After five singles and one album, they broke up in 1984.

Singles
Looks Like A Setup To Me 1981
Georgia Mules And Country Boys 1981/82
Take Like It A Man, Cried Like A Baby 1982
Take A Ride On The Riverboat 1982
Lonely Heart 1983

Album
AFTER TONIGHT 1981

Charlie Chamberlain

Step-dancer and singer Charlie Chamberlain was a popular favorite on TV's *The Don Messer Show* where he wore his bowler hat and shillelagh. His singing partner was the late Marg Osburne.

Charlie's career goes back to 1934 when he was a member of Messer's group, The New Brunswick Lumberjacks, later known as The Backwoods Trio and The Islanders. He died on July 16, 1972.

Albums
SINGS IRISH SONGS n.d.
WITH MY SHILLELAGH UNDER MY ARM n.d.

Cathy Chambers

Born and raised in Welland, Ontario, Cathy Chambers started out in her father's group, The Cooks Mills Ramblers. In 1976 she teamed up with her sister Elaine, and as the Chambers Sisters they won a Fan Fair Talent Contest, sponsored by Welland radio station CHOW.

National exposure for Cathy finally came in 1981 when Galahad Records released her debut single, *Where Could You Take Me*. Her self-titled debut album came out in 1982.

In the mid-1980s she took a hiatus from recording and performing, only to return in late 1989 with the single *Not Even For You* on the Lyons Creek label. In 1990, Elaine and Cathy reunited as The Chambers Sisters and they went on tour.

Singles
Where Could You Take Me 1981
I Fall In Love Everyday 1981
Stay Home Kind Of Woman 1982
I Feel Like Love Again Tonight 1983
Hey Mister Wind 1984
Old Love Affair 1990

Billy Charne

A native of Grand Forks, British Columbia, Billy Charne grew up grooming and excercising horses, roughnecking in the Alberta oil fields, clowning and working barrel on the rodeo circuit in Oregon and Nevada. Not until he was in his late teens did he seriously consider singing as a career when he was asked to sing at a nightclub in Marysville, California in 1964.

Early in 1968 he went to Toronto where he worked for a local talent agency by day and sang at a local nightclub at night. He was later introduced to Gary Buck at Sparton Records. The result was his only single on the label, *No Lonelier Than You.*

Charne later signed an exclusive contract with RCA. His debut release was *Susie's Better Half* in June 1969. He then formed his own band called The Charms. After two more singles, he moved to California where he continued to perform.

In 1995 he released his first record in over twenty years with the independent album, FRESNO RODEO.

Singles

No Lonelier Than You 1968/69
Susie's Better Half 1969
When You Were A Lady 1969
To-Ma-Ray, Tom-O-Ray 1970
Sally In Dallas 1994
Suzannah 1995

CD

FRESNO RODEO 1995

Al Cherny

From Medicine Hat, Alberta, Alexander Peter Chernywech was born on November 1, 1932. At ten years of age he started playing the fiddle. While in high school he formed a country music band that played at fairs and radio shows throughout the Prairies. His first professional appearance was at the 1950 Calgary Stampede. Three years later, he moved to Wingham, Ontario.

On August 5, 1960 he took part in the Annual Ole Time Fiddle contest in Shelburne, Ontario. He was the first Canadian to win both the Old Time and Novelty classes, a feat he repeated in 1961. That same year, he became a regular on CBC-TV's *Country Hoedown,* where he was billed as "Canada's number one fiddling star of CKNX's Barndance." He was later a regular on *The Tommy Hunter Show.* Cherny died on August 23, 1989.

Singles

Sippin' Cider 1959
Shannon Waltz 1972
Mr. Bojangles 1972

Album

OLD TIME FIDDLE CHAMPION 1965
BLUE RIBBON FIDDLE 1966
ON STAGE WITH AL CHERNY 1967
GOLDEN SLIPPERS 1968
THE BIG FIDDLE SOUND OF AL CHERNY 1971
FIDDLE MAGIC 1972
RURAL ROOTS 1974

REEL DE LA POINTE-AU-PIC n.d.
COUNTRY CLUB/HITS OF n.d.
GOLDEN UKRAINIAN MEMORIES n.d.
FIDDLE COUNTRY n.d.
FIDDLE PARTY n.d.
50 ALL-TIME FAVOURITES/A TRIBUTE TO AL CHERNY n.d.

Peter Chipman

Born in Ottawa, Ontario on July 21, 1945, Peter Chipman formed his first folk group The Henchmen while attending the University of New Brunswick. After graduation, he became a stock broker. By 1977 he had devoted himself full time to a music career. Although his stylings were in a folk vein like Gary Fjellgaard's, his songs were charted on country stations. His first single, *Rodeo Road Show Man*, was one of the heaviest played records on country radio in Canada in 1980.

Singles

Rodeo Road Show Man 1980
Four High Cards 1981
Hey Daisy 1981/82
The Singer 1983
I Didn't Ever Really Love You 1983
For All Those Years 1985
She Can Survive 1985

Album

YOU GIRL 1978
I LOVE THE COUNTRY IN YOU 1981
ROMANTICALLY YOURS 1983

Terry Christenson

A native of Nobel, Ontario near Parry Sound, Terry Christenson's musical career started in Toronto in the 1960s where he joined various bands. With his brother Peter, they formed a duo and played in bars and clubs across Ontario. In 1975, Terry formed his own band called Christenson, which played a mixture of middle of the road material with strong country/folk overtones. Their debut album, FIRST VISIT, came out in 1975. It was followed by a solo effort called GHOST OF FORTY THIEVES in 1976. Other albums and singles were released throughout the 1980s, notably *Summer Heart*.

Singles

Goodbye Old Man 1975
Where The Water Meets The Sky Over The Blues 1984
Never Feeling More At Home 1985
Fire In The Snow 1985
Jack Of All Trades 1986
Runnin' With The Blues 1987
Summer Heart 1987
Singin' Blue 1987/88
The Moment I'm Gone 1988

Albums

FIRST VISIT (as CHRISTENSON) 1975
GHOST OF FORTY THIEVES 1976
SPIRIT OF THE NORTH 1978
TAWNA . . . FOREST PHANTOM 1979

IT'S HIGH TIME (as COYOTE) 1980
FIRE IN THE SNOW 1985
SUMMER HEART 1987

Cindy Church

Cindy first made her mark as co-founder of The Great Western Orchestra. From Bible Hill, Nova Scotia, she first started performing when she was seventeen years old. In 1993 she recorded *A Song For Brent,* in honor of Brent Berezay who became a quadriplegic when he was thrown from his horse during a roping event at a rodeo. Proceeds from the recording went to Song For Brent Society that benefits injured quadriplegics.

In 1994 she released her debut album, LOVE ON THE RANGE, which featured the hit, *This October Day*. That same year, she joined Sylvia Tyson, Colleen Peterson, and Caitlin Hanford to form Quartette. (See THE GREAT WESTERN ORCHESTRA, QUARTETTE)

Singles
The Road To Home 1992
A Song For Brent 1993
Rockabilly Heart 1994
Love On The Range 1994
This October Day 1994/95
My Wishing Room 1995
Still A Fool 1995
Never Got Over You 1995/96
Trying To Rope The Wind 1995

CDs
Love On The Range 1994
Just A Little Rain 1995

The City Slickers

GREG LAW ("Wichita") (*vocals, lead guitar*)
ROGER LAW ("Arkansas") (*vocals, bass*)
WILL MCGONEGAL (*vocals, guitar, keyboards, mandolin*)
LARRY SEVERIN ("L.T.") (*vocals, acoustic guitar*)
JIM SHERWOOD ("Slim Jim") (*vocals, drums*)

Based in Kingston, Ontario, The City Slickers started in December 1991 when Larry Severin and Jim Sherwood decided to form their own group. The addition of Joe Brady made it a trio. In 1992 they became a quartet when Duffy King (vocals, lead guitar) joined.

After more personnel changes, they ended up with their present lineup. In 1992 they went to Nashville to record their first, self-titled independent cassette. *G'Day, Workin' Are Ya* and *I'm Going To The Bingo* are two of the group's most requested songs.

Singles
G'Day, Workin' Are Ya 1992
Devil's On The Other Line 1992
I'm Going To The Bingo 1995

Cassette
THE CITY SLICKERS 1992

Terri Clark Terri Clark was born in Montreal, Quebec. Raised in Medicine Hat, Alberta, she first picked up the guitar at age nine. Her maternal grandparents, Ray and Betty Gauthier, were stars of the Canadian country music circuit and opened shows for such *Grand Ole Opry* stars as Little Jimmy Dickens, George Jones, and Johnny Cash.

In 1987 Terri moved to Nashville where she worked as a singer at a club called *Tootsie's.* Longtime friend Keith Stegall, Mercury Records Vice President of A&R, helped get her signed to a recording contract with the label in May 1994. Her self-titled debut album came out in 1995.

Singles *Better Things To Do* 1995 *When Boy Meets Girl* 1995/96

CD TERRI CLARK 1995

Sam Crosby and The Cavalry Born and raised in Port Colborne, Ontario, Sam Crosby was discovered by Canadian-born singer/songwriter/producer Ralph Murphy in a Nashville nightclub called *The Sutler.* Trained in voice, dance and piano, it is her winning personality and vocal demeanor that distinguish Sam's talent. Her debut album, *No Turnin' Back*, was released in 1995.

Singles *What Are You Dreaming Tonight* 1995 *No Turnin' Back* 1995

CD NO TURNIN' BACK 1995

Stew Clayton Born and raised on a farm in Manitou, Manitoba, Stew Clayton sang songs about life on the Canadian Prairies and the lives of people he knew. He received his first guitar at eighteen years of age and taught himself to play it. Growing up he listened to Jimmie Rodgers, the Original Carter Family, Vernon Dalhart, Wilf Carter, and Hank Snow.

In late 1952 he met his future wife and singing partner Marge Redpath at an old-time fiddling contest. Two years later they were married. They have been entertaining audiences with their homespun country music ever since. Sunshine Records gave Stew the title of The Canadian Balladeer.

Singles
Little Arctic Sweetheart 1964
Renfrew Valley 1973
The Canadian Farmer 1979
The Farmer's Alphabet 1987

Albums
THE DYNAMIC 1965
THE MANITOBA BALLADEER 1974
COUNTRY 1975
MY CANADIAN HOME 1973
DOWN HOME COUNTRY 1979
I'M PROUD TO BE COUNTRY 1981
THE CANADIAN BALLADEER STEW CLAYTON SINGS 1985
COUNTRY PICKIN' & SINGIN' (with MARG CLAYTON) n.d.
THE FARMER 1986

Cassettes
THE FARMER VOL. 2 1987
TRIBUTE TO THE STARS 1989
CHRISTMAS MEMORIES 1989
JUST LET ME SING & YODEL 1990
TRADITIONAL COUNTRY OLD & NEW 1991
OLD TIME GOSPEL 1993
TRIBUTE TO WILF CARTER 1994

Don Cochrane

Don Cochrane began playing the guitar in local country bands when he was a teenager. Born in Kingston, Ontario, he started to write songs in 1964 when he met fellow musician Doug Ballard. They collaborated together on two songs, *Whistle On The River* and *Uncle Tom*, which were later recorded by The Mercey Brothers.

Doug and Don later formed The Murney Tower Trio with Diane Kempton. With the addition of Chris Hill, the group's name changed to The Murney Tower Singers. They broke up in 1967.

Don O'Neill, who played bass in Ralph Carlson's backup group The Country Mile, invited Cochrane to join in 1971. After three years, he left to concentrate on a solo career. In 1977 his self-titled debut album was released on Snocan Records. That same year, he formed his own backup group called Sweet Clover. When they disbanded in 1983, Don became a real estate broker in Kingston.

Singles
Manitoba 1977
Country Music Isn't Country Anymore 1977
Sweet Clover 1978
It Takes More Than Love 1978/79
The Eagle (Bobby's Song) 1979

Albums
DON COCHRANE 1977
SWEET CLOVER 1978

Tex Cochrane

Gordon D. (Tex) Cochrane was born in Sweet's Corner, Nova Scotia on June 15, 1914. He first became interested in the guitar from a neighbor named Cecil Flynn, who used to play for old-time country dances with his brother Leslie. The Flynns helped Tex learn to play the guitar, and soon he had his own radio show at CHNS in Halifax. Its success encouraged him to pursue a career in music. He had another radio show on CFCY in Charlottetown which was sponsored by Mother's Own Tea. It was during this time that he met George Chappelle, leader of the Merry Islanders, an old-time dance band. He asked Tex to join them. They toured Prince Edward Island, New Brunswick, and Nova Scotia.

By 1937 he had started to write his own songs, which he recorded for RCA Victor in Montreal. When World War II broke out, he joined the reserve signal unit in Charlottetown and later the regular force. When he retired in 1963, he decided not to resume his country music career, and worked at various trucking companies. He was manager of sales and public relations for M and D Transport in Fredericton when he retired in 1979.

Singles

Twilight Yodel Song 1937
Silvery Moon Guide Me Homeward 1938
Goin' Home In Twilight 1938
The Fate Of My Texas Rose 1939
Echo Yodel Lullaby 1939
My Little Prairie Pal 1939
My Home On The Montana Range 1939
Christmas On The Range 1940

Album

PICKIN', SINGIN' 'N' YODELIN' CANADIAN WESTERN STYLE 1985

Coda The West

CRAIG BIGNELL (*drums*)
BURKE CARROLL (*steel and acoustic guitars*)
WENDELL FERGUSON (*lead and acoustic guitars*)
HELENA KAMEKA (*lead vocals, keyboards, acoustic guitar*)
GORD LEMON (*bass*)

Wendell Ferguson and Helen Kameka were the backbone of Coda The West, a Toronto based group that has gone through several personnel changes since their inception in 1987.

For Ferguson, a self-taught musician, music was a large part of his life. In his native Streetsville, Ontario home he grew up listening to The Beatles and later was a member of the 1970s cover band, Storm Crow. Kameka studied piano for ten years at the Royal Conservatory of Music, Burke Carroll majored in trumpet for his Bachelor of Music at the University of Toronto, Gord Lemon studied jazz at Mohawk and Humber Colleges and York University, and Craig Bignell studied the drums privately and was a quick study on other instruments such as the banjo and acoustic guitar.

Their first of several hits was *Over and Done* in 1992. In 1994 their self-titled debut album came out.

Singles

Over And Done 1992
You Gave Up On Me 1992/93
More Of Me (Less Of Lonely) 1993
Don't Be Like That 1993
The Road I Never Took 1994
Coming Soon (To A Heart Near You) 1994/95
To Have And To Hold 1995

CD

CODA THE WEST 1994

Wade Colt

Born and raised in Hamilton, Ontario, Wade Colt began listening to country music as a boy. In the 1960s and 1970s, he played bass guitar for

Dallas Harms, Buddy Knox, the late Ray Smith, and in various bands. After working for three years at a steel plant in Hamilton, he wrote and recorded the song *Steel City* in 1968 under the name of Dave Waco. It was a number one hit on CKCO, the local radio station. In 1976 he returned to the recording studio to make his second single, *Steel City Man.* He also recorded under the name of Waco Kidd.

As Dave Waco:

Singles *Steel City* 1968
Steel City Man 1976
Bottled Blonde 1983

As Waco Kidd:

Single *Good Ole Coke* 1985

As Wade Colt:

Single *Wrong Direction* 1987

Johnny Comfort

Born John Melanson in Moncton, New Brunswick, Johnny Comfort started out in a band called Southern Comfort. In addition to his talents as a singer/songwriter, he was also a versatile entertainer. Backed by a band that bore his name, his self-titled debut album was released in 1981. Two years later, he captured national attention with the single *Still That Something In Her Eyes,* which was written and produced by Terry Carisse.

Singles *Still That Something In Her Eye* 1983
A Scene From An Old Texas Movie 1984
After Forty Pages 1984
This Time The Lovin's On Me 1985
This Could Be Serious 1985

Albums JOHNNY COMFORT 1981
HANK, YOU'RE STILL THE KING 1982

Tommy Common

Ever since he was a young boy, Tommy Common wanted to be an entertainer. Born in Toronto, he was eight years old when he first joined the Saturday afternoon studio audience of the Microphone Moppets radio show with the hope of being chosen to sing on air. At sixteen he was an engineering student at the University of Toronto, but at night he sang with local bands.

In 1954 he auditioned for CBC-TV's *Pick The Stars* but only made it to the semi-finals. He later was successful in landing a spot on *Arthur Godfrey's Talent Scouts* show in the United States.

Tommy's big break came in 1956 when CBC producer Drew Cossan invited him to join the cast of *Country Hoedown.* During the show's nine-year run, he had 7,000 letters a week and the audiences loved him. His popularity led to appearances on other CBC shows, such as *Juliette* and *Singalong Jubilee.* He also opened a string of Teen Tom record stores. Tommy Common was Canada's answer to Pat Boone.

When *Country Hoedown* ended in 1965, the fame and success stopped. He went through a series of personal and professional tragedies. In 1973 the CBC hired him as host of *It's A Musical World* but it lasted only three years. He then went on the road to make ends meet. During his last years his battle with alcoholism, joblessness, bankruptcy, and mental illness all contributed to his suicide on August 14, 1985 in Calgary.

Albums TOMMY COMMON 1965
TOMMY COMMON SINGS 1966
TOMMY COMMON SINGS COUNTRY CLASSICS 1968
WALK RIGHT IN 1973
THE COMMON TOUCH (COLUMBIA) n.d.

Stompin' Tom Connors

Stompin' Tom was born Tom Charles Connors in Saint John, New Brunswick on February 9, 1936. At fourteen he bought his first guitar and began writing songs. While hitch-hiking across Canada as a teenager, he wrote about the people he met and the places where he lived and worked. He wrote about Martin Hartwell, the northern bush pilot whose plane crashed in the far north in 1972 in *The Martin Hartwell Story*, Saturday nights in Sudbury in *Sudbury Saturday Night*, and hockey in *The Hockey Song.* His nickname "Stompin' Tom" came from waiter Boyd McDonald at the King George Hotel in Peterborough.

Connors recorded a number of songs in 1965 on the CKGB Radio label, which he sold off stage to his fans. His first albums were on Rebel Records, THE NORTHLAND'S OWN (1967) and ON TRAGEDY TRAIL (1969). In 1969 he signed to Dominion Records. His first single was *Bud The Spud.*

In 1971 he started Boot Records with Jury Krytiuk, which helped launch the careers of Canadian classical guitarist Liona Boyd and The Canadian Brass. Disillusioned by the Canadian recording industry, which he claimed supported more American artists than Canadian, Stompin' Tom stopped recording and touring in 1978. He also returned all his Juno Awards.

He returned to the recording studio in 1988. The result was the album FIDDLE AND SONG on EMI. The label also re-released all of his older albums on CD.

St. Thomas University in Frederiction awarded Stompin' Tom with an honorary Doctor of Laws degree in 1990.

Singles *Pizza Pie Love* 1965
Yay Canada 1965
Streets Of Toronto 1965
I Saw The Teardrop 1965

Luke's Guitar 1965
Jingle Jangle 1965
Laura 1965
Movin' On To Rouen 1965
Music For A Winter Carnival 1965
Bud The Spud 1969/70
Big Joe Mufferaw 1970
Ketchup Song 1970
Luke's Guitar 1971
Snowmobile Song 1971
My Stompin' Grounds 1971
Tribute To Wilf Carter 1971
The Bridge Came Tumbling Down 1971
Tillsonburg 1971
Name The Capitol 1971/72
Moon Man Newfie 1972
The Bug Song 1972
Fire In The Mine 1972
The Hockey Song 1972
The Consumer 1973
Prince Edward Island, Happy Birthday 1973
The Martin Hartwell Story 1973
Poor Poor Farmer 1973
Algoma Central No. 69 1973
The Don Messer Story 1973/74
To It And At It 1974
Streaker's Dream 1974
Muk Tuk Annie 1974
New Brunswick Mary 1975
Jack Of Many Trades 1976
Canada Day, Up Canada Way 1989
I Am The Wind 1989
Margo's Cargo 1991
Made In The Shade 1991
Johnny Maple 1992
Alberta Rose 1992
The Football Song 1993/94
Blue Berets 1994/95

Albums/CDs

THE NORTHLAND'S OWN 1967
ON TRAGEDY TRAIL 1969
STOMPIN' TOM SINGS 60 OLD TIME FAVORITES (box set) 1969
BUD THE SPUD 1970
STOMPIN' TOM MEETS BIG JOE MUFFERAW 1970
BEST OF 1970
STOMPIN' TOM SINGS 60 MORE OLD TIME FAVORITES (box set) 1971
LIVE AT THE HORSESHOE 1971
PISTOL PACKIN' MAMA 1971
MY STOMPIN' GROUNDS 1971
LOVE AND LAUGHTER 1972
BRINGING THEM BACK 1972
STOMPIN' TOM AND THE HOCKEY SONG 1972
TO IT AND AT IT 1973
ACROSS THIS LAND 1973
MERRY CHRISTMAS EVERYBODY 1973
STOMPIN' TOM MEETS MUK TUK ANNIE 1974
THE NORTH ATLANTIC SQUADRON 1975
THE UNPOPULAR STOMPIN' TOM 1976
AT THE GUMBOOT CLOGGEROO 1977
STOMPIN' TOM FIDDLE AND SONG 1988
A PROUD CANADIAN 1990
MORE OF THE STOMPIN' TOM PHENOMENON 1991
BELIEVE IN YOUR COUNTRY 1992
KIC ALONG WITH STOMPIN' TOM 1993
DR. STOMPIN' TOM . . . EH? 1994
LONG GONE TO THE YUKON 1995

Patricia Conroy

Born and raised in Montreal, Quebec, Patricia Conroy's dream of stardom began at an early age when she gained singing experience in her family's Irish folk group and later in a bluegrass/folk group in Ontario. She moved to Vancouver in 1980, where she began the long road to stardom.

In 1985 she worked in her first country band, and two years later her first single, *My Heart's On Fire,* was released on Rana Records. A self-titled, seven song EP followed in 1988. Two years later, she signed a recording contract with WEA Music of Canada. Her debut album, BLUE ANGEL (1990), was recorded in Toronto.

During the next five years she earned the reputation as one of Canada's top female country artists. The release of her third album, YOU CAN'T RESIST, in the fall of 1994, established her as an international star.

Singles

My Heart's On Fire 1987
Come On Back 1989
A Thousand Trails 1990
This Time 1990
Take Me With You 1991
Blue Angel 1991
You Can't Resist It 1995
What Else Can I Do 1995
Why I'm Walkin' 1991
Bad Day For Trains 1992
What Do You Care 1993
Blank Pages 1993
Here We Go Again 1993/94
Somebody's Leavin' 1994/95
I Don't Wanna Be The One 1995
Keep Me Rockin' 1995/96

CDs

BLUE ANGEL 1990
BAD DAY FOR TRAINS 1992
YOU CAN'T RESIST 1994

Country Hearts

SHEILA FRIESEN (*lead vocals*)
WANDA FRIESEN (*vocals*)
SANDI KLASSEN (*vocals*)

From Altona, Manitoba, Country Hearts was a vocal trio comprised of sisters Sheila and Wanda Friesen and Sandi Klassen.

They discovered the name of their group while traveling on Highway 101, when they heard a song that had lyrics about "country hearts" playing on the car radio. Their first single was the independent release *High High Hopes* in 1990. They recorded their first album, OFF & RUNNIN', in 1992. It contained the singles *Forever Ends At 8:00AM* and *Lonely Shade of Blue.*

Singles

High High Hopes 1990
Blue Crystal Waters 1991
Forever Ends At 8:00AM 1992
Lonely Shade Of Blue 1993

Album

OFF & RUNNIN' 1992

D

Ted Daigle

Born and raised in Jacket River, New Brunswick on January 16, 1937, Ted Daigle first picked up the guitar when he was in public school. By the time he graduated from high school, he was an accomplished musician, and held two careers as a radio personality and entertainer. His first job as an announcer was at CKBC in Bathurst, New Brunswick in the early 1950s. From 1958 to 1960 he worked at CJLX in Thunder Bay, where he recorded with the Midnighters, a country and rock and roll band.

In 1960 he moved to Ottawa, where he worked at CKOY. A year later, he formed his own backup group The Music Men who were one of the most well-known bands in the Ottawa Valley. He switched from CKOY to CKBY and was instrumental in the latter station becoming full-time country on July 2, 1972.

During this time The Music Men disbanded and Daigle worked full-time as an announcer. In 1988 he was inducted into the Ottawa Valley Country Music Hall Of Fame. He left CKBY in 1995.

Singles
Not Enough To Go Around 1968
Lawley Rae 1975
Before You Leave Today 1976

Albums
TEENAGE TIME WITH TED DAIGLE 1961
12 MILLION MEMORIES 1966
COLOR ME COUNTRY 1968
RUBY 1968
WESTERN HITS — REMEMBER ME? 1969
WESTERN SONGS — IT'S ME, T.D. 1970

Dick Damron

While growing up on his family's farm in Bentley, Alberta, Dick Damron's first exposure to country music was Wilf Carter on the radio. At age five Dick received his first guitar and was soon performing at local talent shows, Christmas concerts, and benefits. He quit school when he was fourteen.

In December 1955 he devoted all his time to music, and three years later he recorded his first single, *Gonna Have A Party*. With his own group The Night Riders he played rockabilly every Saturday night in town halls throughout Alberta until 1961. Four years later, he organized a country group called The Hitch-Hikers.

The 1970 single *Countryfied* established Damron as a country hitmaker, and for the next few years he was in his glory. With the release of the album HIGH ON YOU in 1980, his music became a mature mix of moods and styles, the work of a true country artist. He was inducted into the Canadian Country Music Association Hall of Honor in 1994.

Singles

Gonna Have A Party 1958
The Cold Gray Winds Of Autumn 1968
Countryfied 1970
Rise 'n' Shine 1971
The Long Green Line 1972
Going Home To The Country 1972/73
The Prophet 1973
The Cowboy And The Lady 1974
Bitter Sweet Songs 1974
Mother, Love & Country 1975
Good Ol' Fashioned Memories 1976
On The Road 1976
Waylon's T-Shirt 1977
Susan Flowers 1977
Charing Cross Cowboys 1978
Whiskey Jack 1978
My Good Woman 1978
Silver And Shine 1978/79
High On You 1979
The Ballad Of T.J.'s 1979/80
Dollars 1980
If You Need Me Lord 1981
Midnite Flytes 1981
Reunion 1981/82
Honky Tonk Angels And Good Ol' Boys 1982
Good Ol' Time Country Rock And Roll 1982
Jesus, It's Me Again 1982/83
I'm Not Ready For The Blues 1983
Ridin' Shotgun 1984
A Little More Country Music 1984
Don't Touch Him 1984/85
Last Dance On A Saturday Night 1985
Falling In And Out Of Love (with GINNY MITCHELL) 1985
Rise Against The Wind 1985/86
Masquerade 1986
1955 1987
Hotel Mexico 1987
You'd Still Be Here Today 1987
Cinderella & The Gingerbread Man 1987
St. Mary's Angel 1988
Here We Are Again 1988
The Legend And The Legacy 1989
Ain't No Trains To Nashville 1989/90
Farewell To Arms 1990
Mid-Nite Cowboy Blues 1990
Wild Horses & Honky Tonk Nights 1991
A Rose By The River 1991
Hold On Tight 1992
Free Love 1993
Midnite Madness 1993
As Far As I Can See (duet with BRENT MCATHEY) 1995/96

Albums

DICK DAMRON 1967
LONESOME CITY 1967
COUNTRYFIED 1973
NORTHWEST REBELLION (& ROY WARHURST) 1974
THE COWBOY AND THE LADY 1975
SOLDIER OF FORTUNE 1975
NORTH COUNTRY SKYLINE 1977
LOST IN THE MUSIC 1978
HIGH ON YOU 1980
LIFE STORY 1980
THE BEST OF DICK DAMRON 1981
HONKY TONK ANGEL 1982
LAST DANCE ON A SATURDAY NIGHT 1984
NIGHT MUSIC 1987
DICK DAMRON (RCA) 1988
THE LEGEND AND THE LEGACY 1989

CDs

MIRAGE 1992
WINGS UPON THE WIND 1993
TOUCH THE SKY 1994
DICK DAMRON — THE ANTHOLOGY 1995

Stu Davis

Stu Davis was born David Stewart in 1921 in Boggy Creek, Saskatchewan. At seventeen, he won a radio talent audition, and to avoid embarrassing his family, he changed his name to Stu Davis. In 1939 he teamed up with his brother Fred to form The Harmony Boys. They also hosted their own radio show on CHCH in Regina. With the outbreak of World War II, Stu joined The Royal Canadian Air Force and Fred joined The Canadian Army. An honorable discharge in 1942 allowed Stu to continue his music career, and he returned to CHCH. He moved to Calgary in 1945, where he appeared on *The Buckhorn Ranch Chuckwagon* and hosted his own show on CFCN Calgary. That same year, he met Wilf Carter, who arranged for Stu to record with Sonora Records the following year. His first recordings included the popular *What A Fool I Was,* which was later a big hit for Eddy Arnold in 1948. In 1949 Stu hosted the radio show *Country Corral* on CJCA in Edmonton, Alberta.

Throughout the 1950s he recorded for Apex Records in Montreal and Aragon Records in Vancouver. From 1956 to 1964 he hosted several country shows on CBC, such as *The Stu Davis Show*, *Swing Your Partner*, *Rope Around The Sun*, and *Red River Jamboree.* During Canada's centennial year, Stu recorded THE STU DAVIS CENTENNIAL ALBUM.

In 1987 Cattle Records in Germany released the tribute album LET'S GO BACK TO THE COUNTRY WITH CANADA'S COWBOY TROUBADOUR. Stu Davis retired in the late 1980s.

Singles

What A Fool I Was (To Ever Let You Go) 1946
I Tipped My Hat And Slowly Walked Away 1946
The Bottom Fell Out Of The Sky 1946
Crossroads 1946
Land, Sky And Water 1946
When The Snowbirds Cross The Rockies 1948
The Dude In The Ten Gallon Hat 1948
Too Far Apart 1948
I'm Gonna Leave Town 1948
Crying For You 1948
Deserted 1949
Child Of Divorce 1949
I Looked For Love 1949
In Daddy's Footsteps 1949
Canadian Waltz 1949
Why Should I Send You Flowers? 1949
Fate Of The Flying Enterprise 1950
Lovelorn Heart 1950
Parking Meter Blues 1950
Three Little Secrets 1950
I Went To Your Wedding 1952

Albums

STU DAVIS INVITES YOU TO SADDLE YOUR WORRIES TO A SONG 1957
ROPE AROUND THE SUN 1958
STU DAVIS' CENTENNIAL ALBUM 1967
THE TRAIL RIDIN' TROUBADOUR 1971
LET'S GO BACK TO THE COUNTRY 1987
STU DAVIS SALUTES THE WESTERN STARS VOL I. n.d.
THE TOUCH OF GOD'S HAND— FEATURING STU & FRED & THE HARMONY BOYS n.d.
STU DAVIS SALUTES THE WESTERN STARS VOL II. n.d.
BOOTHILL BALLADS AND SONGS OF THE COWBOY TROUBADOUR n.d.
JUST PLAIN FOLKS n.d.
STU DAVIS IN NASHVILLE HOOTENANNY — FEATURING DUANE ON GUITAR AND BANJO n.d.
STU DAVIS SOUVENIRS — FEATURING DUANE AND THE PATHFINDERS n.d.
STU DAVIS SHOW — DUANE AND THE PATHFINDERS n.d.
SONGS FROM THE HEART OF JOHNNY CANUCK n.d.

The Debenham Brothers

BILL DEBENHAM
DAVE DEBENHAM
JIM DEBENHAM

The Debenham brothers were all born in Toronto, Ontario. When they were in their teens they moved to Renfrew, Ontario, where the trio worked at local events. In 1989 they recorded their first single, *Forever,* on the Altair Four label.

In 1992 they changed their name to Roll 'n' Thunder. The lineup was comprised of Dave Debenham on rhythm guitar and vocals, Derek Gauthier on drums, Dean Lavoy on bass, Phil Denault on lead vocals and lead guitar, and Ted Gerow of The Staccatos and Five Man Electrical Band fame on keyboards and vocals.

As The Debenham Brothers:

Singles

Forever 1989
Dreaming Of You 1989/90
Heart Of Stone 1990
Will My Heart Survive 1990/91
Long Term Lover 1992

CD

IF YOU CAN HEAR ME 1990

As Roll 'n' Thunder:

Singles

I'm Goin' To Fight For You 1993
Summertime In The Country 1993
Flyin' Again 1994
We Owned This Town 1995

Andy Dejarlis

Born in Woodbridge, Manitoba in 1916, Andy Dejarlis learned to play the fiddle when he was fifteen. He won his first fiddling contest when he was seventeen, the same year he moved to Winnipeg. At London Records he recorded more than thirty albums. In 1968 he was awarded the city of Winnipeg's Community Service Award. He died on September 18, 1975.

Singles

Whiskey Before Breakfast 1957
Nobody's Business 1957
Interlake Waltz 1957

Albums

CANADIAN FIDDLE TUNES 1958
ANDY'S CENTENNIAL ALBUM 1967
JOLLY OLD TIME MUSIC n.d.
TRAVELLING WEST n.d.
BACKWOODS FIDDLE TUNES n.d.
RED RIVER ECHOES n.d.
CANADIAN OLD TIME MUSIC n.d.
OLD TIME WALTZES n.d.
HAPPY OLD DAYS n.d.
AND HIS EARLY SETTLERS n.d.
ORIGINAL OLD TIME MUSIC n.d.
LET'S DO TWO STEPS n.d.
FAVORITE OLD TIME TUNES n.d.
SQUARE DANCE CALLS n.d.
TRIBUTE TO JIM MAGILLN.D.
DOMINO LES FEMMES ONT CHAUD n.d.
TOUR DE DANSE n.d.
EARLY SETTLERS OLD TIME TUNES n.d.
GOOD OLD TIME MUSIC n.d.
CHAINEZ LES HOMMES n.d.
RED RIVER ECHOES VOL II n.d.
SQUARE DANCE WITH . . . n.d.
POLKA TIME n.d.
MANITOBA GOLDEN BOY n.d.
FIDDLING FANTASTIC n.d.
SWING YOUR PARTNERS n.d.
TURN OF THE CENTURY n.d.
TRAVELLING WEST n.d.
THE HAPPY OLD DAYS n.d.
WALTZING AT IT'S BEST n.d.

Jack Diamond

Jack Diamond was born Ted Hawkins in Hamilton, Ontario in 1956. His father was a drummer in a marching band, and it wasn't long before young Ted was learning on his own set of coronet drums. By the time he was fifteen, he had made his first public performance at the grand opening of a pizza restaurant. He had also become equally proficient on the guitar.

His first single was a remake of The Hollies' 1972 hit *Long Cool Woman.* Other hits followed such as *Heartwreck* and *Holdin' On For Dear Life.*

Singles

Long Cool Woman 1988
Rescue Me 1988/89
Heartwreck 1989
Stoned To The Bone (with THE BLUES) 1989/90
Love Me Back Together 1990
Holdin' On For Dear Life 1991
The Bottom Line 1992
Money In My Pocket 1992
Hometown Girl 1992
Giving Up On You 1992
Watcha Thinkin' Now 1993
Waiting For A Green Light 1993

CD THE DIAMOND IS JACK 1991

The Dixie Flyers

BERT BAUMBACH (*guitar, vocals*)
MIKE ETHELSTON (*mouth-harp, vocals*)
WALTER MAYNARD (*banjo, vocals*)
KEN PALMER (*mandolin, vocals*)
DAVE ZDRILUK (*bass, vocals*)

Based in London, Ontario, The Dixie Flyers started in 1974 when Bert Baumbach and Ken Palmer wanted to form a band. Included in the original lineup were Willie P. Bennett on harmonica, banjo player Denis LePage, and Brian Abbey on acoustic bass. During the next twenty years there were many personnel changes, with Baumbach and Palmer remaining as the group's mainstays.

On their first two albums (LIGHT, MEDIUM, & HEAVY and CHEAPER TO LEASE), their repertoire consisted of the traditional bluegrass of Bill Monroe and Flatt and Scruggs. By their third album (JUST PICKIN'), they had started to use their own material, which consisted of instrumentals and turning classic country songs like Claude King's *Wolverton Mountain* into bluegrass.

The Dixie Flyers were the first Canadian band to play at the famous Bill Monroe Bean Blossom Festival in Indiana in 1983.

Singles *Sneakin' Chickens* 1978
Gumboot Cloggeroo 1979

Albums LIGHT, MEDIUM, HEAVY 1977
CHEAPER TO LEASE 1978
JUST PICKIN' 1979
FOR OUR FRIENDS 1980
FIVE BY FIVE 1982
NEW HORIZONS 1984
BUSINESS AS USUAL 1987
LIVE AT THE WELLINGTON 1990

Freddy Dixon

Freddy Dixon was born and raised in Perth, Ontario. He formed his first country group, The Diplomats, in 1963. They were a popular group in the Ottawa Valley and later became known as The Friday Afternoon. In 1968 his debut album, A TRIBUTE TO JOHNNY CASH, was released. He signed a contract with Rodeo Records in the early 1970s and scored a hit with the single, *Jim's Used Car Lot*, which was inspired by Dixon's personal experience with used car dealers.

One of his songs, *The Last Fatal Duel* (which was the flip side to the single *All Over Again*) was a story about two law students on the banks of the Tay River in Perth, who challenged each other to a duel over a pretty schoolteacher named Elizabeth Hughes. Stompin' Tom recorded the song on his album, STOMPIN' TOM AND THE HOCKEY SONG.

Singles *Jim's Used Car Lot* 1971
All Over Again 1971
Just Another Step 1972
The Ballad Of Stompin' Tom 1973
Brothers And Sisters 1973
Things Have Changed 1976
Take It From Me 1978
Telecaster Cowboy 1982
Blues In Me 1994

Albums A TRIBUTE TO JOHNNY CASH 1968
FRED DIXON & THE FRIDAY AFTERNOON (SBS 5408) 1972
FRED DIXON & THE FRIDAY AFTERNOON (SBS 5415) 1973
FREDDY DIXON: COUNTRY AND PROUD OF IT 1976
LIVING ON THE EDGE 1994

Donna & Leroy

LEROY ANDERSON
DONNA RAMSAY

As a boy in Belzac, Alberta, Leroy Anderson heard Earl Scruggs' banjo in *The Ballad of Jed Clampett*, the theme of *The Beverly Hillbillies* TV show, and was amazed by its sound. Since there was no one around who could teach him, he taught himself how to play the banjo. He later moved to Calgary, where he worked in a music store by day and played in coffeehouses and pizza parlors as part of a bluegrass duo. In 1968 Gary Buck discovered Leroy and took him to RCA Records. After a demo session, he was signed to the label. He recorded under the name of Lee Roy. Dallas Harms later hired him as a guitarist.

Donna Ramsay was born in Sault Ste. Marie, Ontario. She learned to play the piano as a young girl, and often played with her father on a local TV show. While attending high school she often went to Kitchener to appear on Gary Buck's TV show.

Buck invited her home to meet Leroy, who was then a member of Harms' backup band. After graduating from high school, she worked with The Chaparrels, Roy Warhurst, and Gary Buck before Harms hired her to join his band.

In 1972 Donna and Leroy were married. They soon left Harms to start their own band called Harmony Road, and later became regulars on *The Tommy Hunter Show.* Donna and Leroy released their first album, LIVIN' ON LOVE, in 1981.

As Lee Roy:

Singles *The Sweetest Thing This Side Of Heaven* 1973
Orphan Princess 1974
Lonely Willow 1975
Matthew 1975
Belzac Boogie 1976

As Donna Ramsay:

Singles

I Won't Change For You 1969
Bitter Sweet 1969
Cool Green Waters 1970
I'll Be A Rover 1973
The Familiar Old Way 1976
Before You Say Goodbye 1977

Album COOL GREEN WATERS 1970

As Donna and Leroy:

Singles

I Believe In You 1981
So Much To Be Happy For 1981
Livin' On Love 1981
Sweet Reminder 1983
I've Finally Learned How To Dance 1986
Two Gypsies 1987
You're So Easy To Love 1987/88
I Want You To Wanna Do 1988
Sweet Sensation 1989
Let's Mend It (DONNA ANDERSON) 1990
Love Just Made A Liar Out Of Me (LEROY ANDERSON) 1990
I Need You More Than Ever Now 1990
Street Hearts 1991
Let's Make A Memory 1991
Just Another Miracle (LEROY ANDERSON) 1991/92
Heartaches By The Number 1992
If This Is Freedom (LEROY ANDERSON) 1993

Album LIVIN' ON LOVE 1981

Double Eagle Band

CHARLIE BRENNAN (*vocals, guitar*)
ED DYRDA (*drums*)
KEITH HADDAD (*vocals, guitar*)
MIKE KUZYK (*vocals, guitar*)
GEORGE YOURCHEK (*vocals, guitar, sax*)
GUY DYER (*vocals, bass*)

Originally a sextet, The Double Eagle Band formed in Winnipeg in 1981. Mike Kuzyk left the limelight of the stage to manage the group in 1983. He was also the band's principal songwriter.

Their country/rock/bluegrass sound caught on after the release of their first hit single, *Fiery Feelin'*, in June 1982.

Singles

Fiery Feelin' 1982
Pickin' Chicken Music 1982/83
Play The Ponies 1983
Enough Is Enough 1984
Homegrown 1986
Aimie 1987
God Bless The Farmer 1988/89

Album FIRE ON THE PRAIRIE 1987

Debbie Drummond

Debbie Drummond was born and raised on a family farm near Birchton, a small village in the Eastern Townships of Quebec. At age seven she wrote her first song, and at eighteen formed her own band. In January 1985 she went to Nashville to record her first two singles, *Just Another Song On The Radio* and *Breaking All The Rules.* Two years later, Bookshop Records released her debut album, STARSHINE.

Singles

- *Just Another Song On The Radio* 1985
- *Breaking All The Rules* 1985
- *Your Love Slows Me Down* 1987
- *It's The Lovers Who Give Love A Bad Name* 1988
- *Don't Hang Up* 1988
- *Starshine* 1989
- *You Could Be Dangerous* 1989
- *Making Up For Lost Time* 1990
- *Every Little Thing* 1990
- *Eyes For This Guy* 1991

Album STARSHINE 1987

E

Eagle Feather

JIM AUGUSTINE (*vocals, keyboards*)
KELLY BUOTE (*vocals, lead guitar*)
JIM GALLANT (*drums*)
BRYON SIMON (*bass*)
HUBERT FRANCIS (*lead vocals*)

This sextet from Big Cove, New Brunswick scored in both Canada and the United States with their debut single, *Lady of the Evening*, in 1991. They were discovered by producer/agent Doc Holiday while working at a country club in Prince Edward Island.

Singles

Lady Of The Evening 1991
Rendezvous 1991
Mother Earth 1995

Eddie Eastman

Eddie Eastman was born Edward Rowsell in Terra Nova, Newfoundland. By the time he was seven years old he had learned the guitar. At seventeen he was lead singer in a rock band called The Ducats. When they broke up in 1975, he moved to Mississauga, Ontario, where he became lead singer of The Terra Nova Express, a country band. He later befriended Bob Cousins of Bel Air Records, who suggested Eddie change his last name from Rowsell to Eastman. His debut single on Bel Air was *Eastbound 401* in 1977.

After a string of hit singles that included *Easy* and *Intimate Strangers*, he signed with Artisan Records in Nashville. His debut album, THE WINNING SIDE, in 1985 made him a star.

Singles

Eastbound 401 1977/78
That's All I Want From You 1978
The Other Side Of Town 1978
Easy 1979
Love Is Such An Easy Word To Say 1979
Gone Out In Style 1979
I Think I'll Say Goodbye 1979/80
Lifting Me Up Letting Me Down 1980
Your Used To Be 1980
How Deep In Love Am I 1981
It Will Never Be The Same Again 1981
Nobody Quite Like You 1981/82
Intimate Strangers 1982
From The Barroom To The Bedroom 1982
Loving You, Needing You 1983
Sherida 1983
Lost In Your Love 1983/84
Dreaming All Over Again 1985
Take A Chance On Me 1985
How Close Am I To Losing You (with CARROLL BAKER) 1985
Mountains Too High To Climb 1986
Don't Hold Back 1986
Last Flight To Denver 1986/87
You Have Filled The Days With 1987
Lying In Your Bed 1988
Baby's Got A Brand New Car 1990

Big Fool For Lovin' You 1991
Runaway Heart 1991
Smack Dab (In The Middle) 1991/92
Head Over Heels 1992
Trying To Make A Living 1992
It's Not That Easy 1993
Cowboy Shuffle 1993

Albums EASY 1979
EDDIE EASTMAN 1980
INTIMATE STRANGERS 1982
THE WINNING SIDE 1985
GREATEST HITS 1987

Gerry Edge

Born and raised in Montreal, Gerry Edge first became interested in country music when he attended the University of Prince Edward Island on a football scholarship. After graduation he started playing and writing songs, and later was invited to perform at parties, clubs, and country fairs. In 1994 his self-titled debut album was released on the independent Kee Production label, which was recorded at The Reflections Studios in Nashville, Tennessee.

Singles *Seemed Like The Right Thing To Do* 1994

CD GERRY EDGE 1994

June Eikhard

Canada's "First Lady Of The Fiddle" was born June Marguerite Cameron in Moncton, New Brunswick. Growing up in a musical family, she learned how to play the piano, the accordion, steel guitar, and bass guitar. The Cameron family moved to Sackville, where June met Cecil Eikhard, whom she married in 1952. Together they formed their own band called The Tantramar Ramblers, who toured the Maritime Provinces and played at concerts, dances, and radio shows.

In 1959 June recorded her first album appropriately titled CANADA'S FIRST LADY OF THE FIDDLE, which contained several of her own tunes. A year later she made her second album, JUNE EIKHARD, on Bronco.

June and her family moved to Oshawa in the early 1960s, where she continued to play in various groups as well as record. Her daughter Shirley Eikhard went on to have a successful career in the pop field in the 1970s and 1980s.

Albums CANADA'S FIRST LADY OF THE FIDDLE 1959 (Independent)
JUNE EIKHARD 1960
CANADA'S FIRST LADY OF THE FIDDLE 1969 (Banff)

Carl Elliott

Carl Elliott grew up in the village of Economy in Colchester County, Nova Scotia. With Mrs. Elliott on the piano and organ, the entire family spent evenings singing and learning to play various instruments. Carl and his three brothers played in a square dance band that played in the area.

In 1948 the Elliott family moved to Ontario and Carl played in various country and western groups. He then joined Ramblin' Ross Allen at jamborees and dances and was a featured musician on Allen's 1960 Arc album, MEMORIES OF HANK WILLIAMS. This led to Carl's debut album on Arc called SQUARE DANCE TONITE in 1962. A second Arc album followed in 1964, DOWN EAST DANCIN'.

During the summer of 1972 he moved back to Economy, Nova Scotia, where he still played occasionally. In 1984 he recorded the cassette, DOWN HOME FIDDLE FAVORITES.

Albums

SQUARE DANCE TONITE 1962
DOWN EAST DANCIN' 1964
OLD TYME FIDDLE FAVORITES 1965
GOOD OLD DOWN HOME FIDDLIN' 1972
FIDDLIN' DOWN HOME 1973
MORE FIDDLE FAVORITES 1977
DOWN HOME FIDDLE FAVORITES 1984

Ellis Family Band

BRIAN ELLIS (*rhythm guitar, fiddle, vocals*)
DAVE ELLIS (*lead guitar, vocals*)
RICK ELLIS (*lead vocals, drums*)
STEVE ELLIS (*lead vocals, percussion*)
GREG MACDONALD (*bass, vocals*)

Growing up in their hometown of St. Eleanor's, Prince Edward Island, the Ellis Family Band had a natural talent to perform and all shared a common interest in country music. Their father Russell was a legendary fiddle player, and it was he who added Greg MacDonald to complete the sound of the band.

In 1980 they won a talent contest sponsored by CFQM in Moncton. Three years later, they were in Nashville to record their debut single, *Easy To Love.* It was the first in a string of hits between 1983 and 1990.

Singles

Easy To Love 1983/84
Back On The Bottom Again 1984
Can't You See What You're Doing To Me 1984
I Love You 1985
Don't Tease Me 1985/86
Why Am I Still Crying 1986
Summer Nights Are Made For Lovers 1986
Our Love 1987
She Keeps Pulling Me Back 1987/88
Thank You For Being My Friend 1988
Mother Of Mine 1988
Don't You Cry For Me 1988/89
You Are The One 1989/90
Out Of Control 1991

Albums EASY TO LOVE 1984
SUMMER NIGHTS 1986
HEART ON FIRE 1989

Allen Erwin

Allen Erwin, the youngest of a family of seven, was born in Portal, Saskatchewan. As a young boy he earned extra money playing the fiddle at local dances. When he finished school he went to Peace River, Alberta, where he rode for legendary cattle baron Pat Burns, and apprenticed as a cowboy. Allen was later encouraged to try the rodeo circuit, and his prowess as a bronc-buster earned him the nickname "The Calgary Kid."

While ranching he became interested in cowboy music and demonstrated a natural flair for the guitar. In 1935 he recorded with Cactus Mack and his Saddle Tramps, and in the early 1940s Erwin had his own show on WFAA in Dallas, Texas. He later had a show on CKTB in St. Catharines, Ontario.

Hollywood beckoned and he found himself hired as a stuntman in several "B" westerns. He was also a story consultant with Walt Disney.

In 1943 he published his first song folio, *Stampede of Songs*, which he recorded on a series of Apex 78s. Fascinated by the history of the west, he wrote a biography of legendary frontiersman John Slaughter. Erwin died in Arizona in the early 1980s.

Singles
Why Have You Gone And Broke My Heart?/The Tenderfoot's Warning 1941
Move On, Little Doggies, Move On/Don't Leave Me Heartbroken Alone 1941
Bow River Valley/Darling Please Tell Me Why 1942
I'm A Cowboy That's Never BeenThrown/Punchin' Cowboys On The 76 1943
The Dying Cowboy's Farewell/I'm Sorry We Ever Met 1943
Riders Of Liberty/I'll Never See My Darling Anymore 1944
My Heart Keeps On Yearning For You/The Dude Ranch Cowboy 1944
Old Kentucky Moon/Out On The Western Range 1945
Going Back To Peaceful Valley/My Indiana Moon 1945

As Allen Erwin & His Orchestra:

Single
She's My Little Lady/Rose Of Old Cheyenne 1947

As Allen Erwin & His Frontier Scouts:

Single
The Cowboy's Lament/Way Out Yonder 1947

F

Family Brown

BARRY BROWN (*guitar*)
JOE BROWN (*guitar, vocals*)
LAWANDA BROWN (*vocals*)
TRACEY BROWN (*vocals*)
DAVE DENNISON (*guitar*)
RON SPARLING (*drums*)

The history of The Family Brown goes back to 1968 when Papa Joe Brown decided to form a singing group. He had years of experience as a musician since he started in the late 1940s as a member of The Hillbilly Jewels. When they broke up in the mid-1950s, he moved to Ontario where he organized The Happy Wanderers, who were regulars on *Country Jamboree*, a radio show broadcast live from CHML, Hamilton. During this time Brown also began recording.

The Family Brown consisted of Joe, son Barry, daughters Lawanda and Tracey, guitarist Dave Dennison, and drummer Ron Sparling. In 1971 they recorded their first single, *RR #2*, on MCA Records. The following year they signed with RCA. From 1972 to 1990 they had more than forty hits, including *Family Love*, *If You Keep Throwing Dirt*, *It's Really Love This Time*, and *Til I Find My Love*. Jack Feeney was the group's producer.

On May 30, 1986 Joe died suddenly after finishing a show in Chesley, Ontario. The Family Brown broke up in 1990.

Tracey Brown returned to the studio as Tracey Prescott and Lonesome Daddy, with her husband Randall Prescott and her brother Barry Brown. Their self-titled debut album on Columbia/Sony produced several singles, notably *When You're Not Lovin' Me*, in 1992. They later changed their name to Prescott Brown, and released the album ALREADY RESTLESS in 1994. Barry Brown left in the fall of 1995.

As Family Brown:

Singles

R R #2 1971
Family Love 1972
Yes, Jesus Loves Me 1972
The Feeling's Too Strong 1973
Ninety Acre Farm 1973
Love Is Simple 1974
Kids In The Kitchen 1974
A Touch Of God 1975
I Am The Words 1975
Light At The End Of The Hall 1976
If You Keep Throwing Dirt 1976
Sing A Song Of Love 1977
Jukebox Lover 1977
Lovin' Fool 1977
You're The Light 1978
Love Is A Contact Sport 1978
The Way I Love You 1979
Stay With Me 1979
Love Was On Our Side 1979/80
But It's Cheating 1980
It's Really Love This Time 1980
Ribbon Of Gold 1981
Another Broken Hearted Melody 1981
But It's Cheating 1982
Some Never Stand A Chance 1982
Raised On Country Music 1982
Wouldn't You Love Us Together Again 1986
Memorized By Heart 1983

We Really Got A Hold On Love 1983
Repeat After Me 1984
Did You Know 1984
Straight Forward Love Affair 1984
Comin' From A Blue Place 1985
Feel The Fire 1985
What If It's Right 1986
I Love You More 1987
Overnight Success 1987
Til I Find My Love 1988
Town Of Tears 1988
Let's Build A Life Together 1989
Sure Looks Good 1989
Pioneers 1989/90
How Many Times 1990

Albums THE FAMILY BROWN 1971
PORTRAIT 1972
I AM THE WORDS, YOU ARE THE MUSIC 1976
BELIEVE IN US 1978
FAMILIAR FACES/FAMILIAR PLACES 1979
NOTHING REALLY CHANGES 1981
RAISED ON COUNTRY MUSIC 1982
REPEAT AFTER ME 1984
FEEL THE FIRE 1985
ALWAYS IN REACH (PAPA JOE) 1986
THESE DAYS 1988
BEST OF FAMILY BROWN 1980
LIFE AND TIMES 1982-89 1989
HOW MANY TIMES 1990

As Tracey Prescott & Lonesome Daddy:

Singles *When You're Not Loving Me* 1992
Something Big 1992
If Only You Knew 1993
Lonesome Town 1993

CD TRACEY PRESCOTT & LONESOME DADDY 1992

As Prescott Brown:

Singles *There You Go* 1994
There Ain't Much You Can Do About Love 1994
Broken String Of Pearls 1995
39 Days 1995
Talkin' Love 1995
Christmas Call 1995

CD ALREADY RESTLESS 1994

Farmer's Daughter

ANGELA KELMAN (*vocals*)
JAKE LEISKE (*vocals*)
SHAUNA RAE SAMOGRAD (*vocals*)

Based in Vancouver, British Columbia, Farmer's Daughter started in September 1982 when cousins Jake Lesike and Shauna Rae Samograd joined Angela Kelman to form a trio. Their sweet harmonies contributed to their overall appeal as one of Canada's hottest new country groups of the 1990s.

In December 1993 their debut album, *Girls Will Be Girls*, came out. The first single was the title track. Their 1995 hit, *Son of a Preacherman*, was a remake of Dusty Springfield's pop hit from 1968/69.

Singles
Girls Will Be Girls 1993/94
I Wanna Hold You 1994
Family Love 1994/95
Borderline Angel 1995
Son Of A Preacher Man 1995
Callin' All You Cowboys 1995/96

CD
GIRLS WILL BE GIRLS 1993

Joel Feeney

Born and raised in Oakville, Ontario, Joel Feeney was exposed to country music at an early age, and was later influenced by the country rock sound of the early 1970s bands, such as The Eagles and Poco.

In high school he played in various rock bands. He later went on to work in with several Toronto based rock and pop bands, which led to his first professional job as a member of The Front.

In the late 1970s and early 1980s he concentrated on his songwriting. The American group Pure Prairie League recorded Feeney's *Make Up Your Mind* in the early 1980s. They also offered him a job as a replacement for Vince Gill who left to pursue a solo career. Feeney declined because he preferred to stay in Toronto and work on his songwriting.

Throughout the 1980s he was in demand as a backup vocalist on various Toronto recording sessions. He can be heard on albums by Air Supply, Gordon Lightfoot, Bruce Cockburn, Dallas Harms, Carroll Baker, Cassandra Vasik, and Terry Kelly.

He released his debut album, JOEL FEENEY & THE WESTERN FRONT, in 1991. The Western Front was the name of his backup band. Two years later, MCA Records released his second album, LIFE IS BUT A DREAM.

Singles
It's A Beautiful Life 1991
Poor Billy 1991
Diamonds 1991/92
One Good Reason 1992
If Anything Could Be 1992
Tennessee Hills 1992
Say The Word 1993/94
By Heart 1994
Tears Don't Lie 1994/95
What Kind Of Man 1995
Life Is But A Dream 1995

Albums
JOEL FEENEY AND THE WESTERN FRONT 1991
LIFE IS BUT A DREAM 1993

Shirley Field

Born and raised in Armstrong, British Columbia, Shirley Field started yodeling in 1939 after she heard Jimmie Rodgers on the radio. In 1946 she made her first radio appearance on CFAC in Calgary, Alberta, where she met Stu Davis, one of her idols. In 1950 she became Canada's National Female Yodeling Champion.

She first recorded for Aragon Records in the 1950s with Evan Kemp and sang with him on the radio until she moved to Montreal in the early 1960s. On August 4, 1962 she made a guest appearance on the *Grand Ole Opry*, and on the *Ernest Tubb Record Shop Jamboree* on WSM, Nashville.

Her debut album, THE TWO SIDES OF SHIRLEY FIELD, was released in 1963. *An Illusion* was the first single. In 1968 her second album, YOURS SINCERELY, SHIRLEY FIELD, came out.

Field spent the 1970s and 1980s appearing at benefits and seniors homes. In November 1992 she started to record again. Her first of several cassettes was *Just A Yodel For Me.* In 1993 she became the International Female Yodeling Champion at the Western Music Association Festival in Tucson, Arizona.

Singles

An Illusion 1963
We're Goin' Skiin' 1964
It All Adds Up To You 1968
Mockingbird (with BILLY G. FRENCH) 1973

Albums

THE TWO SIDES OF SHIRLEY FIELD 1963
SINCERELY YOURS, SHIRLEY FIELD 1968
TOGETHER — SHIRLEY FIELD and BILLY G. FRENCH) 1972

Cassettes

JUST A YODEL FOR ME 1992
SEASON OF OUR LIVES 1993
YODELLING MEMORIES 1994
HE TAUGHT ME HOW TO YODEL 1995
THE COUNTRY SIDE OF SHIRLEY FIELD — ON THE OUTSIDE LOOKING IN 1995
THE SPIRIT OF THE COWBOY 1996

Joe Firth

Born in Shelburne, Ontario, Joe Firth grew up on a farm in Keldon, Ontario. In the late 1950s, he formed his first band, Joe Firth and the Rockabillies, with his two cousins, Gord Henry and Grant Middaugh. He switched from playing rockabilly to country in the early 1960s, and his band's name changed to Joe Firth and The Country Gentlemen.

In 1970 he recorded his first album, THE PROMISED LAND. Three years later, the single *Too Many Memories* became a national hit.

By 1974 he realized he could make a living as a country singer and the group's name changed to Joe Firth and The Promised Land. They toured Europe in the early 1980s. In the 1990s he was still playing as Joe Firth & The Promised Land.

Singles

Too Many Memories 1973
Plant The Seeds 1974
Until The Mailman Brings Me The News 1975
You Bring Out The Best In Me 1977
57 Chevrolet 1978
Me And The Old Promised Land 1981
Beer Drinkers, Born Losers And Me 1983
The Rest Of The Night's On Me 1984
Bottle Of Tears 1984
Draggin' That Ball And Chain 1985
You're A Habit 1988
She'll Never Love The Tennessee Out Of Me 1988
I Gotta Run 1989

Albums

THE PROMISED LAND 1970
I'M JUST ME 1971
GETTING TOGETHER (with HONEY WEST) 1972
A FAMILY CHRISTMAS 1972
TOO MANY MEMORIES 1974
THE BEST IN ME 1976
57 CHEVY 1978
JOE FIRTH COUNTRY 1979
ME & THE OLD PROMISED LAND 1981
BOTTLE OF TEARS 1984

Gary Fjellgaard

Gary Fjellgaard (pronounced Fell-gard) is one of Canada's most prolific singer/songwriters. His songs reflect his folk/country roots.

Born in Rose Valley, Saskatchewan in 1937, he began singing at an early age in the church choir. In his teens he moved with his family to Prince George, British Columbia, where he worked as a logger during the day and played music at night. A back injury forced him to abandon logging as a career in 1973, and he concentrated full time on his music, playing at various coffeehouses and bars throughout the west coast.

In 1976 he recorded ME AND MARTIN, the first of two albums on the independent Royalty label. BALLADS AND BEER was released in 1979.

Fjellgaard received a British Columbia Country Music Award for Song Of The Year for *Ten Years Old* and *Barefoot* in 1982. His success brought him to the attention of Savannah Music and its president, Brian Ferriman, who signed Gary in the mid-1980s. NO TIME TO LOSE was his first album on the label in 1986.

Other organizations that have honored Fjellgaard with awards are the Canadian Country Music Association (CCMA), Country Music News, *RPM Magazine*'s Big Country Awards, The Canadian Music Publishers Association (CMPA), British Columbia Country Music Association (BCCMA), and the Dutch Country Music Awards. In

1990 the TMI Fender Humanitarian Award was presented to Gary by the CCMA in recognition of his outstanding contribution to increased environmental awareness through his composition *Somewhere On The Island.*

The year 1988 saw him try his turn as an actor in *The Ranch.* Directed by actress Stella Stevens, he starred as Cody Brewster, a crippled and aging rodeo/cowboy singer who lives at a ramshackle Canadian ranch inherited by a U.S. businessman. *The Ranch* was filmed entirely on location in Calgary.

Singles

Ride Away To The Country 1977
Old Fashioned Cowboy Song 1977
How Much Of Me 1978
Caribou To Nashville 1978
She Makes It Easy 1979
Me And Martin 1979
Ballads And Beer 1979/80
Real Contender 1981
Ten Years Old And Barefoot 1982
Too Much Of A Lady 1983
Never Leave The Farm 1983
Finest Dancer 1983
Alone Again On Sunday 1984
Running Back To Your Heart 1984
Riding On The Wind 1985
She Can Survive 1985
Dancing In The Ring 1986
Heroes 1987
Walk In The Rain Tonight 1987
Once Upon A Time 1988
Tears On Mainstreet 1988
The Moon Is Out To Get Me (with LINDA HUNT) 1989
Cowboy In Your Heart 1989
Heart Of A Christmas Night 1989
The Colour Of Your Collar 1990
Somewhere On The Island 1990
In My Heart (with LINDA KIDDER) 1990
All For You 1990
Dance WithThis Old Cowboy 1991
Cry In The Wilderness 1991
Heart Of A Dream 1991
Drifting Cowboy 1991/92
Fire And Lace (with LINDA KIDDER) 1992
The Last Hurrah 1992
Two Gun Kid 1992
The Winds Of October 1992
Remember When 1993
Never Say Goodbye 1993
Shaganippi Hick 1993
Train Of Dreams 1993/94
Islanders 1994
Trace Back To You (with ANITA PERRAS) 1994
What About Love 1994/95
Dancing Up A Storm 1995

Albums/CDs

ME AND MARTIN 1976
BALLADS AND BEER 1979
NO TIME TO LOSE 1986
TIME AND INNOCENCE 1987
HEART OF A DREAM 1989
WINDS OF OCTOBER 1991
BELIEVE IN FOREVER 1994

Foster Martin Band

LYLE FOSTER (*drums*)
CRAIG FOTHERINGHAM (*keyboards*)
RAY GRENIER (*bass*)
RAY MARTIN (*lead vocals*)
ALAN POPOWICH (*lead guitar*)

Based in Oakbank, Manitoba, the Foster Martin Band started in the early 1980s when Lyle Foster sold a house to Ray Martin. The two realized they had a common bond between them: music. They began writing songs together and decided to form what became known as the Foster Martin Band in 1986. Their first album, WILLY'S BAR AND GRILL, came out in 1993.

Singles

Makin' It 1991
Don't You Dare Go 1991
I May Never Get To Heaven 1992/93
You Can't Two Step (Without A Country Girl) 1993
Rodeo Queen 1994
Willy's Bar And Grill 1994
Stay Out Of The Rain 1994
Brother Joe 1995
I'm The One 1995

CD

WILLY'S BAR AND GRILL 1993

George Fox

From Cochrane, Alberta, George Fox dreamed of becoming a singer while playing in the basement of Brenda Dennis, a high school friend. He was in grade eleven when he formed a 1950s style rock band with some friends. As the lead singer he had to learn the words to the oldies. In a mock concert staged in Brenda's basement, he wore a leather jacket with "The Fox" emblazoned on the back.

His interest in music grew, and while on an exchange trip to Sweden in 1981, he began to like country music. Back home he played at dances and weddings. In 1987 he made a demo tape and sent it to Bruce Allen, who managed Bryan Adams, among others.

A call from Robert Roper, lead music scout at WEA Music, led to a recording contract. Fox's self-titled debut album came out in June 1988. That same year, Leonard Rambeau, who managed Anne Murray and Rita MacNeil, became his manager.

Since 1988, Fox has had many hits to his credit, and has maintained the image of the good old country boy. He is now one of Canada's chief new country stars and has hosted three CBC specials.

Singles

Long Distance 1988/89
RBJ 1989
Goldmine 1989
Jingle Bell Rock 1989
No Trespassing 1989/90
Bachelor Girl 1990
Lime Rickey 1990
With All My Might 1990
Fell In Love (And I Get Out) 1991

I Know Where You Go 1991
Here Today, Gone Tomorrow 1991/92
I Surrender 1992
Clearly Canadian 1992/93
Breakfast Alone 1993
Honest Man 1993
No Hasta La Vista Tonight 1994
Wear And Tear On My Heart 1994
What's Holding Me 1995
First Comes Love 1995
Time Of My Life 1995/96

Albums/CDs
GEORGE FOX 1988
WITH ALL MY MIGHT 1989
SPICE OF LIFE 1991
MUSTANG HEART 1993
TIME OF MY LIFE 1995

G

Rena Gaile

Music came naturally for this London, Ontario native. Her father sang and played guitar, and her sister played the flute and guitar, and sang in local clubs. While in high school, Rena learned to play the flute and guitar.

She then moved to Toronto where she became a honors graduate at Humber College. After graduation she was invited to play keyboards with Major Hoople's Boarding House. After a year-and-one-half, she left to form her own group, The Rena Gaile Band. In 1983 she recorded her first single, *Make Time For Love*. Today, she is still recording and performing.

Singles
Make Time For Love 1983
I Don't Love You Anymore 1989/90
It's Always Love 1990
Golding Out 1990
Country Gold 1991
Now I'm Home 1991
Daddy's School 1992
Let's Not Call It Love, Yet 1993
Better Off Blue 1995
All She Wants 1995/96

CD
OUT ON A LIMB 1995

King Ganam

From Swift Current, Saskatchewan, King Ganam was born Ameen Ganam. The nickname "King" came after he won a contest for King of the Fiddlers. In 1942 he organized the group Sons of the West. Eight years later, he moved to Toronto, where he played every Saturday night in Casa Loma and on radio.

In 1956 the CBC invited him to star on a new country and western show called *Country Hoedown*, which featured then unknown singers Tommy Hunter and Tommy Common. With his riverboat-gambler moustache and trademark wink, Ganam was one of the most recognized faces on Canadian television from 1956 to 1959 when he left the show.

King Ganam died on April 26, 1994 after suffering a stroke.

Singles/78s
Alberta Stomp 1951
Ridin' The Fiddle 1951
Four String Polka 1952
Tomahawk Stomp 1952
Casa Loma Hornpipe 1953
Many Tears Apart 1953
The Farmer's Schottische 1954
May You Never See Sunshine Again 1954
The Maritime Polka 1955
You'll Never Be Satisfied 1955
Dick McDougall's Reel 1957

Albums
KING GANAM'S FIDDLE TUNES 1958
KING OF THE FIDDLE 1966
SQUARE DANCES 1967
SQUARE DANCIN' 1967
RIDIN' THE FIDDLE 1968
REELS & RAGS 1968

CARROLL BAKER
LARRY MERCEY
THE CITY SLICKERS
BEV MARIE

Denise Grant

Denise Grant

STEW CLAYTON
RALPH CARLSON & COUNTRY MILE
MAURICE BOLYER
THE DIXIE FLYERS

Mel Loynd

SMILIN' JOHNNIE & ELEANOR DAHL

STOMPIN' TOM CONNORS

BILLY CHARNE

THE SINGING POST FAMILY

ANNE LORD
J.K. GULLEY
DICK DAMRON
CODA THE WEST

SUZANNE GITZI
JULIE LYNN
MEL LAVIGNE

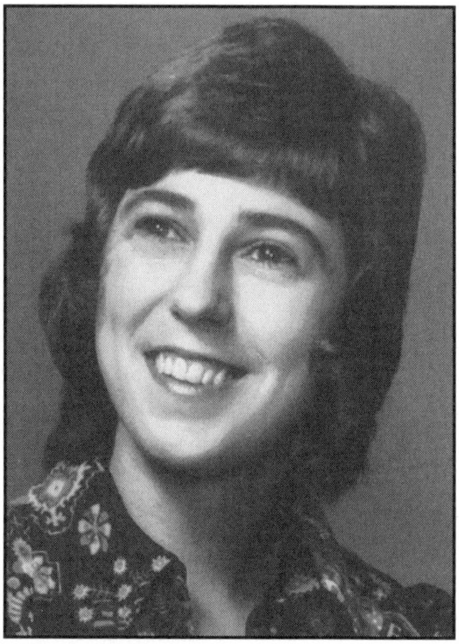

COUNTRY HOEDOWN

DON MESSER'S JUBILEE

SHIRLEY FIELD

Bourbon Gauthier

Growing up in his hometown of Noranda, Quebec, Bourbon listened to country music. His father played the fiddle, while his mother played the piano. At fourteen Bourbon moved with his parents to Sudbury, Ontario, where he learned to play the drums. He also learned everything from the rock sounds of Jimi Hendrix to the country songs of Merle Haggard and Kenny Rogers.

Throughout the 1970s, Gauthier played in several different bands with diverse musical stylings. His debut album, J'AI RIEN POUR ME PLAINDRE, made him a star in his native Quebec. In 1993, he recorded his debut English album, I CAN'T COMPLAIN.

Singles
I Can't Complain 1993
Your Shadow Dances On The Wall 1993
Calling The Shots 1994
Highrise Blues 1994
Camelback Road 1995

CDs
J'AI RIEN POUR ME PLAINDRE 1991
I CAN'T COMPLAIN 1993
CAMELBACK ROAD 1994

Suzanne Gitzi

This Vancouver singer dreamed of a career in showbusiness since she was a young girl. After graduating from high school, she played in a band that played the rock and blues circuit. In 1987 she accompanied Powder Blues founder Tom Lavin and The Wailin' Demons, and by 1990 she had her own R&B/pop/country band. When Doug Bennett of the rock group Doug & The Slugs was looking for a female country singer for his label Tomcat Records, he invited Gitzi to audition. The next day she signed a recording contract. Her debut album, FALLEN ANGEL, was released in October of 1993. The first single was *The Test of Time.*

Singles
The Test Of Time 1993
The Runaround 1993
Look Before You Leap 1994
Fallen Angel 1994
House Without A Soul 1994
Teardrops In The Rain 1995
Judge and Jury 1996

CD
FALLEN ANGEL 1993
DRESSED IN BLACK 1996

Gilles Godard

Cornwall, Ontario-born Gilles Godard is more famous as a songwriter and producer than a singer. At seventeen years of age he was performing in local clubs on the Cornwall and Western Quebec circuit. While working in his father's band, Gilles became interested in the steel guitar.

In 1977 he went to Nashville to attend The Jeff Newman Pedal

Steel Guitar College, where he made various contacts with musicians, studios, and songwriters. A year later, he recorded his self-titled debut album on his own label, Bookshop Records.

His big break as a songwriter came in 1982 when Eddie Eastman recorded two of Godard's songs, *Sherida* and *Last Call.* Eastman changed the latter's title to *From The Barroom To The Bedroom.*

Throughout the 1980s, Gilles built up a solid string of hit singles and albums. He also produced the highly acclaimed ANNIVERSARY SESSIONS album recorded by Tommy Hunter. He continues to write, record, and produce for himself and others.

Singles
Took A Train To Vegas 1982
Dressed To Kill 1983
Tell It To My Heart 1983/84
Call Me An Outlaw 1984
Hold On To What You Got 1985
Nothing Good About Goodbye (with KELITA HAVERLAND) 1984/85
We Won't Ever Say Goodbye 1985
It's Christmas For All 1985
Love Crazy 1986
It's A Fine Line 1986
Tell Me You're Free 1987
I'm Her Melody 1987
En Amour 1987
Baby Makes Me Lose Control 1988/89
She's Good 1989
Have I Got News For You 1993

Albums
GILLES GODARD 1978
TELL IT TO MY HEART 1983
HAVE I GOT NEWS FOR YOU 1985
EN AMOUR 1987

Bruce Golden

A native of Vankleek Hill, Ontario, Bruce Golden was a teenager when he bought his first flat top guitar. He organized his first country band, The Bruce Golden Trio, in 1976. They later added a fourth member and changed their name to Bruce Golden and Country Gold.

In 1983 he decided it was time to record, and chose the self-penned song, *City Lights*, which was produced by Terry Carisse. Golden's other hits include *Midnight Ride* and *Ballad of a Stranger.*

Singles
City Lights 1983
One Night Affair 1984
She Doesn't Love You 1984
Midnight Ride 1984
Loving Your Memory 1985
Is That Your Heart Beating Or Mine 1985/86
Love Fire 1986
When We're Together 1986
Three Broken Hearts 1988
(If You Were) A Turn In The Road 1989
I'll Hold You Forever 1989
Ballad Of A Stranger 1990
If There's No Feeling Left 1991
Forever Eyes 1992
Thumbs Up 1992

Album
MISSING YOU 1985

The Good Brothers

BRIAN GOOD (*guitar, vocals*)
LARRY GOOD (*banjo, vocals*)
BRUCE GOOD (*autoharp, dobro, vocals*)

The Good Brothers hail from Richmond Hill, Ontario. Twins Bruce and Brian began as a traditional folk and bluegrass duo called The Kinfolk. In 1969 they teamed up with Winnipeg guitarist/songwriter James Ackroyd.

In 1971 their first album on Columbia Records, JAMES ACKROYD AND THE GOOD BROTHERS, was released. Two years later, Ackroyd left the band to pursue other musical interests. He was replaced by brother Larry Good.

It was not until 1973 with the acceptance of country rock from such groups as The Eagles and Poco that The Good Brothers began to become popular. One of their most highly acclaimed albums was their two record set, LIVE, on Solid Gold Records.

Over the next eighteen years they became one of Canada's top country and bluegrass bands. In 1991 Larry left to pursue a solo career. He was replaced by Travis Good, Bruce's son. The group then became known as The Goods.

Singles

That's The Kind Of Man I Am 1976
Midnight Flight 1976
Homemade Wine 1977
Good Boogie 1977
Cowboy From Rue St. Germain 1978
Truck Driver's Girl 1978
Let Love Go 1979
Some Kind Of Woman 1979
Brown Eyed Girl 1980/81
Fox On The Run 1981
Weekend Rodeo 1982
Summertime 1982
Hold Out 1983
Person To Person 1983
Celebrate 1984
This Could Be Serious 1986
Better Off Alone 1987
High Rollin' Heart 1987
Gone So Long 1987/88
You Won't Fool This Fool This Time 1988
Live Fast, Love Hard, Die Young 1990
She Told Me So 1990
Inquiring Minds 1991
We Don't Always See Eye To Eye 1991

Albums

JAMES AND THE GOOD BROTHERS 1971
THE GOOD BROTHERS 1976
PRETTY AIN'T GOOD ENUFF 1977
DOIN' THE WRONG THINGS RIGHT 1978
SOME KIND OF WOMAN 1979
THE BEST OF THE GOOD BROTHERS 1980
PERSON TO PERSON 1982
THE GOOD BROTHERS LIVE! 1983
LIVE 'N KICKIN' 1983
DELIVERING THE GOODS 1986
LIVE FAST LOVE HARD 1990

As The Goods:

Singles

That's What Highways Are For 1994
I Really Dug Myself A Hole 1994/95
The Shape I'm In 1995
Don't Know Much About Love 1995/96

CD

SO MANY ROADS 1994

Michael Dee Graham

Michael Douglas Graham was born in Toronto, Ontario on October 3, 1944. His music career goes back to Montreal in the late 1950s when he started a rock and roll group called M.G. and The Roadrunners. He was also in The Rockatones before going country in 1965. He first called himself Michael Dee Graham when he recorded his first hit, *No Pity For A Fool,* on Rodeo Records in 1970.

In the late 1970s he called himself "Canada's Rockabilly King" and his songwriting became more vibrant. He had a string of hit singles from his MISS MISUNDERSTOOD album in 1979, the first of which was *Till The Minute You Go.*

By the mid-1980s he had become Michael Dee, and recorded the singles *Oh Carol* and *Party Shoes.* He also became popular with country fans in Southwestern Ontario.

Graham gained international fame in 1991 when his song, *If The Jukebox Took Teardrops,* was a Top Ten hit in the U.S. for Billy Joe Royal.

On August 18, 1993 he died after a lengthy battle with cancer. He was 48 years old.

Singles

No Pity For A Fool 1970
She Always Lets Me Down Easy 1970
These Things 1970
Love Kept On 1970/71
Skip A Rope 1971
I'd Better Not See Her Again 1972
Mama Bake A Pie 1972
Redemption City 1972
Lock, Stock & Teardrops 1972/73
Yonder Comes A Train 1973
Lonely Cabdriver 1973/74
Lately I'm Afraid It's Gone Too Far 1974
Country Bound 1974
Battle Of New Orleans 1974
Ghost Story 1974
Shadow Of A Man 1976/77
Would You Still Love Me 1977
Then Came You 1977
Do Right Woman 1978
Who Will The Next Fool Be? 1978
Loving You 1979
Till The Minute You Go 1979/80
This Travelin' Life 1980
Cuddle Up 1982
Hello Lonesome Town 1983
Oh Carol 1985
Party Shoes 1986

Sea Of Heartbreak 1986
Heart Of Mine 1987
I'm Sorry 1988
If The Jukebox Took Teardrops 1989
I Can't See Me Without You 1989
It's Quittin' Time 1989/90
Mountain Right 1990
Where The Sun Don't Shine 1990
Steal Of The Night 1990
Since I Met You Baby 1992
Outta Sight 1994
The Greatest Love 1995

Albums SKIP A ROPE 1971
HERE I AM AGAIN 1971
FRIENDS 1972
MIKE GRAHAM 1973
COUNTRY REFLECTIONS 1974
PEOPLE MUSIC 1977
MIKE GRAHAM SINGS PEOPLE MUSIC 1977
MISS MISUNDERSTOOD 1979
DEE ONE 1986
SORRY I HAVEN'T WRITTEN FOR SO LONG 1988
STEAL OF THE NIGHT 1989
MOMENTO OF MANITOULIN n.d.
LONELY CAB DRIVER n.d.

As The Rockatones:

Singles SHADDIA 1963
SUBMERGE 1963
SHAKE HANDS 1964
BAD GIRL/I'M A MAN 1965
FOR MY OWN 1966

Susan Graham

Born in Calgary, Alberta but raised on a dairy farm outside Didsbury, Susan Graham started singing in church choirs and performing at local community functions. Before her dream of a career in music came true, she became a licensed beautician and drove a 170 ton truck for an oil company. Her big break came in 1989 when Charlie Lamb, a veteran talent promoter and manager, liked her voice enough to help get her started. She opened for Michael Martin Murphey and made a guest appearance on *Nashville Now* (on The Nashville Network), where she was interviewed by host Ralph Emery.

Her first hit was *Take The Keys To My Heart* in 1992, from the four song CD of the same name. In 1995 her first full CD, SOMEWHERE IN BETWEEN, was released.

Singles *Take The Keys To My Heart* 1992
Blue All Over You 1993
If He Ever Knew 1993
Man With A Mission 1994
The Beating Of My Heart 1995
The Greatest Love 1995/96

CDs TAKE THE KEYS TO MY HEART 1992
SOMEWHERE IN BETWEEN 1995

Curtis Grambo

Curtis Grambo was one of the top premier club acts in Western Canada in the late 1980s and early 1990s. Born in Prince Albert, Saskatchewan, he was raised in Crystal Springs and graduated from Crocus Hill High School in Brandon, Manitoba. After playing a weekend engagement at the North 40 Saloon in Brandon, he decided to forsake a career in the Canadian Air Force and became a country singer. He fronted the band C.C. Rider and developed a local following. In 1993 he went to Maddock Studios in Winnipeg, where he recorded his debut album, BIG NEWS BACK HOME, which came out a year later.

Singles
Can't Make No Sense 1994
Give Her My Number 1994
Don't Leave Me In Love 1994
Big News Back Home 1995
Me, Myself & I 1995

CD
BIG NEWS BACK HOME 1994

Great Western Orchestra

CINDY CHURCH (*vocals*)
STEWART MACDOUGALL (*vocals, guitar*)
NATHAN TINKHAM (*guitar*)
DAVID WILKIE (*mandolin, vocals*)

Formed in the late 1980s, The Great Western Orchestra of Southern Alberta were a traditional group founded by David Wilkie and Cindy Church. When she and Nathan Tinkham left to pursue solo projects in 1990, Wilkie and Stewart MacDougall carried on as the new edition of the group.

In 1990 they released the album, THE WIND IN THE WIRE. It was followed by BUFFALO GROUND four years later. (See CINDY CHURCH)

Singles
Train Of Life 1989
Ride On 1989/90
Vagabond 1990
Cactus Swing 1991

Album
GREAT WESTERN ORCHESTRA 1989
WIND IN THE WIRE 1990
BUFFALO GROUND 1994

Ray Griff

Raymond Griff was born on April 22, 1942 in Vancouver, British Columbia. At age eight he played drums in The Winfield Amateurs, a family band from Winfield, Alberta. He went on to master the guitar and piano, and fronted his own group in the 1950s called The Blue Echoes.

His big break came in 1959 when one of his songs, *Mr. Moonlight,* was recorded by the late Johnny Horton. Another song, *Where Do I Go From Here*, was recorded by Jim Reeves, who was instrumental in bringing Griff to Nashville in 1964. His hopes of a recording deal were dashed when Reeves was killed in a plane crash in July 1964. In 1965 Ray recorded his first single, *That Weepin' Willow Tree,* on Groove Records. He later signed to RCA.

By 1970 he finally began to be noticed as a singer and had a string of successful singles and albums right into the 1980s. He also established himself as a first rate producer with Jack Bailey's KEEP ME album in 1973.

Singles

That Weepin' Willow Tree 1965
Don't Lead Me On 1965
Golden Years 1965
Your Lily White Hands 1967/68
The Sugar From My Candy 1968
Wanderin' Through The Valley 1969
The Entertainer 1969
Patches 1970
Ain't Nowhere To Go 1970/71
The Mornin' After Baby Let Me Down 1971
It Rains Just The Same In Missouri 1972
A Song For Everyone 1973
What Got To You 1973
Darlin' 1973/74
That Doesn't Mean (I Don't Love My God) 1974
The Hill 1974
If That's What It Takes 1975
You Ring My Bell 1975
If I Let Her Come In 1976
I Love The Way That You Love Me 1976
That's What I Get 1976
The Last Of The Winfield Amateurs 1977
A Passing Thing 1977
Cold Day In July 1977
Raymond's Place 1977/78
What Can I Say 1978
Canada 1978/79
Betty Mitchell 1979
Friends & Neighbours 1979
Maple Leaf 1980
Jimmy, Luke & Me 1981
Draw Me A Line 1981/82
Things That Songs Are Made Of 1982
If Tomorrow Never Comes 1983
Gone 1983
You Can Count On Me 1983
So Close 1984
Diamond In The Rough 1984
Light In The Window 1985
I Did 1985
What My Woman Does To Me 1986
It Doesn't Make A House A Home 1986
Reelin' Rockin' Rollin' 1986/87
I Can't See Me 1987
Dividin' My Time 1987
That Old Montana Moon 1987/88
Calgary, Calgary 1988
Honest To Goodness Amigos (& RONNIE PROPHET) 1988
Shiny (& SUSAN JACKS) 1988/89
Snow Covered Mountains 1989
Moonlight (& TERRY CARISSE) 1989
Damned If I Do, Damned If I Don't 1989
Mama Made Christmas Shine For Me 1989
Flames 1989/90
Daybreak 1990
Someday 1991
It's Not The Right Time 1995

Albums

A RAY OF SUNSHINE 1968
THE ENTERTAINER 1969
RAY GRIFF SINGS 1972
SONGS FOR EVERYONE 1973
EXPRESSIONS 1974
RAY GRIFF 1976
LAST OF THE WINFIELD AMATEURS 1976
WORLD OF RAY GRIFF 1977
RAYMOND'S BAR AND GRILL 1977
RAYMOND'S PLACE 1978
CANADA 1979
MAPLE LEAF 1980
THE GREATEST HITS OF RAY GRIFF 1981
ADAM'S CHILD 1981
YOU CAN COUNT ON ME 1983
YOU 1983
THE SKY'S THE LIMIT 1985
MY KIND OF COUNTRY 1987
RAY GRIFF & FRIENDS 1988
HONEST TO GOODNESS AMIGOS 1988
CANADA-MY NATIVE LAND 1989
THERE'LL ALWAYS BE CHRISTMAS 1989
THROUGH THE YEARS VOL I & II 1992

J.K. Gulley

John Kenneth Gulley was born in Toronto and raised in Elmvale, a small community near Barrie, Ontario. He was inspired by his father Kenneth who taught him to play the guitar at age fourteen. After graduating from high school in the mid-1970s, he played lead guitar in The Country Kings. The latter part of the decade saw him form his own band, Dusty Road, tour Eastern Canada with Ronnie Prophet, and play lead guitar on CBC-TV's hit show, *Funny Farm.*

In the early 1980s, Gulley moved to Nashville, where he toured with Billie Joe Spears and Freddie Hart. J.K. also became known as a songwriter when Cindy Hurt recorded *Talk To Me Loneliness* in 1982. The following year he returned to Canada and joined The Mercey Brothers as guitarist and vocalist. After several tours he left them to pursue a solo career. His first single was *Stay Lady Stay* in August 1984.

Throughout the 1980s and 1990s he established himself as one of Canada's top singer/songwriters and producers.

Singles

Stay Lady Stay 1984
Stop Hidin' Your Heart 1985
Come To Me 1985/86
Gettin' Tired 1986
Sweet Dreams (& WENDY DAVIS) 1986
One Step Closer 1987
Don't Turn Me Away 1987/88
You're Gonna Lose That Lady 1988/89
Blue Jeans Boy 1989
If He's Like Me 1989
Coming Out Of Your Eyes 1989/90
We Can Dream 1990
Leah 1991
Blue Mountain Memories 1992
If She Only Knew Me 1995

Albums Dusty Road 1978 · Under Cover 1986 · Blue Jeans Boy 1988

Larry Gustafson

Born in Grand Prairie, Alberta, Larry Gustafson first wanted to be a major league hockey player, but at fifteen he was diagnosed with a rare bone disease, and changed his career goals. He became interested in music and became a leader of a local Edmonton band. About this time he started writing his own songs. One he co-wrote with friend Stu Mitchell was *Sweet Alberta Woman*, which was recorded by R. Harlan Smith on the 1975 album, SON OF A COUNTRY MAN.

In 1977 Gustafson recorded his debut album, LONG TIME LAYIN' DOWN, which contained the hit *Tulsa Turnaround.* By the early 1980s he had formed his own backup band called Hot Spur.

Singles
Long Time Layin' Down 1977
Tulsa Turnaround 1977
High Steppin' Woman 1978
Red River Valley 1978
Cold On A Feeling 1979
Fiddle & A Bow 1981
Pennsylvania Flower 1982
Too Much Of A Lady 1983
Where Do I Go 1991

Albums LONG TIME LAYIN' DOWN 1977 · COLD ON A FEELING 1978

H

Albert Hall

Albert Hall was born Chris Hughes in Wolverhampton, England. After coming to Canada in the early 1960s, he was in a British cover band called Rocking Horse. He later gave up his music career and established his own advertising agency in Toronto. It was not until the early 1980s that he returned to music.

He was inspired by the music of Willie Nelson. Hughes changed his name to Albert Hall after the renowned English playhouse of the same name. His debut album, COWBOY ROCKER, came out in 1981. It contained *Sentimental Part Again*, the first of a string of hits for this Toronto-based singer/songwriter.

In 1990 he established his own record label, Custer Music, and was honored by fellow songwriter Brian Levi who named his cafe in Whitehorse, Yukon, The Blue Moon Cafe, after Hall's 1985 hit album and single. Under the name Chris Hughes, he was president of the CCMA from 1992-94.

Singles

Sentimental Part Again 1981
Modern Day Love Song 1982
Face In The Mirror 1983
Song For Davey 1984
Once Upon A Marriage 1984
Blue Moon Cafe 1985
Blue Umbrella 1986
I Want You 1988
There Will Never Be Another 1989
Rosanne 1990
Music Of A Memory 1991
Why Don't You Hear Me 1992

Albums

COUNTRY ROCKER 1981
AMAZING STRANGER 1984
ONCE UPON A MARRIAGE 1984
BLUE MOON CAFE 1985
COURAGE/THE MUSICAL CHOICE OF THE NATIONAL ALPINE SKI TEAM 1988
KING OF THE COUNTRY WALTZ 1993

Dyanne Halliday

Discovered by Mel Shaw, Toronto-born Dyanne Halliday first sang in a church pageant at age four. She and Canadian country/folk artist Tom Kelly recorded the duet *Any Kind of Man (Any Kind of Woman)* in 1990. That same year, she released her debut single, *Crazy In Love With Your Man.*

In 1991 her debut album, HOW SWEET IT IS, featured the famed Jordanaires on background vocals. She moved to Nashville in 1993 and the following year recorded the song *Small Town Texas*. She also made a six cassette package called MOMENTS OF MEANING, which combined music and narration by Halliday on such subjects as family relationships, understanding of others, and a positive personal life outlook.

Singles
Any Kind Of Man (Any Kind Of Woman (with Tom Kelly) 1990
Crazy In Love With Your Man 1990
Don't Worry Be Happy 1991
Small Town Texas 1994

Album
HOW SWEET IT IS 1991

Dallas Harms

Originally from Janzen, Saskatchewan, Dallas Harms moved with his family to Ontario in the late 1930s. His music career started in 1953 when he played in local clubs in the Hamilton area. Two years later, he starred on the Main Street Jamboree on CHML with Jack Kingston. In 1957 Harms met the late Conway Twitty, who invited him to audition for Sun Records in Memphis. Although nothing came of it, Dallas did tour Arkansas.

In 1959 he had the chance to record for Quality Records. His debut single was called *You Mean The World To Me.* Four years later, he went to Nashville to record his second release, *Chain Gang,* for Sparton Records. For his third, *She's Gone*, in 1968, he used his own backup band, The Coulson Brothers, which later became Deep Creek.

Dallas' next big break came in 1972 when he signed with Columbia Records. His first single with the label was *In The Loving Arms of My Marie*. He is still performing with a band in the Hamilton area.

Singles
You Mean The World To Me 1959
Chain Gang 1963
She's Gone 1968
In The Loving Arms Of My Marie 1972
Old Ira Gray 1972/73
Little Annie Brown 1973
Ruby's Lips 1974
Paper Rosie 1975
Georgia I'm Cheating On You Tonight 1976
Julie I Think It's Going To Rain 1977
It's Crying Time For Me 1977
Master Of The Classical Guitar 1978
The Fastest Gun 1978
I Picked A Daisy 1978/79
Ballad Of The Duke 1979
Lean On Me 1979
Rendezvous For Lovers 1979
Shelley's Last Request 1980
You're A Memory 1980
Painter Of Words 1980
Country Fever 1983
Honky Tonkin' All Night Long 1983
Foolin' With Fire 1983
Get Along Little Doggie 1984
Driving You Out Of My Mind 1984
Never Been To Spain 1984

Albums PAPER ROSIE 1975
THE FASTEST GUN 1978
PAINTER OF WORDS 1979
THE BEST OF DALLAS HARMS 1979
OUT OF HARMS WAY 1982

Ken Harnden

From Belleville, Ontario, Ken Harnden's musical career goes back to 1973 when he was a member of the gospel group The Proverbs. By the late 1970s he wanted to broaden his musical interests and worked with several club bands. In 1980 he formed his own band, Cedar Creek. After it disbanded in 1984, he was offered a contract as a solo artist in Nashville. His first of several hits was *She Can't Say No* in 1988. (See CEDAR CREEK)

Singles *She Knows I Can't Say No* 1988
Leanna 1988
It's Love In The Long Run 1988/89
You Broke All The Rules 1991
It Won't Be Me And You 1992
Take Her To Heart 1993

Kelita Haverland

A native of the ranchland area of Claresholm, Alberta, Kelita Haverland drew upon characters she invented as a teenager to enhance her stage act, such as the gossipy Sophelia Flannigan and Honky Tonk Queen Dixie Lee. As singer/songwriter her inspiration came from looking at the positive side of three traumatic events in her life, the loss of her father, mother, and older brother.

In 1983 she recorded her debut single, *I Don't Care,* on Boot Records. She continued to have hits into the early 1990s when she went under the name of Kelita.

Singles *I Don't Care* 1983
Where Is Love 1983
Could It Be Lo 1983
My Only 1983/84
New Love 1984
I'm So In Love 1985
Too Hot To Handle 1985
Pour Me Another 1986
Saturday Night Dancing 1987
Neighbours Of The World (with DUNCAN MEIKLEJOHN) 1987
I've Been A Lonesome 1987
Love On Her Lips 1988
Stay At Home Lady 1989/90
For Crying Out Loud 1991
Merry Go Round 1991
I Can't Get Close Enough (with BOBBY LALONDE) 1992

Albums KELITA 1983
TOO HOT TO HANDLE 1986

Harvey Henry

Since he was a youngster, Harvey Henry has been singing and playing guitar. In his teens he played with various groups, such as The Royal

Polka Kings, Banshee, and Masquerade.

In 1973 he and his brother Len formed The Henry Brothers. Four years later they recorded the hit *Ramblin'*. Early in 1978 they broke up. Harvey went on to play with Midnite Ryder and the Downs Show Band before forming The Harvey Henry Band in 1979. In the mid-1980s he recorded with Donna Henry.

As The Harvey Brothers:

Singles *My Woman, My Wife* 1974
Ramblin' 1977

As Harvey Henry Band:

Singles *Jenny* 1979
Springtime Lovers, Autumn Strangers 1980
Nellie 1982
Linda 1982
Reach Out And Touch Her 1986

As Donna & Harvey Henry:

Singles *Mystery Lover* 1985
No Other Love 1986

Len Henry

Len Henry was born in Boggy Creek, Manitoba. His first professional job was in a band called Burt Todd's Firestrings. They later became The Mystics, who played in and around Winnipeg from 1959 to 1972. With brother Harvey, he formed a duo called The Henry Brothers. When they split up in 1977, Len went solo and formed his own backup band, The Good Company.

Singles *My Woman, My Wife* 1974
What's It Like To Live In Texas? 1978
Cold Wind On Mountain 1981
Poor Man's Railroad Line 1981
Ramblin' 1982
Love Has Made A Fool Of Me Again 1983
Happy Ever After 1983
You're Driving Me Up To The Wall 1984
The Devil Offered More 1983/84

Albums DON'T GIVE A DAMN KIND OF MAN 1978

Bill Hersh

From Minton, Saskatchewan, Bill Hersche (he changed the spelling to Hersh) was the youngest of eight children. Born on November 1, 1947, he spent his first ten years on the family farm, where he listened to Hank Williams Sr. on the radio and played accordion. When the family moved to Regina, Bill liked the rockabilly sound of Jerry Lee Lewis and others. He also bought his first guitar at Simpson's for $70.00.

In 1968 he became a member of The Sandmen. When this band broke up, he joined a trio with Barry Whitmore, formerly of Ian and Sylvia's

Great Speckled Bird, and Jimmy Pock, who used to play drums with Joe Vargo and The Dynamics. They became Blue Train, Bill's backup band.

Veteran producer and manager Don Grashey helped Bill get his own TV show in Regina, *A Place Called Home*, which was also the name of his first single in 1975. He moved to Edmonton, Alberta in 1976, where his career continues to flourish.

Singles

A Place Called Home 1975
Our Little Girl 1976
It Sure Looks Good On You 1976
Good Old Time Country Rock And Roll 1977
All Nite Country Party 1979
Take Me To The Country 1979
Satisfied Mind 1981
White Lightning (& GARY DARE) 1981
Country Gold 1981/82
I Am Your Fire 1982
Hello Operator 1982
She Learned Everything She Knows 1983
From A Cheating Man 1983
By And By (with MEL DEGEN) 1983
Babysittin' With The Blues 1983
Happy Hour 1984
Paint Me Blue 1984
It Won't Be Much Like Christmas 1984
Midnight Train 1989

Albums

TAKE THE TIME 1981

Kenny Hess

Kenny Hess was born in Outlook, Saskatchewan. He first toured Canada as part of the pop/rock band The Boys Next Door. In the mid-1980s he switched to country music. His 1993 album, BACK TO REALITY, received national critical acclaim.

Harlan Howard, a veteran songwriter in Nashville, signed Hess to his publishing firm. In 1994 his second album, WELCOME TO LONELINESS, was released.

Singles

The Good Life 1993
Nature Of The Beast 1994
Crazy About Me 1994
Welcome To Lonesomeville 1995
Until We're There 1995

CDs

BACK TO REALITY 1993
WELCOME TO LONESOMEVILLE 1994

Earl Heywood

Like many of his generation, Earl Heywood listened to the likes of Gene Autry, Jimmie Rodgers, Wilf Carter, and others on the radio. Born on a farm near Exeter, Ontario, Earl decided that he wanted a career in country music. He received his first guitar at age ten, took lessons from a neighbor, and played and sang with his sister at local events.

In 1940 he started to write his own songs. One of them was *Living In The Army,* which was written to the tune of *The Strawberry Roan.* The army camp where he was serving acclaimed it as their official marching song.

On Christmas Eve, 1941 at the Patricia Theatre in London, Ontario, he took part in an amateur contest. The theatre manager, Tom McNight, introduced him as "Canada's Number One Singing Cowboy" and the title has stuck ever since.

Earl joined radio station CKNX in Wingham in 1942, and for the next twenty-one years he was the star of Canada's largest traveling barn dance. He also hosted a weekly program called *Serenade Rance Radio Show.*

In 1949, Heywood was signed to RCA-Canada. His debut release was the two-sided *There's A New Love True Love In My Heart* and *Down In Lily Valley.* His second hit record was *The Alberta Waltz,* which became one of the biggest hits of his career. Some of his other hits include *Picking Flowers* (1950), *Tears of St. Anne* (1951), and *Isle of Campobello* (1954).

Rodeo/Banff Records released the album, AN INTRODUCTION TO EARL HEYWOOD AND FAMILY, in 1960. Earl and his wife Martha, daughter Patricia, and son Grant were the first family to make commercial recordings in Canada. Grant was also the youngest Canadian ever to record at Rodeo.

In the 1960s Earl's fame spread to Australia, where he had a fan club of over 1,000 members. On November 1, 1989 he was inducted into the Canadian Country Music Hall Of Fame.

Singles

There's A New Love True Love In My Heart 1949
The Alberta Waltz 1950
Broken Down Merry-Go-Round 1950
Picking Flowers 1950
Tears Of St. Anne 1951
A Bad Penny Always Returns 1951
Three Roses and An Orchid 1951
Isle of Campobello 1953
Old New Brunswick Moon 1953
I Want To Be Your Only Ray Of Sunshine 1957
Nellie Rey 1957
This Little Gospel Light Of Mine 1960
Single Girl 1960
The Donnelly Circle 1970
Three Candles In The Window 1970

Albums

THE HEYWOOD FAMILY 1960
EARL HEYWOOD AND FAMILY 1960
AN INTRODUCTION TO EARL HEYWOOD AND FAMILY 1960
EARL HEYWOOD SOUVENIRS 1960
EARL HEYWOOD SINGS 1968
TALES OF THE DONNELLY FEUD 1970
GOOD OLD COUNTRY SINGIN' 1972
EARL HEYWOOD'S ORIGINAL GOLDEN HITS 1974

Cassettes

EARL HEYWOOD & THE GOLDEN PRAIRIE COWBOYS 1947
EARL HEYWOOD SINGS GOLDEN COUNTRY HITS 1975
EARL HEYWOOD AND THE SERENADE RANCH GANG 1978
GOOD OLE COUNTRY SINGIN' 1979
EARL HEYWOOD COUNTRY 1979
EARL HEYWOOD'S TALES OF THE DONNELLY FEUD 1980

Dixie Bill Hilton

William Dixon Hilton was born on October 25, 1920 in Bjorkdale, Saskatchewan. In his teens he began singing and playing the guitar and he became a popular radio show performer on CKIB in Prince Albert and CJVI in Victoria, British Columbia.

During World War II he served as a wireless air-gunner in the Royal Canadian Air Force. After the war he formed the first edition of The Calgary Range Riders, who made several recordings on Aragon Records. During the early 1950s they recorded in Toronto on the Apex label.

In 1956 Hilton retired from performing and moved to Calgary, Alberta, where he died on February 1, 1991.

Singles

Ramblin' Man 1952
What A Waste (Of Good Corn Likker) 1952
Thousand Miles At Sea 1952
Reward 1952
Careless Ways 1953
Dear Dad 1953

Albums

CALGARY RANGE RIDERS 1952
DIXIE BILL HILTON AND THE CALGARY RANGE RIDERS 1986

Gary Hooper

Born in the village of L'Etete, New Brunswick, Gary Hooper worked at various jobs before he decided on a career in music in the early 1960s. He played at various hotels and taverns in and around Toronto and was a featured guest on many TV shows in Ontario. In 1969 he recorded his first album on Paragon, ALL I HAVE TO OFFER YOU IS ME. The title track of his second album, I WOULDN'T TAKE A MILLION DOLLARS FOR A

SINGLE MAPLE LEAF, was a big hit in 1970. Some of his other hits are *The Miracle* and *Selling Our Country Down The Drain.*

Singles

I Wouldn't Take A Million Dollars For A Single Maple Leaf 1970
She's Not You 1971
The Miracle 1971
22 Dollars From Dallas 1971
Answer Calls For Rose 1971
Selling Our Country Down The Drain 1972
Where The Blue Waters Foam 1994

Albums

ALL I HAVE TO OFFER YOU IS ME 1969
I WOULDN'T TAKE A MILLION DOLLARS . . . 1970
JUST ONE ANGEL ON MY MIND 1972

D. J. Hopson

A native of Oshawa, Ontario, D.J. Hopson (a.k.a. Diamond Jim Hopson) came to music naturally. His father Howard was a fiddle player in 1940s and was a member of the group, The Canadian Ramblers. In the 1930s they were one of the first touring bands in Canada. They also hosted their own live radio show in Quebec's Eastern Townships.

Jim was eight-years-old when he started singing and playing the guitar. Until he was fourteen he played at the Bowmanville Jamboree. He later switched to pop music and was in several bands before he returned to country music. When he realized he could not make a comfortable living as a musician, he became a successful businessman. By 1986, he was playing country music again, and in March 1989 his debut single, *I Only Sing The Sad Ones Anymore,* was released on his own Double Barrel Records label.

Singles

I Only Sing The Sad Ones Anymore 1989
Lost In Her Love 1989
Cold Front 1990
Where There's A Will There's A Way 1990
I Must Be Out Of Your Mind 1991
Have A Heart 1991
Half A Mind To Go Crazy 1992
Someone To Write Home About 1993
Baby's Leavin' 1994
I Got The Car 1994
But She Loves Him 1995
Trouble In Paradise 1995

Albums

A DAY IN THE LIFE 1992
NO TURNIN' BACK 1994

Tommy Hunter

Born in London, Ontario on March 20, 1937, Tommy Hunter knew music was the career path for him after he had seen a traveling Grand Ole Opry Show when he was nine years old. His parents enrolled him in the Edith Hill Adams Academy in downtown London so he could learn the guitar.

Although he listened to other country greats, his favorite was Hank Williams Sr. because his songs were simple yet powerful, and his recitations as Luke The Drifter were unforgettable.

Hunter received his first dollar as a professional performer when he was thirteen. His early days as a singer were spent in movie theatres where he entertained between shows. He also played with a magician and his wife as the Royal Heads of Magic.

On CFPL in London, Ontario and CKDA in Victoria, British Columbia, he was a featured guest. He later joined The Golden Prairie Cowboys who played in Toronto at the famous club, The Olympia.

In June 1956 King Ganam invited Tommy to join the cast of *Country Hoedown* on CBC TV. The first song he sang was *Sixteen Tons.* Two years later, he had his own radio show on the CBC. It featured The Rhythm Pals, who had just arrived in Toronto from Vancouver.

Teenage Love Is A Losing Game was his first hit single in 1957, recorded at RCA studios in Hollywood.

Hunter remained with *Country Hoedown* until it went off the air in 1965. That same year, he was given his own TV show which ran until 1992. He remains one of Canada's best known and most influential country artists.

Singles

Teenage Love Is A Losing Game 1957/58
Penny Wishes 1963
Cup Of Disgrace 1967
The Battle Of The Little Big Horn 1967
Mary In The Morning 1967
Half A World Away 1968
Nowhere Bound With Greyhound 1968/69
Can't Find A Space 1969
Walk With Your Neighbour 1969/70
Wait For Sunday 1970
Travelin' Man 1970
Bill Jones General Store 1971/72
The Departure 1974
Born To Be A Gypsy 1974/75
Love Of A Good Woman 1975
The Great Mail Robbery 1978
Dance With Me Molly 1982
Fool Enough To Fall In Love Again 1982
The Man of 87 1989/90
Couldn't See The Gold (& JANIE FRICKE) 1990
Name The Time And Place 1990

Albums

TOMMY HUNTER 1964
TRAVELLING WITH TOMMY HUNTER 1968
TIME SLIPS AWAY 1971
GREATEST HITS 1973
TOMMY 1982
TOMMY HUNTER 1983
GOSPEL READINGS & RECITATIONS 1983
THE ANNIVERSARY SESSIONS 1989

Cassette SINGS FOR YOU 1993

CDs TIMELESS COUNTRY TREASURES 1994
TIMELESS COULNTRY TREASURES VOL. 2 1995
SONGS OF INSPIRATION 1995

Ron Hynes

Ron Hynes started playing in the early 1960s in his hometown of St. John's, Newfoundland and graduated to the coffeehouse circuit in Toronto and Montreal. In 1972 he released his first solo album on Audat Records, DISCOVERY. Four years later, he wrote *Sonny's Dream*, which has been recorded by more than thirty artists, including Emmylou Harris.

In 1978 he returned home and co-founded The Wonderful Grand Band. They later changed their name to CODCO. Hynes played the lead role in *Hank Williams: The Show He Never Gave in St. John's*, and starred in a fifteen week run of the Opry Show in Prince Edward Island with other country singers. Ron also palyed a role in *A Secret Nation*, a film about Newfoundland's confederation with Canada. He wrote the song, *The Final Breath*, which won a Genie Award, the equivalent to the Oscar in Canada, for Best Song.

His next album, *Wild Card*, came out in 1990. It was followed three years later by his major label debut on EMI with CRYER'S PARADISE.

Singles
Story of My Life 1989/90
Roy Orbison Came On 1990
Sonny's Dream 1991
Cryer's Paradise 1993
Man of A Thousand Songs 1993
Atlantic Blue 1994
No Kathleen 1994
Roy Orbison Came On (Re-release) 1994/95

Albums/CDs
DISCOVERY 1972
WILD CARD 1990
CRYER'S PARADISE 1993

J

P.J. Jackson

P.J. (Peter John) Jackson was born on September 30, 1956 in Milton, Nova Scotia. At an early age he became inspired by the music of Merle Haggard. After leaving home at fifteen, he worked at various day jobs, and at eighteen he enlisted in the Canadian Army for three years. After his discharge he was a logger in British Columbia before he turned to singing country music.

His self-titled debut album on Stony Plain Records came out in 1992.

Singles
Hand In Hand 1992
Walking In A Hard Rain 1992
Walkin' Tall 1993
Step Back 1993
Here Comes Monday Morning 1993
Love Boogie Walk 1994
Mr. Misery 1994

CD
P.J. JACKSON 1992

Jimmy James

Jimmy James was born James Heinz in Verdun, Quebec, and became a teenage sensation in 1958 after Columbia Records released his debut single, *Teen-Age Beauty*. He hosted his own TV show on both CFCL in Timmins, Ontario and CHLT in Sherbrooke, Quebec.

His second hit was *Marjolaina,* in 1958, which Arc Records re-released in 1965. By the late 1960s he had devoted some of his time and effort to support the causes of the North American Indian.

Singles
Teen-Age Beauty 1958
Marjolaina (COLUMBIA) 1958
In The Middle Of A Dream 1963
Everybody's Laughing At My Heartaches 1965
Victim Of Love 1965
Bottoms Up 1965
Marjolaina (ARC) 1965
They Used To Come Home Laughing 1969

Albums
WALKIN' THE FLOOR OVER YOU 1963
I REMEMBER YOU 1965
WITH A SONG FOR YOU 1966
EDDY ARNOLD SONGBOOK 1966

Elaine Jarvis

From Brampton, Ontario, Elaine Jarvis grew up in a musical environment. Her father was leader of his own dance band, The Generation Gap, and when she was a teenager she sang in the band. With a solid background in vocal training, dancing, and acting, her dream was to sing professionally. Her big break came in 1983 when Bob Cousins, President of Bel Air Records, signed her. That same year, she recorded her first hit, *I'll Meet You in the Middle of the Bed.*

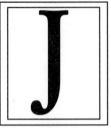

Singles

I'll Meet You In The Middle Of The Bed 1983
I See Somebody Else 1983/84
Last Chance Dance 1984
Why Don't You Give Me A Ring... 1988/89
Walking Angel 1990
The Day That You Walked In 1993/94
Country Town 1994
I Can See The Lights 1994

CD

COUNTRY TOWN 1994

Jerry & Jo'anne

JO'ANNE MOREAULT
JERRY ROBITAILLE

The Quebec duo of Jerry & Jo'Anne impressed both English and French audiences with their country/pop stylings when they were at their peak in the 1970s. The two of them met in Sherbrooke, Quebec, Jo'Anne's hometown, in 1968 during a television show hosted by Levis Boulianne. Jerry was accompanying Boulianne on the banjo, steel guitar, and electric guitar, while Jo'Anne was giving her first solo performance. A year later, the two began to have a professional relationship.

From 1971 to 1976 they recorded several albums and singles to meet the increasing demand for their music. They also formed their own label, Daisy Records.

Singles

We Were Made For Each Other 1971
Down Home 1971/72
Diggy Liggy Lo 1975/76
Drop Some Silver In The Jukebox 1976
Dream Love 1978
That Easy Loving Song 1980
Will You Love Her In The Morning 1981

Albums

ON EST FAIT L'UN POUR L'AUTRE 1971
DOWN HOME 1972
WE WERE MADE FOR EACH OTHER 1971

Johner Brothers

BRAD JOHNER (*vocals*)
KEN JOHNER (*vocals*)

From Midale, Saskatchewan, the Johner Brothers did not attract national attention until 1990 with the release of their debut single, *Why Did I Mistake You.*

Younger brother Brad was the first to record in 1983 after he won a talent contest in his native province. The song on Sunshine Records was *Everyday Strangers*, which The Mercey Brothers included on their self-titled MBS album in 1982.

By the latter half of the 1980s, Brad and Ken became a duo and spent the next few years working the club circuit. *Why Did I Mistake You* in 1990 was their fist single release.

Singles

Why Did I Mistake You 1990
Merry Christmas From Me 1990
Goodbye For Good 1991
Old Gang 1991
Right On Time 1991
Stranded In Love 1992
Where The Highway Divides 1992
My Brother And Me 1993
To Keep The Country Boy Alive 1993
One Horse Town 1993/94
If I Had Us 1994
Smooth Bottom Autumn 1994
Light In My Life (with LISA BROKOP) 1994/95
Starting Right Now 1995
If I Had Us (re-released) 1995

CDs

SOME KIND OF MAGIC 1991
ONE WINTER'S NIGHT 1991
MY BROTHER AND ME 1993
TEN MORE MILES 1995

Lynn Jones

Born in Toronto, Ontario, Marilyn Jones appreciated all types of music. Through her high school and university years she appeared in operettas, played in jamborees, and sang gospel in church. She played drums in several pop groups until she realized she felt more comfortable with country music. By 1967 she had signed with Capitol Records. Her debut single and album were both called *Take The Bad With The Good.*

Singles

Take The Bad With The Good 1967
Gonna Put Some Lovin' On You 1968
Applesauce 1968
Wishing Tree 1969
Only Way To Cry 1971
Total Destruction/Same Old Song 1972
Clap Your Hands 1972
Roses & Candy To Please Me 1973
I Love Your Kind Of Lovin' 1974
Pasedena's On My Mind 1975

Albums

TAKE THE BAD WITH THE GOOD 1967
ROSES AND CANDY 1973

Lori Jordan

A native of North Bay, Ontario, Lori Jordan moved to the west coast at age five. Now a resident of Langley, British Columbia, one of her main musical influences was Anne Murray, who almost recorded a Jordan original, *I Must Be Losing Your Touch.*

In 1988 she recorded her debut single, *Up To No Good,* on Brainchild Records. After a short hiatus in the early 1990s, she returned with the independent album ONE NIGHT in 1994.

Singles *Up To No Good* 1988
I Must Be Losing Your Touch 1989
Another Rainy Day In My Heart 1990
Money Talks 1994

CD ONE NIGHT 1994

K

Ronnie Kartman

Born in New York City, Ronnie Kartman's first musical experience was in a teenage band that won the World's Fair prize as top group. After graduating from the University of Oklahoma, he wrote jingles for radio and television. In 1972 he moved to Canada and became a landed immigrant. The following year he had a minor hit with the song *Strawberry Wine.*

He formed his own record label, Kansas City Records, in 1976. *Honest Love* was the first release in 1976. Although he had other hits, he never really attained star status.

Singles

Strawberry Wine 1973
Honest Love 1976
Can't You Stay At Least Until The Morning 1976
She's Back In Manhattan 1979
You're Never Gonna Find Another Man 1979
You And Me Were Meant To Be 1979
Louisiana 1980
My Love Kept Me Hanging On 1980
April 1981
Babe 1982
California 1984

Album

HONEST LOVE 1977

Carl Kees & The Golden Fiddle Music Co.

CARL KEES (*fiddle, banjo, mandolin, vocals*)
DAVE LEWIS (*drums*)
AL MANNING (*lead guitar, vocals*)
DOUG "SHAKY" WALTERS (*bass*)

Formed in 1979 in Woodstock, Ontario, Carl Kees and The Golden Fiddle Music Co. maintained a high profile when it came to playing a country date. They have played at the International Plowing Match, the Royal Winter Fair, the Canadian National Exhibition, the Calgary Stampede, and on Caribbean cruises.

Kees' career began at age nine when he played on his very first radio show. He then became a member of the group The Chaparrals, and backed up The Good Brothers from 1975 to 1979.

Previous members of the group included Bobby Martin, Leigh Schott, and Glenn Schafer.

Singles

Ain't Drinkin' Whiskey 1984
Honky Tonk Saturday Night 1989/90
Applejack Wine 1992
Have A Drink On Me 1992

Terry Kelly

A native of St. John's, Newfoundland, Terry Kelly was diagnosed with retina blastoma, a cancerous condition that left him blind at the age of one-and-a-half. His parents sent him to the Halifax School For The Blind when he was seven.

Growing up he loved a challenge whether it was sports or music. He was a double silver medalist at the 1979 Canadian Track Competition, and carried the Olympic Torch as part of the Cross Canada Torch Relay for the 1988 Olympics.

He learned to play the accordion, clarinet, guitar and piano. His recording career began in high school when he released five albums with The Stringbusters, an instrumental band.

In 1984 his debut solo album, ON THE MOVE, was released. The first single was *Driving To Mexico* in 1985. Three years later came his second album, FACE TO FACE. His third, DIVIDED HIGHWAY (1992), featured the hit *River of No Return.*

Singles

Driving To Mexico 1985
The Swinger 1985
Old Tyme Christmas 1985
Mama Likes To Rock And Roll 1988
In My Father's House 1992/93
We Can Do Nothing (with KELITA) 1993
There Goes The Fire 1993
River Of No Return 1994
The Girl Is On A Roll Tonight 1994/95
Heart Set On You 1995

Albums

ON THE MOVE 1984
FACE TO FACE 1988
DIVIDED HIGHWAY 1992

Evan Kemp

Born in Vancouver, British Columbia in 1928, Evan Kemp was accidentally rendered blind as a young boy by windblown cedars in a railway yard. For almost a year he could barely distinguish shapes, but something happened that changed his life. He discovered radio — and Wilf Carter and Eddy Arnold. By listening to them he was able to learn to yodel. Wearing a tall hat he yodeled at the cafes and restaurants on Granville Street in Vancouver.

Bill Rea, a disc jockey at CKNW, heard Kemp and invited him to perform on radio. By the time he was twelve he was a radio star, and had become friends with The Rhythm Pals and other country singers.

Evan began working with his first band, the B.C. Ranch Boys, who later became The Trail Riders. He began recording for Aragon Records in the early 1950s. One of his early hits was the *Jessica Waltz.*

Throughout the 1950s and 1960s, he played on radio and at community dances, appeared on the *Grand Ole Opry*, and became good friends with the late Jim Reeves and Loretta Lynn. Kemp also recorded with Alberta Slim and Shirley Field.

The 1970s saw Kemp host his own television show, *Circle 7 Ranch*, which ran over the CTV network. Although he was sidelined by a debilitating stroke in 1989, he was still making guest appearances in the 1990s.

Singles

Jessica Waltz 1952
Santa Got Stuck In The Chimney 1953
On The Golden Shore 1953
Our Old Rockin' Chair 1953
The Beautiful Nicola Valley 1953
Laughing Horse (with ALBERTA SLIM) 1953
Brother You're Not Dead (with ALBERTA SLIM) 1953
Try A Prayer 1953
We Two (with SHIRLEY FIELD) 1953
Cattle Call 1954
1901 Polka 1954
4-H Club Song 1954
Rootie Tootie 1954
My Home By The Fraser 1955

Albums

EVAN KEMP & THE TRAIL RIDERS 1958
EVAN KEMP & THE TRAIL RIDERS 1959
EVAN KEMP IN HOLLYWOOD 1960
REMEMBER ME 1966
IN THE BLUE CANADIAN ROCKIES 1967
PLAIN COUNTRY: EVAN KEMP & FRANK O'CONNELL 1979
COUNTRY COOKIN' n.d.
VELVET COUNTRY n.d.
TRY A PRAYER n.d.

Joan Kennedy

Born in Minto, New Brunswick and raised in Douglas Harbour a few miles away, Joan Kennedy grew up in a musical family. In the late 1950s her parents were in a group called The Golden Guitar Boys. When she was in school, she sang in the church choir. In high school she was in the country band Mutiny.

She entered and won a talent contest sponsored by the Canadian Country Music Association in 1983. That same year she signed with MBS Records, the Mercey Brothers label. *I'm A Big Girl Now* was her first hit. Four years later, she had signed to Destiny Records. FAMILY PRIDE was the name of her first single and album with the label.

On stage she was backed up by Country Clover, a group from Sussex, New Brunswick. They left Joan during the production of FAMILY PRIDE.

By 1990 MCA Records had expressed interest in Joan. Her debut album, CANDLE IN THE WINDOW, came out in February, 1991. Two years later, her second, HIGHER GROUND, was released.

Singles

I'm A Big Girl Now 1984
You're A Stranger 1984
If I'm Wrong 1985
Tell The Boys No 1986
Family Pride 1987
Don't Look In My Eyes 1987
This Time 1988
Mothers And Daughters 1988
Sweet Nothins 1988/89
The Trouble With Love 1990/91
Never Met A Liar 1991
Just Can't Let Go 1991
Candle In The Window 1991/92
Sometimes She Feels Like A Man 1992
If You Want Love 1992
I Need To Hear It From You 1992/93
Talk To My Heart 1993
Breakin' All Over Town 1993
Dream On 1993
Circle Of Love 1994
You Said It 1994

CDs

I'M A BIG GIRL NOW 1984
A CHRISTMAS TO REMEMBER 1986
FAMILY PRIDE 1987
CANDLE IN THE WINDOW 1990
HIGHER GROUND 1993

Bob King

Bob King was born in Joyceville, Ontario on January 6, 1934. He began his music career when he was a teenager. After he won a talent contest in Ottawa, he was invited to join Mac Beattie and the Ottawa Valley Melodiers. Ottawa radio personality 'Long' John Corrigan gave King the nickname "Mr. Sunshine" because of his smile.

In 1954 he signed with RCA Victor. His debut single, *Laurel Lee,* attracted national attention. Its success led to an invitation to tour with bluegrass musicians Wilma Lee and Stoney Cooper and their Clinch Mountain Clan in Wheeling, West Virginia.

Two years later, King returned to Canada where he toured with Wilf Carter, and joined the CFRA Happy Wanderers, who were one of the Ottawa Valley's prominent country acts.

Throughout the 1960s he continued to record and tour with his wife Marie, a singer in her own right, right up to his untimely death on January 20, 1989.

Singles

Pretty Little Girl In Blue 1957
Hey Honey 1958
My Petite Marie 1958
If The Things They Say Are True 1959
Lonely City Park 1959
That's What's On My Mind 1959
The All Canadian Boy 1959
I Dreamed About Mom Last Night 1959
No Parking Here 1959

My Home By The Fraser 1960
Rose Of Old Pawnee 1960
Laurel Lee 1960
Give My Love To Rose 1960
Waltz of Two Broken Hearts 1960
Going Back To An Old Love Affair 1960
Why Don't You Leave Me 1960
Be Careful Of Stones That You Throw 1960
She Went Without Saying Goodbye 1960
Pray For Me Mother Of Mine 1960
Let's Make A Fair Trade 1960
Just Call On Me 1961
Bluest Man In Town 1962
Cowboy 1962
Jimmie Brown The Newsboy 1962
Little Tom 1962
Train Of Memories 1962
French Canadian Girl 1962
Road Paved With Heartaches 1962
It Breaks A Mother's Heart 1962
Once More 1962
Coconut Joe 1962
Boy With A Future 1963
I've Been Dreaming (with MARIE KING) 1963
It's Goodbye And So Long To You 1963
You And My Old Guitar 1963
The Little Shirt My Mother
Made For Me 1963
Between Our Hearts (with MARIE KING) 1963
Patanio, The Pride Of The Plains 1963
Mommy, Please Stay Home With Me 1963
I'm Just Here To Get My Baby Out Of Jail 1963
On The Banks Of The Old Ponchartrain 1963
When The Works All Done This Fall 1963
An Old Log Cabin For Sale 1963
Strawberry Roan 1963
Rockin' Alone In An Old Rockin' Chair 1963
I've Been Down That Road Before 1963
The Ballad Of The Chapeau Boys 1963
Mary Ann Regrets 1963
Memories Of You (*Marie King*) 1963
Rescue From The Moose River Gold Mine 1963
When It's Lamplighting Time In The Valley 1963
The Cat Came Back 1963
The Ballad Of Jed Clampett 1963
Texas Leather & Mexican Lace 1965
Girl With The Sad Lovely 1965
Goodbye My Friend 1965/66
Rambling Shoes 1966
Working On The Country Road 1966
Blue Day 1967/68
Good Times 1968
The Revenuer's Daughter 1969
Let's Make It A Fair Trade 1977
Louisiana Swampmen 1977

Albums

SING WITH BOB KING AND THE COUNTRY KINGS 1958
SING A COUNTRY SONG WITH BOB KING AND HIS COUNTRY KINGS 1959
BOB KING AND HIS COUNTRY KINGS SING FOR LAUREL LEE 1959
JUST ME AND MY OLD GUITAR — BOB KING 1962
SINGS SONG THAT TELL A STORY 1962
BY REQUEST VOL. 2: BOB KING SINGS SONGS THAT TELL A STORY 1963
BOY WITH A FUTURE 1964
THE BEST OF BOB KING 1965
A KING IN THE COUNTRY 1965
SONGS OF A COUNTRY FAN 1966
THE VERSATILE BOB KING SINGS 1968
24 GOLDEN GREATS 1970
KEEPIN' IT COUNTRY 1977
THE BLUEGRASS SIDE OF ME n.d.
25 ANS DE MUSIQUE WESTERN (& MARIE KING) n.d.

CD

BOB KING AND THE COUNTRY KINGS 1993

Scott Kyle King

Scott Kyle King was born in Thunder Bay, Ontario and raised in Regina, Saskatchewan. His father was Fred King, a country disc jockey and former president of the Canadian Country Music Association.

Growing up Scott spent twelve years in the family band. In 1990 he recorded his first single, *Only Time Will Tell,* on Sunshine Records. The following year, he recorded the single *Dark Eyes* as part of the prize he won in the 1991 Bud Country Talent Search. In 1994 his first album, LITTLE BY LITTLE, was released.

Singles

Only Time Will Tell 1990
Dark Eyes 1992
Till I See You Again 1992
Someday 1993
A Brand New Day 1993
Straight From You 1994
Little By Little 1995

CD

LITTLE BY LITTLE 1994

Jack Kingston

Born on October 4, 1925 in St. Catharines, Ontario, Jack Kingston started singing in the church choir. At age six he marked his radio debut with the song, *Springtime In The Rockies,* on CKTB, the local station.

In 1945, he formed his first group, the Kingston Brothers, which was comprised of Jack on vocals and guitar, his brother Art on bass, and friend Alex Dalgleish on steel guitar and fiddle. They broke up in 1946 when Alex suddenly died.

He joined the CKNX Travelling Barn Dance as singer and bass player in 1949, and in 1950 he became the first Canadian country singer to sign with Capitol Records. His first two singles on the label were *Yodeling Cowboy* and *A Love That's True.*

From 1959 to 1963 he lived in Nashville, where he appeared on the *Grand Ole Opry* with Hank Snow. When Jack returned to Canada, he formed a trio with Les Wamboldt and Jimmy King. Jack continued to work in radio and television. He recorded some of his old songs on the 1971 album, SPRINGHILL MINE EXPLOSION.

Singles
Yodeling Cowboy 1951
A Love That's True 1951
Dear Mother 1953
How Far Is She Now? 1954
Alabama Jubilee 1955
Springhill Mine Explosion 1956
Hey There, Baby 1957/58
Road of Broken Hearts 1958
Go Away 1959
Don't Trade 1960
It Never Rains 1960
Cajun Cutie 1962
Snug As A Bug In A Rug 1963
Bye Bye Love 1963

Albums
MAIN STREET JAMBOREE 1962
THE SPRINGHILL MINE EXPLOSION 1971
HAPPY BIRTHDAY DARLING 1974

Chris Krienke

A native of Thunder Bay, Ontario, Chris Krienke (pronounced Krinkee) played a mean banjo and won several titles, including Jr. Canadian National Banjo Champion (1981), Jr. World Banjo Champion (1981), and National Grand Champion (1982).

He recorded his first album, PICK-A-WAY, in 1983. Four years later came his second, GOOD STUFF.

Singles
Honey You Ain't So Tough 1985
She's A Cold Hearted Woman 1986
You're Not Giving Me Much 1987
Good Stuff 1987
Watching Angelina Dance 1988

Albums
PICK-A-WAY 1983
GOOD STUFF 1987

L

Mark Laforme

Mark LaForme was born on the New Credit Indian Reserve near Hagersville, Ontario, and started playing music when he was eleven years old. While in high school Mark played in several rock bands.

He also started writing songs and collaborated with Dallas Harms on the hit *Get Along Little Doggie,* which Gene Watson recorded on his 1985 album, MEMORIES TO BURN.

That same year, LaForme released his debut single, *Here Comes Love or Here Comes Trouble*, but it was his second release, *I Don't Love You Anymore,* that gave him the big break. He continues to have hits in the 1990s.

Singles

Here Comes Love or Here Comes Trouble 1985
I Don't Love You Anymore 1985
Nashville Dream 1987
Long Gone 1988
Nothing Can Stop Me Now 1988
The Road I Walk 1989
Blackbird 1990
Makin' It Easy 1991
Easy For You To Say 1993
I'll Comfort You 1993

Bobby Lalonde

Born on May 22, 1958 in Fournier, Ontario, Bobby Lalonde began performing at age nine with his three brothers in a group called The Four Sons. His main influence in those early years were the fiddle stylings of the late Johnny Mooring.

In the 1970s he won the title of North American Junior Fiddle Champion at the Shelburne Fiddling Competition, which led to an appearance in the Canadian film, *Across This Land* (1973), featuring Stompin' Tom. That same year, Bobby's first self-titled album came out.

After winning the National Fiddling Championships in Ottawa in 1975, Bobby was invited to perform with The Earl Scruggs Revue Band. The Bobby Lalonde Band was organized early in 1981. A year later, Bookshop Records released Lalonde's debut single, *Forty Shades Of Blue.*

Singles

Forty Shades Of Blue 1982
Forget It 1983
Play Old Man 1983
Breezy Nights 1984
Rosin' Up (with VASSAR CLEMENTS) 1984
Lisa 1985
Lovers Will 1987
Long Lonely Nights 1988
She Got Away With Love 1988
If Your Love Ran Out Tomorrow 1988/89
Thanks To You 1989
Somebody Painted My Hometown 1991
Zydeco 1992
Fiddle Man 1993
Cuttin' The Strings 1993
Reinvented Love 1995

Albums BOBBY LALONDE 1973 · FORTY SHADES OF BLUE 1985 · LONG LONELY NIGHTS 1988 · FIDDLE MAN 1993

Ned Landry

Born Frederick Lawrence in Saint John, New Brunswick on February 2, 1921, Landry grew up in a family of musicians. He taught himself to play the violin as a boy, and at fifteen he performed with the New Brunswick Lumberjacks on CBC Radio.

His recording career began in 1950 when he signed a contract with RCA. One of his early hits was *Red River Rag.*

Known as Canada's number one oldtime fiddler and most recorded, Landry received the Order Of Canada in 1992.

Singles/ 78s

Big John McNeil 1950
Newfoundland Breakdown 1950
Ragtime Annie 1950
Red Wing 1950
Soldiers' Joy 1950
Mockingbird 1951
The Bride of the Wind Jig 1952
Lumberjack's Special 1952
Dill Pickles 1952
Red River Rag 1953
Cotton-Eyed Joe 1953
Angus Campbell 1953
MacDougall's Polka 1953
Logger's Breakdown 1954
Johnny Wagoner 1955
Silver and Gold Reel 1957
Ned's Favorite Reel 1958

Albums

NED LANDRY AND HIS FIDDLE 1964
SATURDAY NIGHT BREAKDOWN 1965
MORE NED LANDRY FAVORITES 1965
CANADIAN OLD TIME FIDDLIN' FAVORITES 1966
OLD TIME FIDDLIN' 1966
BOWING THE STRINGS 1966
NED LANDRY 1966
FIDDLE CENTENNIAL TOUR 1967
LIGHTNIN' FIDDLE 1967
ME & MY FIDDLE 1967
FIDDLIN' AROUND 1968
BEST OF NED LANDRY 1968
THE SINGING FIDDLER 1977
CANADA'S OLD TIME FIDDLING CHAMP n.d.
CANADIAN OLD TIME FIDDLE TOUR n.d.
FIDDLIN' & OTHER FUN n.d.
SILVER ANNIVERSARY n.d.
PLAYS & SINGS n.d.

k.d. lang

Born in Consort, Alberta, k.d. (Katherine Dawn) lang is one of Canada's most controversial recording artists. Until 1988 when *Crying*, a duet with Roy Orbison from the soundtrack of the film *Hiding Out*, became a hit, her music was largely unknown to a majority of Canadians and rarely played on Canadian radio stations. Her second album, ANGEL

THE MERCEY BROTHERS

IAN TYSON

TOMMY HUNTER

SHIRLEY FIELD
RON SCOTT

THE RHYTHM PALS

PRAIRIE OYSTER

Mark Tucker

PRESCOTT BROWN

Denise Grant

ANNE MURRAY
CARROLL BAKER

CHARLIE MAJOR

WITH A LARIAT, leaned more toward rural folk or country than pop. Her first single release in 1983 entitled *Friday Dance Promenade* was pressed on white vinyl and is now considered a collector's item.

Her singing style has been deliberately modeled on Patsy Cline's recordings. Owen Bradley, Cline's producer, came out of retirement to produce lang's 1988 album, SHADOWLAND.

In concert she wowed audiences with her frenetic performance and vocal stylings. At the closing ceremonies of Calgary's Winter Olympics in 1988, she led a rousing square dance. That same year, *Chatelaine* magazine chose her as their woman of the year. In 1989 she made her sixth appearance on *The Tonight Show Starring Johnny Carson*, and performed at New York's Radio City Music Hall at the invitation of Barbara Orbison, Roy Orbison's widow.

She admitted publicly in the early 1990s that she was a lesbian and offended her critics when she became a spokesperson in a "Meat Stinks" campaign.

Her 1992 single, *Constant Craving*, reached Billboard's Hot 100.

Singles

Friday Dance Promenade 1983
Hanky Panky 1984
Crying (with ROY ORBISON) 1987/88
Rose Garden 1987
Tune Into My Wave 1987
Diet Of Strange Places 1987
I'm Down To My Last Cigarette 1988
Lock, Stock & Teardrops 1988
Busy Being Blue 1988/89
Full Moon Of Love 1989
Trail Of Broken Hearts 1989
Pulling Back The Reins 1989
Three Days 1989/90
Luck In My Eyes 1990
Big Boned Gal 1990
Ridin' The Rails (K.D. LANG & TAKE 6) 1990
So In Love 1991
Constant Craving 1992
Miss Chatelaine 1992
The Mind of Love (*Where Is Your Head Kathyrn?*) 1992
Just Keep Me Moving 1993
Hush Sweet Lover 1994

Albums/CDs

A TRULY WESTERN EXPERIENCE 1984
ANGEL WITH A LARIAT 1986
SHADOWLAND 1988
ABSOLUTE TORCH AND TWANG 1989
INGENUE 1992
EVEN COWGIRLS GET THE BLUES 1993
ALL YOU CAN EAT 1995

Willie Lamothe

For more than thirty-five years, Willie Lamothe was one of the pioneers of Quebec's country music scene. He composed all the words and music to his songs, and translated American country hits by

Johnny Cash, Merle Haggard, and others from English into French. Lamothe's first record on RCA Victor in 1946 was *Je suis un cowboy canadien.* Another hit that same year, *Je chante a cheval,* was equally successful.

In 1954 and 1955 he co-starred in Gene Autry's show at the Montreal Forum. During Canada's centennial year (1967), he sang in French at the *Grand Ole Opry Show* at the North American Disc Jockey's Convention in Nashville, Tennessee.

The 1970s marked Willie's TV debut on Tele-Metropole's *Le Ranch à Willie.* The National Film Board documentary on his life as a performer won first prize at the Canadian Film Festival in Toronto.

He continued to record until 1991, and died on October 19, 1992.

Singles

Je suis un cowboy canadien 1946
L'amour des roses 1946
Je chante a cheval 1946
Je chante au clair de lune 1947
Mon reve 1947
Le joyeux cowboy 1947
Giddy-Up Sam 1948
L'amour d'une cowgirl 1948
Je suis un as du rodeo 1948
Quand je regarde tomber la pluie 1948
Allo Allo, petit Michel 1948
Histoire de l'est canadien 1949
L'eglise de mon village 1949
Je suis un vrai cowboy 1950
Une guitare et un cowboy qui chante 1950
Mon passage en Gaspesie 1950
Au petit trot 1950
La samba des cowboys 1950
Dans mon beau pays 1951
Je suis un cowboy fantaisiste 1951
Allo cowboy 1951
Pour un cowboy 1952
Le long du Mississippi (with RITA GERMAIN) 1952
Ma prairie si jolie 1953
Jambalaya 1953
A cheval dans Montreal 1953
Le chant du draveur 1954
Quand vous aurez 20 ans 1954
Coeur brise 1955
Mon palamino 1955
J'suis un cowboy qui a de la veine 1955
Une vie brisee 1955
Dans une caresse 1956
Sous le ciel bleu de ma prairie 1956
Nos artistes canadiens 1956
Le train du Tennessee (with RITA GERMAIN) 1956
Rock & Roll a cheval 1956
Pourquoi ma cherie 1957
Y'a pas d'cowboy a la TV 1958
Ma Mimi 1959
Pourquoi m'as-tu delaisse 1959
Tu partis un jour 1960
J'ai les bleus quand il pleut 1960
Oh ma cherie 1962
Pourquoi donc as-tu brise mon coeur 1963
Oh ma cherie — J'ai perdu ton amour par ma faute 1964
Cinq minutes pour t'aimer 1965
Cherie, tu me demandes si je t'aime 1967
Tant mieux 1969

Telephone-moi 1969
A cause de toi 1970
Papa Willie 1970
Suis-je facile a oublier 1971
Puisque tout est fini 1972
La fin d'un amour 1972
Mes voyages en Louisiane 1972
Willie r'viendra 1972
Y'a toujours moyen de moyenner (with DOMINIQUE MICHEL) 1973
La blond a Willie 1974
Mustang 1975
Quand le soleil dit bonjour aux montagnes (with DENIS NIQUETTE) 1976
Y'a un mur qui nous separe 1983
Willie r'viendra (re-release) 1991

Albums

WILLIE LAMOTHE ET SES CAVALIERS DES PLAINES 1954
WILLIE LAMOTHE ET RITA GERMAIN 1959
WILLIE LAMOTHE ET SES CAVALIERS DES PLAINES (WITH RITA GERMAIN) 1960
15TH ANNIVERSARY 1961
CHANSONS D'HIER ET D'AUJOURD'HUI 1962
WILLIE LAMOTHE (MB 103) 1963
WILLIE LAMOTHE (MB 135) 1963
WILLIE LAMOTHE (DS 2010) 1964
SUCCES DES ANNEES 1940 ET 1950, VOL 2 1965
WILLIE LAMOTHE: MES PREMIERES CHANSONS 1965
JE CROIS EN MON ETOILE 1967
LES GRANDS SUCCES DE WILLIE LAMOTHE 1970
WILLIE LAMOTHE (SDS 5062) 1971
WILLIE LAMOTHE A L'HARMONICA 1971
PENSE A MOI CUPID ON TANT MIEUX 1971
LES DISQUES D'OR DE WILLIE LAMOTHE 1971
LES DISQUES D'OR VOL 2 1972
LE SOLEIL SE LEVE AVEC PAPA WILLIE 1972
UN PEU DE TOUT 1973
20 SUCCES SOUVENIRS 1974
ALBUM SOUVENIR 1974
MUSTANG 1975
30 ANS. DUIS NASHVILLE 1976
MA VIE 1983
JE REVIENS 1991

Iris Larratt

Born in Lloydminster, Saskatchewan and raised in Sardis, British Columbia, Iris Larratt's first experience with music was through her mother who wrote children's songs. At five Iris sang in front of an audience for the first time. After graduating from high school, she moved to Prince George with a friend who helped her find work as a singer. At The Hut, a local club, she first sang solo and then was invited to play in the house band.

In 1970 she joined Bitterwind in Calgary, Alberta. They later changed their name to Iris and The Bitterwind and then broke up. She joined another group called Celebration. When it, too, broke up, she played in various house bands.

She recorded her debut single, *You Can't Make Love To A Memory,* in 1979 on Infinity Records. The following year her self-titled debut album was released on RCA.

Singles

You Can't Make Love To A Memory 1979
She Won't Love You 1980
Sorry Doesn't Always Make It Right 1979/80
Only Tomorrow Knows 1981
I've Gotta Cowboy In The Saddle 1981/82
Ease My Mind 1982
Don't Give Up On Him Now 1983
You Thrill Me 1983/84
Don't Rush Me 1984

Albums

IRIS LARRATT 1980
OUT OF MY HEART 1983

Mel Lavigne

Mel Lavigne was born and raised in Midland, Ontario. An accomplished fiddler, piano, and saxophone player, he joined *The Canadian Army Show* during World War II, and played a Command Performance for Wilhelmina, Queen of the Netherlands. He was a regular member of the *CKNX Barn Dance* in Wingham, Ontario in the early 1950s, and became the first old time fiddler to win the Canadian Open Championship at the International Old Time Fiddle Contest in Shelburne, Ontario in 1951. He later formed his own band, The Bluewater Boys, and became a producer at CKVR TV in Barrie, Ontario. He died on February 10, 1994.

Cassette

FIDDLE TUNES 1989

Claudette Lefebvre & The Country Jewels

MAURICE CHARRON (*fiddle*)
FLORAM DESJARDINS (*bass*)
CLAUDETTE LEFEBVRE (*rhythm guitar, vocals*)
ROLLAND PLOUFFE (*accordion*)

Born in Ottawa, Ontario in 1940, Claudette Lefebvre joined CFRA's Happy Wanderers in 1952. While in high school she formed her first band called The Country Jewels. The original lineup consisted of Lefebvre, Maurice Charron, Rolland Plouffe, and Floram Desjardins. In 1957 they became a trio comprised of Lefebvre, Jean Desmond on fiddle, and Billy O'Boie (real name: William F. Paradosky) on lead guitar and vocals. O'Boie was taken from Buddy Holly's hit *Oh Boy,* and he had previously been in a high school band called The Melody Ranch Boys in his native Winnipegosis, Manitoba.

In 1965 they teamed up with Slim Gordon and later recorded the single *I Can't Lose These Blues.* Claudette and Billy released a French album in 1969 on the Rustique label, CLAUDETTE LEFEBVRE & BILLY O'BOIE.

By the early 1970s the group was a trio comprised of O'Boie, Claudette, and Jean Desmond on fiddle. David Austin Lemay (known to his friends as Tim) became their new bass player in 1972. That same year Cynda Records released the album CLAUDETTE LEFEBVRE AND THE COUNTRY JEWELS.

Singles

As Claudette Lefebvre:

Oceans of Love 1966

As Billy O'Boie:

I Love My Gal 1966

As Claudette Lefebvre & The Country Jewels

Ain't You Ever Gonna Sing My Song 1972

La Chanson Des Bles D'Or 1972

Albums

As Claudette Lefebvre & Billy O'Boie:

CLAUDETTE LEFEBVRE & BILLY O'BOIE 1969

As Claudette Lefebvre & The Country Jewels:

CLAUDETTE LEFEBVRE & THE COUNTRY JEWELS 1972

Diane Leigh

Toronto-born Diane Leigh started singing when she was fifteen. Her idol was 1950s star Joni James. It was while singing to one of her records that Diane's cousin Ted overheard her. He arranged for her to sing with the Toronto pop group, The Sapphires. She later joined a small dance band as an unpaid singer, and met Vic Siebert of the Sons of the Saddle, who introduced her to country music. In the early 1960s she was invited to join Siebert's group and record with them.

In the fall of 1963 she went to Nashville to record her first single, *Little Boy Lost*, which was released in early 1964. Her second single, *Biggest Hurt Of All,* came out later that same year.

She was a regular cast member on *Carl Smith's Country Music Hall* on CTV from 1965-69, and in 1965 signed a recording contract with Capitol Records. Her debut single was *Shadows of Your Heart.* By 1977 she had retired from the limelight.

Singles

Little Boy Lost 1964
Biggest Hurt Of All 1964
Shadows Of Your Heart 1965/66
Why Can't He Be You 1966/67
Mr. Jukebox/The Sound That Makes Me Blue 1967
The Wife You Save May Be Your Own 1968
Keep The Home Fires Burning 1968/69
I'm Gonna Let George Do It 1969
I'm A One Man Woman 1969/70
I'm Your Puppet 1970
Devil To Angel 1972
Sing Happy 1972
Long Lonely Road 1972
I'll Count Every Hour 1972
Cape Breton Colors 1973
Blind Jonathan/Make It Over The Hill 1973
His Kind Of Woman 1974
God's People Are One 1974/75
Go Gently 1976

Albums

SHADOWS OF YOUR HEART 1965
DIANE . . . COUNTRY QUEEN 1972
TWO SHADES OF BLUE 1973
CHRISTMAS AT HOME 1973
GOD'S PEOPLE ARE ONE 1975
COUNTRY TUNES I REMEMBER 1977

Vic Levac

Vic Levac was born and raised in Timmins, Ontario. He credits his Uncle Oscar Laframboise for introducing him to the fiddle. At six years of age, Vic made his first public performance over Timmins radio station CFCL.

In his teens he took up the guitar and often performed in his uncle's band on the Northern Ontario circuit. Vic later moved to Hamilton where he worked with many Southern Ontario groups, such as Kolor of Tyme, The Alley Cats, and The Impalas.

By the 1980s he had honed his talents as a songwriter and written over two hundred songs. His debut album, YESTERDAY'S GONE, came out in 1987.

Singles

Open Up The Door 1987
Go Slow 1987/88
Yesterday's Gone 1988
Magic Highway 1988
The Vision 1993
Golden Years 1993

Album

YESTERDAY'S GONE 1987

The John Lindsay Band

At an early age, John Lindsay developed an interest in music. Born on a farm in Sonningdale, Saskatchewan, he was ten years old when he started writing lyrics. At twelve he received his first set of drums and joined a country group. He later played rock and roll in a high school band, but went back to country when he graduated. In 1986 he put together a touring band and, a year later, recorded his first single, *Only You.*

Singles

Only You 1987
If I Know You 1987/88
Am I The Only One 1989
Homecoming Christmas 1989
Way Back When 1991

Bill Long

Born in Albuquerque, New Mexico, Bill Long came to Canada in 1948 and settled in Hamilton, Ontario. While in Toronto in 1953 he met Harold Moon, who arranged for him to appear on CHML's *Main Street Jamboree.* He would take over as foreman of the show, and appear on two other CHML shows, *Bar II Ranch* and *Fireside,* a religious show for children. In 1953 he recorded *Redheads, Blondes, and Brunettes* on the Apex Record label. Two years later, he recorded *What A Waste (Of Good Corn Likker)* on King Records, which Dixie Bill Hilton recorded first in 1952.

Long met his future wife Rose Jackson in 1955 and they were married the following year. They performed together in clubs and on TV. He recorded several 78s and one album for Arc in 1965 called MY FAVORITE SONGS.

Singles

Redheads, Blondes & Brunettes 1953
Bleeding Heart 1953
What A Waste (Of Good Corn Likker) 1955/56
Relax, Relax, Relax n.d.
Ranch of the Golden Rule (with the YONGE STREET CHILDREN'S CHOIR) n.d.

Albums

MY FAVORITE SONGS 1965

Anne Lord

A native of Birmingham, England, Anne Lord is based in Vancouver. She rose to fame as a country singer in the 1980s after years of experience in rock and folk groups. She and her husband Roger wrote songs, played in a band, and performed as a duo called Meadow from 1972 to 1979.

Under the name of Anne Attenborrow, she had two hits on Polydor Records, *We Will Find You* (1970) and *I Shall Be Released* (1972).

Her debut country single as Anne Lord was *Without You (What Will I Do)* in 1982. A year later she was signed to Comstock Rocks in the United States. *Hung Up On You* was the first of several hits she has had on the label.

As Anne Attenborrow:

Singles

We Will Find You 1970
I Shall Be Released 1972

As Anne Lord:

Without You 1982
Hung Up On You 1983
Endlessly 1983
Nobody Said 1984
Up The Wall 1984
Rainbow 1984/85
Stars In My Eyes 1985
Forget About Me 1985/86
Don't Cry For Me 1986
I'll Never Get Over You 1986
True Blue 1987
Seventh Heaven 1988
Takes One To Know One 1988
Blue Rain 1989
Cherokee 1990
Because Of You 1991

Album ENDLESSLY 1984

Myrna Lorrie

As a teenager in the 1950s, Myrna Lorrie was one of Canada's top female stars. In November 1954 the Fort William, Ontario (now Thunder Bay) native recorded her first single called *Are You Mine*, a duet with Buddy DeVal. She was managed by Don Grashey, who helped launch the career of Loretta Lynn in Canada in the early 1960s. He also looked after many others, such as Carroll Baker and Cindi Cain.

In 1963 Lorrie headlined a country music show at the Atlantic Winter Fair, and later made guest appearances on such national CBC-TV shows as *Tommy Hunter* and *Don Messer*. She was invited to appear on the CBC TV show *Countrytime* out of Halifax, Nova Scotia in 1969. In 1970 she became the show's co-host with Don Tremaine.

After a long hiatus she returned to the spotlight in 1988. Now managed by her brother Dave Petrunka, they formed a new label together called Sibley Records. Her first single was *Blue Me.* In 1989 she was inducted into the Canadian Country Music Hall of Fame.

Singles

Are You Mine (with BUDDY DEVAL) 1954
I'm Your Man (with BUDDY DEVAL) 1955
Tears Amid The Laughter 1955
Life's Changing Scene 1955
That's What Sweetheart's Do 1957
Teenager's Breakup 1957
I'll Be Lonesome When You're Gone 1958
On A Little Bamboo Bridge 1958
Do You Wish You Were Free 1965
Can't Live With Him 1965
The Longest Day This Year 1966
Your Special Day 1966/67
Turn Down The Music 1968
Changing Of The Seasons 1968
Tell Me Not To Go (COLUMBIA) 1968
Tell Me Not To Go (MCA) 1970
Bringing Mary Home 1971
Don't Take Away Your Love 1975/76
It's Too Late 1977
Blue Blue Me 1989
Sometime 1989/90
Our Love Keeps Coming Back 1990

Albums MYRNA LORRIE n.d.
IT'S COUNTRY TIME n.d.

Sharon Lowness

From Halifax, Nova Scotia, Sharon Lowness grew up in a musical family. In her teens she met her future husband Chuck Lowness, who discovered her potential. Sharon and Chuck later fronted their own group, Chuck and The Chicks, later known as The Teddy Bears. In 1972 Sharon recorded her first single, *Same Old Memory.*

Singles
Same Old Memory 1972
Flowers of the Darkness 1972
Flying East 1972/73
God Made Me A Woman 1973
You Do It Again 1973/74
He's My Morning Sunshine 1978
Hang Up Your Rhinestone Suit 1979
Two Timin' Man 1979
There's A New Moon Over My Shoulder 1981

Album BROOMSTICK HORSE COWBOY 1973

Julie Lynn

The daughter of a French-Canadian mother and an Irish father, Julie Lynn was born in Gaspé, Quebec in 1948. Her real name was Julia Catherine Flynn. When she was a youngster, she moved to Fort Coulonge, Quebec, and at sixteen she worked at a local sawmill splicing wood. About this time she was asked to sing at a local club, and liked it enough to form her own band, which played a mix of rock and country. In 1970 she signed a recording contract with Dominion Records, and her biggest hit, *Good Morning World,* was released in late 1970.

Singles
The Great Pretender 1970
Good Morning World 1970
Why Did You Love Me Yesterday 1971
Travelin' On 1972
Shanty Girl 1974
Love Is Hard To Find 1975
The Sweetest Thing This Side Of Love 1976
I Don't Care 1976
I Wanna Be Bad 1976
I Want To Be Loved 1977
My Little One 1977
To Hear The Family Sing 1977/78
Love Made A Honky Tonk Woman 1978
Played Me For A Fool 1979
Easy Does It 1980

Albums
PUT A LITTLE LOVE IN YOUR HEART 1970
LOOK WHAT THEY'VE DONE TO MY SONG 1971
IN A WINDOW PANE 1971
THE NICKEL SONG 1972
JULIE LYNN SHOW n.d.
JULIE LYNN n.d.
MANY MOODS OF JULIE LYNN n.d.

M

Harold Macintyre

Growing up in the little town of Sugarcamp near Port Hawkesbury in Cape Breton, Nova Scotia, Harold MacIntyre often sang for his father, sisters, and aunts. He didn't start to sing professionally until he went to Toronto in 1967. By day he worked at General Electric, and by night he played and sang at various honky tonks.

It all started when George and June Patrick, a husband and wife duo in Duffy's Tavern in Toronto, asked Harold to come up and sing. He later met another musician named Albert MacDonald, and the two of them were in several country bands, such as Harold's Super Service. In 1973 he recorded his first album, MY COUNTRY WAY, on Condor Records.

He went to Sudbury where he appeared on the TV show, *Area Code 705*, which later became the name of his backup band. Signed to Burco Records, his first single on the label was *George* in 1980. That same year the album AREA CODE 705 was released.

In 1985 he left the group to concentrate on a solo career. Backed by the Harold MacIntytre Band, he put out two single releases in 1994, *I Am What I Am* and *To Drink Or Not To Drink.*

Singles

George 1980
Margie 1980
The Newfie Sheik 1981
Too Much Woman 1981
Honky Tonk Fever 1981
That's How Long I'll Love You (& MARJI LEA CODY) 1981/82
Possum 1982
That Don't Mean I Love You Less 1982
Till The Day I'm Gone 1983
Roads And Other Reasons 1983/84
Pressures Of Progress 1983
Heaven's Almost As Big As Texas 1984
Too Much Woman 1984
To Drink Or Not To Drink 1994
I Am What I Am 1994

Albums

MY COUNTRY WAY 1973
AREA CODE 705 1980
HONKY TONK FEVER 1981
TRAGIC ROMANCER 1983
THE HORSE AND THE RIDER 1984

Brent McAthey

Brent McAthey was born in Calgary and raised on a farm in Water Valley, Alberta. His interest in poetry led to a love of songwriting. By the time he was twenty-years-old, he had launched a professional career. He later met Dick Damron, who helped him develop as an artist. After several singles, Brent's debut album, WAITIN' FOR THE SUN, came out in 1994.

Singles *I'm In Love* 1989
Dreamer 1990
Here I Go Again 1990/91
You And The Ocean 1991
Not Much Left To Say 1993
Will She Remember 1994
She Wants To Fly High Again 1995

Album/CD WAITIN' FOR THE SUN 1994

Jason McCoy

Born in Minesing, Ontario on August 27, 1970, Jason McCoy's first exposure to country music was through his parents' record collection. By age seven he had started to learn the guitar, and he wrote his first song, *Greatest Times Of All,* when he was twelve. After he won a talent contest in Toronto in 1988, he went to Nashville with Ray Griff to record an independent album called GREATEST TIMES OF ALL on the Airstrip Music label.

In 1994 MCA Records released his debut album, COUNTRY . . . CLOSER TO THE EDGE. *Your Mama Warned You 'Bout Me* and *Take It From Me* were the first two singles.

Singles *Slow This World Down* 1989
How Could You Hold Me 1989
She's My Wife 1991
Your Mama Warned You 'Bout Me 1994
Take It From Me 1994
Ghosts 1995
This Used To Be Our Town 1995
Learning A Lot About Love 1995
Candle 1995/96

CD GREATEST TIMES OF ALL 1989
JASON MCCOY 1994
JASON MCCOY (MCA) 1995

Fred McKenna

Born in Fredericton, New Brunswick in 1934, Fred McKenna was blind at birth, but by the time he was seven years old, he was showing an interest in music. After moving to the Halifax School For The Blind, he was discouraged from playing the piano because his fingers were not long enough. At twelve his parents bought him a Spanish guitar, which he laid across his knees and picked Hawaiian style.

In his teens he toured the Maritimes, where he played in community halls. He first appeared on *Don Messer's Jubilee* in 1958 and, three years later, he became a regular on the show. Other shows he appeared on were *At The Caribou* and *Country Time.*

At the time of his death on November 18, 1977, he had been working as musical director of *The George Hamilton IV Show.*

Singles *Sad Songs That Tell A Story* 1973
Moonlight Time (& GEORGE BECK) n.d.
I'm Afraid To Go To Sleep (& GEORGE BECK) n.d.
Millie's Mine n.d.

Albums DOWNEAST MUSIC OF FREDDIE MCKENNA 1958
FRED MCKENNA OF CBC-TV SING ALONG JUBILEE 1964
HANK WILLIAMS' SONGBOOK 1966
STEEL RAIL BLUES 1967
PLAIN OLD THREE CHORD HURTIN' COUNTRY SONGS 1972

Ron McLeod

An accomplished accordion player, Hamilton, Ontario-born Ron McLeod was fifteen when he won a gold medal at the Waterloo Music Festival. He was later hired by Slim Gordon, who gave him his first taste of country music.

In the early 1950s he was hired to play in the Johnny Davidson Band, which became the house band on *Main Street Jamboree* on CHCH-TV in Hamilton. While on the show, Ron gave up the accordion for the guitar and began to sing.

He formed his own band in 1958, The Rock-A-Billies, and three years later, he recorded his first album on Sparton Records, *Thanks A Lot.* In the 1960s he formed another group called The Lincoln County Boys, and recorded for Arc and Quality Records.

Singles *Suicide* 1963
Ashes To Ashes 1964
Big Red Jimmy 1973
Baby's Got This Thing About 1976

Albums THANKS A LOT 1961
ON TOP OF THE WORLD WITH COUNTRY MUSIC 1966
ON THE ROAD 1967
OKEEFANOKEE 1973
BEST OF/A ROYAL FLUSH 1974

Ron McMunn

Born and raised on a farm in Almonte, Ontario, Ron McMunn began playing music with his parents and two sisters. He apprenticed with Charlie Finners and the Hay Shakers. While working as a ranchhand in Arcola, Saskatchewan, he played with Ollie and The Playmates on weekends. By the mid-1950s McMunn had returned to Ottawa and formed his own group called The Country Cousins, who had their own weekly radio show on CJET in Smith Falls, Ontario. In 1959 Rodeo Records released their debut album, COUNTRY MUSIC WITH RON MCMUNN AND THE COUNTRY COUSINS. In 1986 McMunn was inducted into the Ottawa Valley Music Hall Of Fame.

Single *Peter Smokey Jones* 1972

Albums
COUNTRY MUSIC WITH RON MCMUNN AND THE COUNTRY COUSINS 1959
SING 'M GOOD 'N COUNTRY 1961
BLUE GRASS CANNONBALL WITH RON MCMUNN AND THE COUNTRY COUSINS 1962
RON MCMUNN AND SHIRLEY THOMAS SING COUNTRY 1964
THE SILVER FOX CUTS COUNTRY 1966
RESERVE ME A TABLE 1975
LIVE, THE SILVER FOX, MISSISSIPPI COUNTRY 1977
THANKS FOR THIRTY YEARS 1981

Larry Magee

Born and raised on a farm near Flesherton, Ontario on February 22, 1954, Larry Magee was a fourteen-year-old when he learned to play the guitar. He came from a musical family. Grandpa Magee played the fiddle, and Dad played guitar. When he finished high school, Larry bought the family business (Magee's Gas Bar) but still found time to practice and play on weekends.

His first two albums, WHO WILL HE LEAN ON and WE'LL FIND OUR WAY, were both produced by Gary Buck in Nashville.

Singles
I'd Rather Be Alone 1991
I Never Saw It Coming 1992
Who Will He Lean On 1992
Stepping Out Of The Picture 1992
Anybody's Guess 1993
I Take The Fifth 1993
No Turning Back 1994
Grandma's Purple Flowers 1995

CDs WHO WILL HE LEAN ON 1991 WE'LL FIND OUR WAY 1994

Charlie Major

Born on New Year's Eve, 1954 in Aylmer, Quebec, Charlie Major started making a living with his music in the late 1970s when he played the coffeehouse circuit in Western Quebec and Eastern Ontario.

In the early 1980s, he went to Alberta to eke out a living as a country singer, but the novelty wore off and he returned home to Ottawa. Songwriting remained his forté and he honed his craft while working at various day jobs. He worked in a sawmill in British Columbia and as a contruction worker.

His music career started in 1987 when he entered and won the CKBY-FM Ottawa Talent Contest. The win provided him with an opportunity to make his first record, *Back in '73/Crazy In The Night.*

In 1988 Matt Minglewood had a Top Ten hit with *Someday I'm*

Gonna Ride In A Cadillac, a Charlie Major original. Another Major original, *Walk Away*, was recorded by Patricia Conroy and included on her BLUE ANGEL album. The one song that made Major famous was *Backroads*, which Ricky Van Shelton recorded in 1991.

Two years later, BMG Music Canada released his debut album, THE OTHER SIDE, which he recorded in Nashville. The first single was *I'm Gonna Drive You Out Of My Mind.*

Singles
Back in '73/Crazy In The Night 1987
I'm Gonna Drive You Out Of My Mind 1993
I'm Somebody 1993
Nobody Gets Too Much Love 1994
The Other Side 1994
It Can't Happen To Me 1994
I'm Here 1994/95
Running In The Red 1995
(I Do It) For The Money 1995
Tell Me Something I Don't Know 1995/96

CDs
CHARLIE MAJOR 1993
LUCKY MAN 1995

Bev Marie

Born and raised in Bobcaygeon, Ontario, Bev Marie started singing with her brother Malcolm, sister Donna, and father Robert as part of the Bradt Family, who were popular in the Kawartha area. She then moved to Oshawa, where she resumed her career and appeared at various jamborees, and worked with Bud Roberts and Con Archer.

In October 1970 Paragon Records released her debut album, COUNTRY GIRL. Two years later, she had formed her own group, The Canadian Showband. One of her early hits was *Life Is Like A Merry-Go-Round* in the fall of 1972.

Bev went into semi-retirement in 1973. She made appearances at fairs, telethons, jamborees, and charitable events until the early 1990s when she retired from the music business entirely.

Singles
There's A Little Town (Bobcaygeon) 1971
Life Is Like A Merry-Go-Round 1972
Brand New Me 1987
Jessie's Tragedy 1987
Family Love n' Country 1987
Could This Be Love 1988
Your Love Is Here To Stay 1989
I Remember 1989
Alive And Loving It 1990

Albums
COUNTRY GIRL 1970
SPIN IT COUNTRY 1973

Shelley-Lou Marie

Born in Winnipeg, Manitoba in 1960, Shelley Lou-Marie (Morrisseau) was influenced by her parents while growing up on the family farm.

Her father, who was in a band in Portage La Prairie, taught her to play the guitar. At six years of age she began competing in local talent shows, and was heard in on a series of Rotary Club Amateur Shows broadcast over radio station CFRY in Winnipeg. From this experience she met Dusty Lee Rivers, her manager, record producer, and future husband. In 1981 her first single, *Breaking and Entering,* was released on the MCC label.

Singles *Breaking And Entering* 1981 — *I Love Making Love To You* 1981

Jim Matt

Born on January 18, 1964 in Englehart, Ontario, Jim Matt grew up in a musical family. At age six he learned his first country song, Hank Snow's *Little Buddy.* By the time he was sixteen, Matt was working at high school dances and honing his skills as a songwriter. His exposure at the 1991 Bud Country Talent Contest led to his first single release, *Vince Gill, Ricky Skaggs & Me,* in 1992. Two years later, he signed a contract with Little Dog Records. His debut album, ALL MY WILD OATS, was released in 1995.

Singles
Vince Gill, Ricky Skaggs & Me 1992
A Better Place To Live 1995
This Old Guitar 1995

CD ALL MY WILD OATS 1995

The Mercey Brothers

From Hanover, Ontario, The Mercey Brothers started out in 1957 as a duo comprised of Larry and Ray Mercey. Their first single, *Just The Snap of Your Fingers,* on Chateau Records was a pop hit in late 1961 and early 1962. Brother Lloyd joined his two brothers to make the group a trio in February of 1966.

They signed with Columbia Records that same year, and had four number one hits on the RPM Country Chart: *Whistling On The River* (1966), *Uncle Tom* (1967), *Who Drinks My Beer When I'm Gone* (1969), and *Old Bill Jones* (1970). In 1970 they signed with RCA and their chart success continued with two consecutive number one hits, *Hello Mom* and *Who Wrote The Words* (both 1971).

Two years later, they opened their own recording studio in Elmira, Ontario, and in 1975 started their own record label, MBS Records, that helped launch the careers of Terry Carisse, Marie Bottrell, Joan Kennedy, and others. In June 1980 the Mercey Brothers Studio closed. Later that same year, Ray left the group to start his own carpentry business.

During the 1980s the group went through some personnel changes. George Ogilvie and Darrell Scott were added in 1981. They were replaced by J.K. Gulley and Greg Smith in 1983, and John Dymond and Eric Mahar in 1986.

The Mercey Brothers broke up in 1989. That same year they were inducted into the Canadian Country Music Hall Of Fame.

Singles

Just The Snap Of Your Fingers 1961/62
Whistle On The River 1966
Uncle Tom 1967
Absent Minded Me 1968
What's A Guy To Do 1968
Who Drinks My Beer When I'm Gone 1969
Ordinary Peeping Tom 1969
My Song For You 1970
Pickin' Up The Pieces 1970
Goodbye 1970
Old Bill Jones 1970/71
Knockin' Down The Hard Times 1971
Hello Mom 1971
Who Wrote The Words 1971
The Day Of Love 1971/72
Kentucky Turn Your Back 1972
It's So Easy To Please Me 1973
Meant To Be With Me 1973
I Heard Bells 1973
California Lady 1974
Our Lovin' Times 1974
Did You Hear My Song 1975
Loving You From A Distance 1975/76
Old Loves Never Die 1976
If I Believed In Myself 1976/77
Jamie 1977
You Know It Felt Good 1977
Home Along The Highway 1978
Comin' On Stronger 1978
Stranger 1978/79
Hell Bent For Mexico 1979
I Wish You Could Have Turned My Head 1979/80
Your Eyes Don't Lie To Me 1980
Makin' The Night The Best Part Of My Day 1980
Sweet Harmony 1981
The Same Eyes That Drove Me Crazy 1981
Maybe It's Love This Time 1982
Starting All Over Again 1982
I've Already Left You In My Mind 1982/83
The Day That You Walked In 1983
Anytime Down 1983
The Leader Of The Band 1984
Love At Last Sight 1984
You Lifted Me High Enough 1985
Love Is The Reason 1985
Take A Little Chance On Love 1986
A Pretty Diamond Ring 1986
Heroes 1986/87
Raised By The Radio 1987
Straight To Your Heart 1988

Albums

THE MERCEY BROTHERS (COLUMBIA) 1968
MY SONG FOR YOU 1969
THE MERCEY BROTHERS (HARMONY) 1969
NATURALLY 1970
THE MERCEY BROTHERS (CTL/COLUMBIA) 1970
HAVE MERCEY 1971
MERCEY BROTHERS COUNTRY 1972

THE MERCEY BROTHERS (RCA) 1973
DID YOU HEAR MY SONG 1975
BEST OF THE MERCEY BROTHERS 1975
HOMEMADE 1976
MERCEY BROTHERS RADIO SHOW 1976
COMIN' ON STRONGER 1977
COMMAND PERFORMANCE 1980
THE MERCEY BROTHERS (MBS) 1982
LATEST AND GREATEST VOLUME 1 1984
LOVE IS THE REASON 1985
LATEST AND GREATEST VOLUME 2 1988

CDs THE MERCEY BROTHERS 30 GREATEST: THEIR HITS AND MORE (VOL. 1 & 2) 1990

Larry Mercey

After The Mercey Brothers broke up at the end of 1989, Larry Mercey decided to continue as a solo act. He released his first independent album, FULL SPEED AHEAD, in 1990. It contained *You're Still In These Crazy Arms Of Mine,* which went to number one on the Cancountry Hit Chart in *Country Music News* in May 1991. That same year, he was nominated for Country Male Vocalist at both the Juno Awards and the Country Music Awards. In 1994, Rodeo Records released Larry's second album, LET'S DEAL AGAIN.

Singles
She Feels Like A New Man Tonight 1990
Full Speed Ahead 1990
You're Still In These Crazy Arms Of Mine 1991
True Blue 1991
Hold That Thought 1991/92
Keepin' Up With The Joneses 1992
I Love You Canada 1992
I Might Be Down (But I Ain't Out Yet) 1993
If I'm Only Good For One Thing 1993/94
Wild West Show 1994
Quarters For The Jukebox 1995

CDs FULL SPEED AHEAD 1990
LET'S DEAL AGAIN 1994

Don Messer

For thirty years, first on radio and then on television, Don Messer was a household name. Each show began with the familiar phrase, "And now it's time for the Down East music of Don Messer and His Islanders," accompanied by *The Fireman's Reel,* followed by the Islanders theme, *Going To The Barndance.*

The youngest of eleven children, he was born in Tweedsmuir, New

Brunswick in 1909. He began playing in public when he was seven. His first radio show was on March 19, 1929 over the Canadian Radio Commission, now CHSJ in Saint John. Don's group, the New Brunswick Lumberjacks, became famous. He later disbanded it, and only Duke Neilsen and Charlie Chamberlain remained as the Backwoods Breakdown.

In 1938 they moved to Prince Edward Island and the group became known as The Islanders. From 1939 to 1965 they became a radio institution with their fifteen minute broadcasts on Wednesday and Friday nights over CFCY and broadcast coast to coast over the CBC Radio network.

Besides Messer, Neilson, and Chamberlain, the Islanders band included Rae Simmons as Master of Ceremonies and on clarinet and saxophone; Cecil McEachern on fiddle bass and guitar; Warren MacCrae on drums. Marg Osburne joined in 1947, and Waldo Munro on piano and trombone was added later.

Don was invited to have his own television show on CBC in 1956 as a summer replacement. However, its success led to a regular spot on the Maritime Network, and in 1959 it was seen coast to coast on the entire CBC network. It was first called *The Don Messer Jubilee Show*, then *The Don Messer Show.* Ten years later it was canceled, but it found an audience in syndication for another three years.

He died on March 26, 1973.

Singles

Big John McNeill/ Dusty Miller's Reel/Don Messer's Breakdown/Johnny Wagoner's Breakdown 1941
Favorite Polka/By The Fireside/ Souris Lighthouse/Mouth of the Tobique 1941
Goin' Back/Broken Down Piano (with CHARLIE CHAMBERLAIN) 1941
Medley of Londonderry and London Hornpipes 1942
Flanigan's Polka 1945
Little Burnt Potato 1945
Angus Campbell 1946
Monkey's Wedding 1946
Atlantic Polka Change 1 1946
Atlantic Polka Change 2 1946
Atlantic Polka Change 3 1946
Atlantic Polka Change 4 1946
Rambler's Hornpipe 1946
Rustic Jig 1946
The Dawn Waltz 1946
Flop Eared Mule 1946
Flowers Of Edinburgh 1947
St. Anne's Reel 1947
Hill Lilly 1947
When Paddy McGinty Plays His Harp 1948
Valley In The Sky (with CHARLIE CHAMBERLAIN) 1948
Billy Wilson's Clog 1948
Half Penny Reel 1948
Belfast and Cock-O-The North 1948
Silver and Gold Two Step 1949
Roll Away Hornpipe 1949

Jack The Sailor 1950
Mississippi Sawyer 1950
Durang's Hornpipe 1950
Anne Marie Reel 1950
Logger's Breakdown 1950
It's The Same Old Shillelagh (with CHARLIE CHAMBERLAIN) 1950
Clancy Lowered The Boom (with CHARLIE CHAMBERLAIN) 1950
The Country Waltz 1950
Silvery Bell 1950
Shenanigins (with MARG & CHARLIE) 1950
Gypsy Hornpipe 1950
Guitar Boogie Breakdown 1950
Goose Feathers 1950
Abegweit Reel 1951
Bride Of The Wind 1951
The Weather Beaten White Washed Church 1951
The Woodchopper's Breakdown 1951
Norwegian Waltz 1951
The Wreck of the John B (vocal by MARG OSBURNE) 1951
Silver Threads Among The Gold 1951
Balken Hills 1951
Cec McEachern's Breakdown 1951
Alley Crocker Reel 1951
Mac's Polka 1952
Cotton-Eyed Joe (with WALDO MUNRO) 1952
The Spud Island Breakdown 1952
The Opera Reel 1952
Carnival Hornpipe 1957
Uncle Henry's Reel 1957
Snowflake Breakdown 1958

Albums

DOWN EAST DANCIN' VOLS. 1-4 1957
25TH ANNIVERSARY ALBUM 1958
CANADA'S DON MESSER AND HIS ISLANDERS 1966
DON MESSER'S CENTENNIAL SOUVENIR ALBUM 1967
HELLO NEIGHBOUR 1969
DON MESSER'S BACK 1969
THE DON MESSER FAMILY 1971
THE EVERLASTING . . . DON MESSER & HIS ISLANDERS 1971
DON MESSER'S TV FAVORITES n.d.
DON MESSER'S HOUSE PARTY n.d.
THE DON MESSER QUARTET PLAYS COUNTRY MUSIC n.d.
THE DOWN EAST DANCE MUSIC OF DON MESSER n.d.
MORE DOWN EAST DANCIN' n.d.
MORE OF DON MESSER & HIS ISLANDERS n.d.
OLD TIME WALTZ NIGHT n.d.
GOIN' TO THE BARN DANCE TONIGHT n.d.
DON MESSER'S JUBILEE n.d.
DOWN EAST n.d.
CHRISTMAS WITH DON MESSER & HIS ISLANDERS n.d.
THE BEST OF DON MESSER — P.E.I. SERIES (VOLS. 1-6) n.d.

Midnite Rodeo Band

AL HILDEBRAND (*steel guitar*)
JESS LEE (*bass, lead vocals*)
ED MOLYSKI (*lead guitar*)
CHRIS VOLKAERT (*drums*)

Based in Surrey, British Columbia, The Midnite Rodeo Band formed in September 1980. Ed Molyski, its acknowledged leader and principal songwriter, had been in such groups as Ray McAuley and Wild Country,

Nashville Touch and Showdown (not Gary Lee And Showdown). In Showdown, Ed was teamed with Jess Lee, a former rodeo rider and singer. The other two members, Hildebrand and Volkaert had experience in other B.C. groups.

Signed to RCA, their first single came out in the summer of 1981, *Nashville Just Wrote Another Cheatin' Song,* which turned out to be their biggest hit.

Singles

Nashville Just Wrote Another Cheatin' Song 1981
(Livin' On) Fast Love 1981/82
She Was Lady (I Was Cowboy) 1982
Everybody's Going Country 1982/83
Cowboy From The 40s 1983
Rocky Mountain Opry 1983
Slow Lovin' 1984
Love Comes In Two's/Bicycle Sunday 1984
Never Got Over Loving You 1985
Liona 1986
Boppin' In The Hall Again 1987/88
Yellow Pages Of Texas 1988
Midnite Eagle 1988/89
When You're Not Around 1989/90
Dream Maker 1990

Albums

THE MIDNITE RODEO BAND 1982
MRB 2 1984
MIDNIGHT EAGLE 1988

The Mighty Mohawks

GEORGE HILL (*rhythm guitar, vocals*)
BETTY BENOIT (aka Princess Moonbeam) (*snare drum, vocals*)
BERNIE GOGUEN (*bass, vocals*)
VINCENT HICKEY (*fiddle, guitar*); replaced by WALLY MOON

Organized in 1949 by George Hill, a real Mohawk and leader of the band, the Mighty Mohawks were one of Canada's most colorful groups. Their clean country sound and extensive wardrobe made them unique. During Canada's Centennial year they played at Expo 67 in Montreal.

Album

THE MIGHTY MOHAWKS CAPTURE COUNTRY 1966

Vic Mullen

Vic Mullen was born in Woodstock, Nova Scotia and raised in the farm areas of Yarmouth and Digby counties. In 1949 he started traveling with road bands as a mandolin and guitar player. He joined the Rainbow Valley Boys on radio station CJLS in 1951.

In the mid-1950s he worked at CKVR-CKRB TV and radio in

Barrie, Ontario. He returned to the Maritimes in 1957 to tour with the Country Harmony Boys. A year later, he became a regular member of the Kidd Baker Show that toured New Brunswick.

By the fall of 1958 Vic formed the Birch Mountain Boys bluegrass band. They toured the Maritimes until 1960.

During the 1960s he worked on the CTV network as bandleader on various shows, then on *Don Messer's Jubilee* on CBC. Vic left the show in 1969 to form The Hickorys for the CBC show *Countrytime.*

The 1970s saw Mullen become host of CBC radio's *Country Road.* He also started several bluegrass festivals, notably the Nova Scotia Bluegrass and Oldtime Music Festival.

Since 1980 he has toured across Canada and made guest appearances at concerts, dances, festivals, and exhibitions. He won the Fiddle Player of the Year Award at the Eastern Canada Bluegrass Music Awards in 1991, 1992, 1993, and 1994.

Singles

Bringin' Mary Home 1971
Railway Tracks From Halifax 1973
Who Do You Think You're Foolin' 1973

Albums

BLUEGRASS BANJO 1963
MR. COUNTRY SINGS 1964
SWINGIN' FIDDLE 1965
IT'S COUNTRYTIME 1970
VIC MULLEN PRESENTS THE HICKORYS 1973
THE COUNTRYTIME SHOW WITH VIC MULLEN 1973
MAC WISEMAN "LIVE AT REBECCA COHN" WITH VIC MULLEN AND MEADOWGREEN 1976
JUST US 1986
25 YEARS OF VIC MULLEN COUNTRY 1987
DANCE TO A DIFFERENT FIDDLER 1989

Anne Murray

Anne Murray was Canada's first international female singing star. Since 1970 she has sold over twenty-two million albums, earned four Grammys, and almost thirty Junos. The Canadian Recording Industry Association honored her as the Female Recording Artist of the Decade in 1980. In addition to her numerous awards in both the pop and country fields, her 1988 CBC-TV *Christmas Special* was the most widely viewed program of the decade. Capitol Records released her thirtieth album in September of 1991, and early in 1992 a greatest hits album came out.

The story of Anne Murray's rise to the top of the music charts began in Springhill, Nova Scotia, where her parents had her take piano and vocal lessons. Born Morna Anne Murray on June 20, 1945, she made her first TV appearance on Moncton's CKCW-TV's *Supper Club,* where she sang *Moon River.* Her first professional audition was in 1964 for the CBC TV show *Singalong Jubilee*, where she met her future husband, Bill Langstroth, whom she married in 1975. She became a regular on CBC-TV's *Let's Go* in Halifax and later returned to *Singalong Jubilee.*

Brian Ahern, the musical director of *Singalong,* produced Anne's first ten albums. He invited her to record an album for Arc Records, and in 1968 WHAT ABOUT ME was released. She later signed a contract with Capitol Records, where she stayed for the next twenty-two years. Anne's first major hit on Capitol was Gene MacLellan's *Snowbird.* On *The Merv Griffin Show* in November 1970, she became the first female artist from Canada to receive a U.S. gold record for *Snowbird.*

Her manager was Leonard T. Rambeau, who guided her career from 1968 until he died in 1995. He was in a youth group in Dartmouth, Nova Scotia called *Club '45* when he discovered Anne. At the 1995 Juno Awards he was given the Global Achievement Award by the Canadian Academy of Recording Arts and Sciences (CARAS).

Over the next two decades she received numerous awards, including four Grammys, and more than 20 Junos. She was made an Officer of the Order of Canada in 1975.

Anne returned to EMI Records in 1993. Her first album for the label was *Croonin,'* a collection of 1950s torch songs. The Anne Murray Centre, a museum of her life and career, opened in 1989 in her hometown of Springhill.

Singles

What About Me 1968
Bidin' My Time 1970
Snowbird 1970
Sing Hi, Sing Low 1970
A Stranger In My Place 1971
It Takes Time 1971
Talk It Over In The Morning 1971
I Say A Little Prayer/By The Time I Get To Phoenix (with *Glen Campbell*) 1971
Cotton Jenny 1972
Robbie's Song For Jesus 1972
Danny's Song 1972/73
What About Me 1973
Send A Little Love My Way 1973
Love Song 1973/74
He Thinks I Still Care 1974
Son Of A Rotten Gambler 1974
You Won't See Me 1974
Children of My Mind 1974
Just One Look 1974
Day Tripper 1974/75
Uproar 1975
Sunday Sunrise 1975
The Call 1976
Golden Oldie 1976
Things 1976
Sunday School To Broadway 1977
Walk Right Back 1978
You Needed Me 1978
Hey Daddy 1978/79
I Just Fall In Love Again 1979

Shadows In The Moonlight 1979
Broken Hearted Me 1979
Daydream Believer 1979
Why Don't You Stick Around 1979/80
Lucky Me 1980
I'm Happy Just To Dance With You 1980
Could I Have This Dance 1980
Blessed Are The Believers 1981
It's All I Can Do 1981
We Don't Have To Hold Out 1981
Another Sleepless Night 1982
Hey! Baby! 1982
Somebody's Always Saying Goodbye 1982/83
A Little Good News 1983
That's Not The Way It's Supposed To Be 1984
Just Another Woman In Love 1984
Nobody Loves Me Like You Do 1984
That's Not The Way 1984
I Don't Think I'm Ready For You 1985
Time Don't Run Out On Me 1985
Who's Leaving Who 1986
Now and Forever (You And Me) 1986
My Life's A Dance 1986
Are You Still In Love With Me 1987
Anyone Can Do The Heartbreak 1987
On And On 1987
Perfect Strangers (with DOUG MALLORY) 1988
Flying On Your Own 1988
Slow Passin' Time 1988/89
Who But You 1989
I'll Be Your Eyes 1989
If I Ever Fall In Love Again (with KENNY ROGERS) 1989
Feed This Fire 1990
Bluebird 1990
Everyday 1991
Si Jamais Je Te Revois 1991
I Can See Arkansas 1992
Are You Still In Love With Me 1992
Make Love To Me 1993
The Wayward Wind 1994
Born To Be With You 1994
Over You 1994/95

Albums/CDs

WHAT ABOUT ME 1968
THIS WAY IS MY WAY 1969
SNOWBIRD 1970
HONEY, WHEAT & LAUGHTER 1970
STRAIGHT, CLEAN & SIMPLE 1971
TALK IT OVER IN THE MORNING 1971
ANNE MURRAY/GLEN CAMPBELL 1971
ANNIE 1972
DANNY'S SONG 1973
LOVE SONG 1974
COUNTRY 1974
HIGHLY PRIZED POSSESSION 1974
TOGETHER 1975
KEEPING IN TOUCH 1976

THERE'S A HIPPO IN MY TUB 1977
LET'S KEEP IT THAT WAY 1978
NEW KIND OF FEELING 1979
I'LL ALWAYS LOVE YOU 1979
A COUNTRY COLLECTION 1980
SOMEBODY'S WAITING 1980
GREATEST HITS 1980
SOMETHING TO TALK ABOUT 1986
HARMONY 1987
ANNE MURRAY'S COUNTRY HITS 1987
AS I AM 1988
CHRISTMAS 1988
GREATEST HITS VOLUME II 1989
YOU WILL 1990
YES I DO 1991
FIFTEEN OF THE BEST 1992
CROONIN' 1993
THE BEST . . . SO FAR 1994
NOW AND FOREVER (box set) 1994
THE BEST OF THE SEASON (reissue of Christmas albums) 1994

N

Don Neilson was born Neil Donnell in Noranda, Quebec and raised in Montreal. He supplied background vocals on albums by Matt Minglewood, Rita MacNeil, Joan Kennedy, The Goods, Patricia Conroy, Terry Kelly, and others.

In 1992 Sony Music released his debut album, THE OTHER SIDE OF YOU. His second, BASED ON A TRUE STORY (1994), featured the smash hit *Country In The City.*

Don Neilson

Singles

Still In The Game 1992
The Other Side Of You 1992
You're My Hometown 1993
Let Me Be The One 1993
Country In The City 1994
Tell Me The Lie 1994/95
Rusted Hinges 1995
Easy To Say 1995

Albums

THE OTHER SIDE OF YOU 1992
BASED ON A TRUE STORY 1994

Dick Nolan

A native of Cornerbrook, Newfoundland, Dick Nolan began singing country music in the late 1950s. He moved to Toronto, Ontario where he recorded for Arc Records and played in the houseband at the famous Horseshoe Tavern. In 1965 he had his first hit, *Golden Rocket.*

In the early 1960s he was an original member of the group, The Blue Valley Boys. (See THE BLUE VALLEY BOYS)

Dick moved back to Newfoundland in 1968 and signed a recording contract with RCA. He had a smash hit in 1972 with *Aunt Martha's Sheep*. Other albums and singles followed, notably WELCOME ABOARD on Boot Records in 1985, which was a collection of songs about Atlantic Canada.

Singles

Golden Rocket 1965
The Fool 1967
Aunt Martha's Sheep 1972
Home Again This Year 1972
Me And Brother Bill 1973
Japanese Gin 1974
Old Newfie Outhouse 1975
Piece Of Bologna 1975
Newfoundland That's What You Mean 1981

Albums

DICK NOLAN SINGS 1964
I WALK THE LINE 1964
TRUCK DRIVING MAN 1965
ATLANTIC LULLABY 1965
I'SE THE BYE WHAT CATCHES DA FISH 1966
MOVIN' OUT 1967
BE TRUE NEWFOUNDLANDER 1967
FOLSOM PRISON BLUES AND OTHER JOHNNY CASH SONGS 1968
HAPPY ANNIVERSARY, NEWFOUNDLAND n.d.
HAPPY NEWFOUNDLANDERS n.d.
HOME OF THE BLUES n.d.
LUKEY'S BOAT 1968
NEWFIE HITS 1968
I WANT TO LIVE 1968
ATLANTIC CHRISTMAS 1968
COUNTRY (with MARLENE BEAUDRY) 1969
DUET (with MARLENE BEAUDRY) 1969

HOME AGAIN THIS YEAR 1972
DICK NOLAN'S GREATEST HITS
BEST OF
NEWFOUNDLAND 1980
DICK NOLAN n.d.
DICK NOLAN n.d.
ECHOES OF THE ATLANTIC n.d.
SIDE BY EACH (& ROY PAYNE) n.d.
GREATEST HITS OF
NEWFOUNDLAND n.d.

O

One Horse Blue

GORD MAXWELL (*lead vocals, bass*)
LARRY PINK (*keyboards*)
MICHAEL SHELLARD (*vocals, acoustic guitar, harmonica*)
ROCKO VAUGEOIS (*vocals, drums, percussion, acoustic guitar*)

This quartet from Edmonton, Alberta began as Pickens, a commercial rock band who had only one hit record in 1977, *We All Want To Live*. They changed their name in 1978 to One Horse Blue, which came from a song written by Paul Cotton of the folk/rock group Poco.

They continued to be a rock band and in the late 1970s and early 1980s scored with such hits as *Cry Out For The Sun*, *Deliver Me,* and *Crazy Fool.*

By the early 1990s they had switched from rock to country and moved to Vancouver. In 1991, 1992, and 1993 they won Group of the Year honors at the BCCMA Awards. Signed to Savannah Records in 1993, their first release was the CD single *Starting All Over Again*, previously recorded in 1979.

Singles
Cry Out For The Sun 1978
Deliver Me 1979
Bring My Love Around 1979/80
Crazy Fool 1980
One Man Walks Alone 1990
Colors Of Love 1990
Ride The Wind 1991
Starting All Over Again 1993
Love's Looking For Me 1993/94
Baby Don't Cry 1994
Everything Money Can Buy 1994
Hopeless Love 1994/95
Bringing Back Your Love 1995

Albums
ONE HORSE BLUE 1979
BITE THE BULLET 1980
ONE HORSE BLUE 1993

Marg Osburne

Verna Marguerita Osburne was born in Moncton, New Brunswick on December 29, 1927. Reared in a musical family she learned hymns and folk songs, and sang in a church choir. On a five dollar bet from a cousin she auditioned and won a part in a country and western show that aired on radio station CKCW Moncton.

In 1947 Don Messer heard Marg on one of the shows and hired her. For the next twenty-five years she received more fan mail than any other member of the Messer band. One of her most requested songs was *Little Arrows*.

She died suddenly on July 16, 1977 after finishing a concert in Rocklyn, Ontario.

Singles
That Easy Rockin' Chair 1957
Alberta County Soil 1972
Lonesome City 1974
Blues Comin' Round 1974
City Of Tears 1974/75

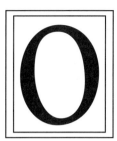

Albums

- BY REQUEST (with CHARLIE CHAMBERLAIN) 1958
- A CENTURY OF FOLK SONGS 1960
- MARG OSBURNE 1963
- NEARER MY GOD TO THEE 1963
- MARG OSBURNE/CHARLIE CHAMBERLAIN 1963
- THAT LONESOME ROAD 1963
- I BELIEVE 1965
- SING FAVORITE HYMNS 1966
- SONGS OF FAITH 1966
- THE BEST OF MARG OSBORNE 1966
- MARG OSBURNE AND CHARLIE CHAMBERLAIN 1967
- SING FAVORITE SACRED SONGS 1967
- THE GOLDEN ERA OF MARG OSBORNE 1970
- MY KIND OF COUNTRY 1972
- COUNTRY GOSPEL 1973
- OLD GOLD & NEW 1974
- MARG OSBURNE 1976
- THEY NEVER GROW UP (with CHARLIE CHAMBERLAIN) n.d.
- BEST OF (PARAGON) n.d.
- BEST OF (CORAL) n.d.
- BEYOND THE SUNSET (with CHARLIE CHAMBERLAIN) n.d.
- SONGS YOU KNOW AND LOVE (with RAY CALDER) n.d.
- I BELIEVE (with RAY CALDER) n.d.
- HE/SONGS OF REVERENCE (with RAY CALDER) n.d.

Al Oster

Born in a one room tar paper shack in Vanguard, Saskatchewan, Al Oster grew up on the farm. He spent most of his youth punching cows, bronc busting, and working the lumber camps. During the Depression, he and a friend named Roy traveled across the Prairies on freight trains. Whenever they were short of money, they brought out their guitars and sang.

Until his big break in the music business came in 1957, Al was a military policeman. He was a judo expert and a master rifleman and pistol shot. When he was discharged from the army, he began writing and singing his own songs. He wrote about the Alcan Highway in the Yukon in *918 Miles*, and the boat at Skagway, Alberta that brought supplies to the Yukon in *Next Boat*. The latter became his first single in 1960. His first album, YUKON GOLD, was released in 1961.

Throughout the 1960s he continued to record. He also represented the Yukon at the Canadian Pavilion at Expo 67 in Montreal. In the 1970s he left the music business when he was appointed Economic Development Officer for the Yukon Department Of Indian Affairs. His only major public appearance was in 1977 on the *Stompin' Tom Connors Across Canada* series on CBC TV.

Oster retired from federal services and moved to Salmon Arm, British Columbia. In 1981 Hank Carr, a musician and friend, recorded a tribute album of Oster's songs.

Singles

Next Boat 1960
Yukon Gold 1960
Waltz of the Yukon 1961
One Of These Days 1961
Klondike Cattle Drive 1962
Sourdough Rendezvous 1962
Twilight In The Yukon 1962
Kee-Bird Song 1962
Beautiful Alaska 1965
Out In The Great Northwest 1965
In My Book Of Yukon Memories 1965
The Alaska Earthquake 1966
Call Of Alaska 1966
Buckets Of Steel 1967

Albums

YUKON GOLD 1961
NORTHLAND BALLADS 1962
ALASKA STAR 49 1965
ECHOES OF THE YUKON 1966
ALASKA 1966
THE YUKALASKA SPELL 1987
THE YUKON BALLADEER 1987

P

Jerry Palmer

Long before Jerry Palmer (whose real name was Jerry Godick) was a country star, he was a rock and roller. He was discovered by Don Grashey, who managed the careers of Myrna Lorrie and Carroll Baker.

In the early to mid-1960s Jerry had such hits as *Walkin' The Dog* and *Travelin' Shoes*, and played with Bobby Vee, Gene Vincent, and many others.

By 1975 Palmer had switched to country, and a year later had a number one hit with *One Way Ticket To A Lady.* Two years later his self-titled debut album on RCA was released. It contained the hit *Last Will and Testament,* and a duet with Carroll Baker on *Are You Mine*, Myrna Lorrie's 1954/55 hit.

Singles

Oh Lucky Me 1961
Travelin' Shoes 1961
Gotta Learn To Twist 1961
Come Along With Me 1962
Gotta Love 1963
Walking The Dog 1966
Ooo Mama 1975
One More Song 1975
One Way Ticket To A Lady 1976
Mule Skinner Blues 1976
Did I Forget To Tell Her 1976
Does The Rain Only Fall On My Mansion 1978
The Joker Of It All 1979
A Picture's Worth A Thousand Words 1980
Not Living, Not Dying 1980/81
Last Will And Testament 1981
Did I Forget To Tell Her (re-release) 1981
Mother Nature 1982
The Hitman 1983/84
Good Lookin' Woman With The Devil In Her Eyes 1984

Albums

STRING OF HITS 1963
COUNTRY SOUND 1969
ON MY WAY 1969
LOVIN' COUNTRY 1975
JERRY PALMER 1977
THE HITMAN 1982

Rae Palmer

Raymonde Poliquin (a.k.a. Rae Palmer) was born in Hearst, Ontario and raised in Thunder Bay, Ontario. At age three she performed with the family band, The Ray Poliquin Trio. She played the accordion and sang in both English and French.

In 1976 she moved to Ottawa, where she was exposed to the music of the Ottawa Valley. Five years later, her husband Bob Palmer encouraged her to compete in a local singing contest, which she won. In 1982 she recorded her first of several hit singles, *Kaw-Liga.*

Singles

Kaw-Liga 1982
Corner Of Walk And Don't Walk 1983
Everybody Gets Lonely 1983
Keep On Walking 1984
Stuck On Love 1985

It's Just A Matter Of Time 1985
Stuck On Love 1985/86
Call Me Up 1986
Broken Hearts 1986
You Can Count On Me 1987
Does Anybody Need A Broken Heart 1987

Album A DREAM COME TRUE 1986

The Panio Brothers

DAVE PANIO (*vocals, bass, saxophone*)
JOHN PANIO (*vocals, rhythm & bass guitar*)
VLADIMIR PANIO (*vocals, accordion*)
JIM EDEL (*vocals, drums*)
ALEX KRALL (*vocals, violin*)
BILL LEWCHYSHYN (*vocals, bass & rhythm guitar*)

The Panio Brothers started out in 1970 in their native province of Saskatchewan John, Dave, and Vladimir Panio were born and raised in Ituna, Saskatchewan, while Alex Krall came from Punnychi, and both Jim Edel and Bill Lewchyshyn from Regina. On stage they entertained audiences with their own style of Ukranian music. They put out five albums, including CELEBRATE SASKATCHEWAN which paid tribute to the province's 75th anniversary. In 1987 they broke up.

Singles *I Once Had A Girl* 1970
It's Trudeau (with FATHER LUZNEY) 1970
Christmas Is Near (with THE SINGING GEMS) 1983

As The Panio Brothers:

Albums SONGS OF JOY 1971
SONGS OF SENTIMENT 1972
PRESENT DANCE MUSIC 1977
CELEBRATE SASKATCHEWAN 1980

As Vlad Panio:

UKRANIAN COUNTRY 1987
SINGS TRADITIONAL UKRANIAN SONGS 1994

Terry Parker

Known as "Canada's Yodeling Sweetheart," Terry Parker was born in North Bay, Ontario, on July 20, 1933. When she was six years old, she wanted to become a country singer. She made her national debut on CBLT-TV's *Holiday Ranch* program. It led to appearances on *Don Messer's Jubilee* and other top rated radio and TV shows across Canada and the Maritimes.

In 1961 her debut album, CANADA'S YODELING SWEETHEART, was released on Rodeo Records.

Albums CANADA'S YODELING SWEETHEART 1961
THE YODELING SWEETHEART 1965
YODELING FAVORITES n.d.

George Pasher

From New Waterford, Nova Scotia, George Pasher strummed his first guitar at fourteen, and gained experience playing at hospital benefits and other charity events. In 1955 he formed his own band, The Country Playmates. They stayed together until 1972 when he wanted to pursue a solo career. He also became a regular performer at The Diplomat, a Toronto club. During his forty-year career he made a few recordings, some with his wife June.

Singles *Are You Mine* (& JUNE PASHER) 1964
I Take A Lot Of Pride 1968
Apple Time n.d.

Albums YOUR CHEATING HEART (JUNE PASHER) 1961
ARE YOU MINE (GEORGE & JUNE) 1964
I TAKE A LOT OF PRIDE (GEORGE PASHER) 1968
ROUNDERS AND ROMANTICS (GEORGE PASHER)1993

Greg Paul

Based in Edmonton, Greg Paul began his career singing cover tunes by The Eagles, John Denver, Merle Haggard, and Bob Seger. Managed by R. Harlan Smith, Paul has had a dozen singles and three albums released on Royalty Records between 1989 and 1994.

Singles *Donna Lee* 1989
Old Broken Heart 1989
Never Be Sorry 1989/90
Can't Get Over Losin' You 1990
Lady Of The Water 1990
Under Your Cover 1991
Feeling Guilty 1991
Texas On My Mind 1992
Papa 1992/93
This Old Heart Of Mine 1993
If It Hadn't Been For You 1993
Love Will 1993/94
All The Colors In My Rainbow 1994
Hey Emmylou 1994

Albums MOMENTS IN BETWEEN 1988
WHEN I SEE YOU AGAIN 1991
LOVE WILL 1994

Roy Payne

From Trout River, on the west coast of Newfoundland, Roy Payne was a "Jackytier," a colloquialism for someone who is part Indian, part French, and part Celtic. He began writing songs while in the army. One of them, *I Wouldn't Take A Million Dollars For A Single Maple Leaf,* was a big hit with the Canadian contingent there. By the late

1960s he had quit the army and headed for Toronto, where he recorded some albums and played at The Horseshoe Tavern, a local club. One of Payne's biggest hits was *There's No Price Tag On The Doors of Newfoundland.*

Singles

Little Boats Of Newfoundland 1971
Goofie Newfie 1971
Pal Of Mine 1971
D.J. 1972/73
One Step Forward Two Steps Back 1973
Sweet Jesus 1974
Whisper To Me Tina 1974
That's Why I'm In Love 1974/75
Willie's Yellar Pick Up Truck 1975
Outlaw Heroes 1976
Lady From Boston 1979
The Old Fishing Hole (with DICK NOLAN) 1981

Albums

ROY PAYNE 1970
NO PRICE TAG ON THE DOORS OF NEWFOUNDLAND 1971
ROY PAYNE'S COUNTRY 1971
LOVE & HATE & WOMEN'S LIB 1972
NEWFIE BOY 1973
ONE STEP FORWARD 1974
WILLIE'S YELLAR PICK UP TRUCK 1975
OUTLAW HEROES 1976
I WOULDN'T TAKE A MILLION DOLLARS FOR A SINGLE MAPLE LEAF 1980

Anita Perras & Tim Taylor

Anita Perras was born in Sudbury, Ontario and was a celebrity at age eleven when she sang at amateur shows, local jamborees, and TV telethons. In the 1970s, Anita was the star of her own TV series, *Anita*, on the mid-Canada TV Network. With her own band named after herself, she was in demand on the club circuit.

Tim Taylor was born in Bowmanville, Ontario. He worked with the country rock band Buckshot and later formed his own band called Red Wing, later known as The Tim Taylor Band.

Anita Perras and Tim Taylor first met in 1978 and three years later they were married. Their first single was *You're Not Sure* in 1980, an answer song to the Jim Ed Brown and Helen Cornelius duet hit, *I Don't Want To Marry You.*

Between 1980 and 1988 they established themselves as a duo with such hits as *Lucky In Love* and *This Is Our Night.* They have also had individual solo careers.

As Anita Perras and Tim Taylor:

Singles

You're Not Sure 1980
Lucky In Love 1981
We Get By 1984
This Is Our Night 1985
Something Good Is Gonna Come Of This 1986
Headed In The Right Direction 1986/87
Isn't That The Strangest Thing 1987/88
You're Too Much 1988

Albums

BOUGHT & PAID FOR 1982
THIS IS OUR NIGHT 1985
ANITA & TIM 1987

As Anita Perras:

Singles

Over The Line Again 1981
You Never Looked At Me That Way 1982
Somebody Said It Was Me 1983
You Got What You Want 1983/84
How's A Girl To Know 1984/85
Mutual Acquaintance 1985
Heads You Win (Tails I Lose) 1986
I've Found Someone Too 1987
One Smokey Rose 1988
Hello Again 1989
The Tip Of My Fingers 1989
Touch My Heart 1989/90
Here Comes My Baby 1990
After All 1990
I've Got A Travelin' Heart 1991
Can't You Just Stay Gone 1992
Somewhere Under The Rainbow 1992
It Might As Well Be Me 1993
If I Didn't Have You In My World 1993
Way Beyond The Blue 1993
When Love Comes Around The Bend 1995
This Country's Rockin' 1995

Albums

TOUCH MY HEART 1989
WAY BEYOND THE BLUE 1993

As Tim Taylor:

Singles

Nice Night To Be Lonely 1982
When I Close My Eyes 1983
Love Along The Line 1983
Three Little Words 1984
Say When 1987
Brown Eyes Best 1988
Talk To A Lonely Man 1989
Having A Real Good Time 1989/90
Farewell Ave. 1990
You Just Pretend You're Asleep 1991
It Goes Without Saying 1991
Look Who's Loving You 1992
Wild One 1992
Big Plans 1993

Albums

FAREWELL AVE. 1990
BIG PLANS 1992

Colleen Peterson

Born in Peterborough, Ontario in 1950, Colleen Peterson started playing when she bought her first guitar with Lucky Green stamps at age thirteen. While still a teenager she moved to Ottawa, where she performed as a folk singer and also as lead vocalist in various rock bands. While Three's A Crowd was playing in Ottawa, Colleen was invited to fill in for Donna Warner as the group's lead singer, and later went on to become a full-fledged member.

In 1970 she moved to Kingston and with singer Mark Haines became half of the duo Spriggs and Bringle. They toured Canada and the United States for the next four years.

BEGINNING TO FEEL LIKE HOME was the name of her first album in 1976. Released on Capitol Records, it contained *Souvenirs*, which became her signature song.

In the late 1970s she recorded two more albums for Capitol, COLLEEN and TAKIN' MY BOOTS OFF.

The next decade saw her perform at the Mariposa Folk Festival and Expo 86. She also released a series of hit singles, including *I Had It All*, *Weather The Storm*, and two duets with singer Gilles Godard, *I Still Think Of You* and *Life Is Just A Holiday*.

Colleen joined Sylvia Tyson, Cindy Church, and Caitlin Hanford to form the group QUARTETTE in 1993. (See QUARTETTE)

Singles

Souvenirs 1976
I Had It All 1986
Basic Fact Of Life 1987
What A Fool I'd Be 1987
Gently Lay Me Down 1988
I Still Think Of You (with GILLES GODARD) 1988
Mr. Conductor 1988/89
Weather The Storm 1989
Life Is Just A Holiday (with GILLES GODARD) 1990
If You Let Me Down Easy 1990
No Pain No Gain 1991
Hearts Still In Love 1992
I'm Not Just Another April Fool 1992
Code Of The West 1993
Deeper Waters 1993
Crazy 1993
Let's Try Love Again 1993/94
Love Scares Me 1994
Souvenirs (re-released) 1994
What Goes Around Comes Around 1995

Albums

BEGINNING TO FEEL LIKE HOME 1976
COLLEEN 1977
TAKIN' MY BOOTS OFF 1978
BASIC FACTS 1988
LET ME DOWN EASY 1993

CDs

BEGINNING TO FEEL LIKE HOME 1994
WHAT GOES AROUND COMES AROUND 1995

Stu Phillips

Stu Phillips was born on January 19, 1933 in Montreal, Quebec. He taught himself to play the guitar, and while in school he formed his own band. During the early days of his musical career, he toured his home province. At sixteen he moved west to Edmonton. During the trip he wrote *Travelin' Balladeer*, which later became his theme song. On CFRN, Edmonton he hosted his own radio show, *Stu For Breakfast.* He continued to be in demand as a radio and TV host. In 1961 he succeeded Stu Davis as host of CBC-TV's *Red River Jamboree.* In the mid-1960s he recorded several hits for RCA, such as *Cathy Keep Playing* and *The Great El Tigre.* He also recorded for Capitol, Columbia, and Banff/Rodeo.

He has since settled in Nashville, Tennessee. In 1993 he recorded the album DON'T GIVE UP ON ME.

Singles

Champlain and St. Lawrence River 1957/58
Bill Miner 1958
This Heart Of Mine 1964
Here She Comes Again 1964
If Loving You Means Anything 1965
Cathy Keep Playing 1965
Bracero 1966
The Great El Tigre 1966
Walk Me To The Station 1967
Vin Rose 1967
Juanita Rose 1967
Note In Book #9 1968
The Top Of The World 1968
Bring Back Love Into Our World 1968/69
Rio Tijuana 1993

Albums

ECHOES OF THE CANADIAN FOOTHILLS 1957
A VISIT TO OLD QUEBEC 1957
A VISIT TO BRITISH COLUMBIA 1958
OLD SONGS FOR OLD FOLKS 1960
FEELS LIKE LOVIN' 1965
SINGIN' STU PHILLIPS 1966
GRASSROOTS COUNTRY 1967
OUR LAST RENDEZVOUS 1968
BORN TO BE A MAN 1980
EARLY STU PHILLIPS FOLK SONGS n.d.
HAVE A NICE DAY n.d.
BIG CANDY MOUNTAIN n.d.

CDs

DON'T GIVE UP ON ME 1993

The Post Family

(See THE SINGING POST FAMILY)

Prairie Oyster

JOHN P. ALLEN (*fiddle, mandolin*)
JOAN BESEN (*keyboards*)
RUSSELL DECARLE (*vocals, bass*)
DENNIS DELORME (*pedal steel*)
KEITH GLASS (*guitar, vocals*)
BRUCE MOFFET (*drums*)

The history of this sextet goes back to 1974 when Russell deCarle, Keith Glass, and Dennis Delorme joined together with Alastair Dennett, the group's original drummer, to form Prairie Oyster. Dennett's mother gave them that name when they didn't know what to call themselves.

After four years they split up because things were not happening for the group. In 1982 they realized that people wanted to hear them again, so they reunited. During the next two years they added keyboardist Joan Besen and fiddle/mandolin player John Allen. They also had minor success with two singles, the double sided *Jukejoint Johnny/ Give It A Little More Time* and *Rain Rain.*

By 1986, Bruce Moffet had joined the band and they had signed with Stony Plain Records, who released their first and only album on the label, OYSTER TRACKS.

In 1989 they signed with BMG Music Canada. Their debut album was DIFFERENT KIND OF FIRE (1990), which also marked their U.S. debut. Their success continued into the 1990s with such hits as *Will I Do (Til The Real Thing Comes Along)*, *One Precious Love*, and *Louisiette.*

Singles

Jukejoint Johnny/Give It A Little More Time 1984
Rain, Rain 1985
Till The Real Thing Comes Along 1986
Man In The Moon 1986
Play Me Some Honky Tonk Music 1987
You Got A Way 1987/88
Goodbye, So Long, Hello 1990
I Don't Hurt Anymore 1990
Lonely You, Lonely Me 1990
Christmas In Jail 1990
Something To Remember You By 1991
Did You Fall In Love With Me 1991/92
Will I Do (Till The Real Comes Along) 1992
Everybody Knows 1992
Here's To You 1992/93
One Precious Love 1992
Just For Old Times Sake 1993
Such A Lonely One 1994
Louisiette 1994
Black Eyed Susan 1994/95
Don't Cry Little Angel 1995
Only One Moon 1995
Ancient History 1995

Albums

OYSTER TRACKS 1986
DIFFERENT KIND OF FIRE 1990
EVERYBODY KNOWS 1991
ONLY ONE MOON 1994

Prescott Brown

(See FAMILY BROWN)

Irwin Prescott

Irwin Prescott was born in Widdifield outside North Bay, Ontario on January 17, 1932. At nine years of age he called at square dances, and at seventeen played the guitar and sang.

On radio station CFCN in North Bay he had his own show. He also appeared with most of the top country acts of the day. His first hit was *The Auctioneer* in 1966 on Melbourne Records. He died on August 8, 1977.

His son Randall Prescott went on to become a successful producer and singer/songwriter in The Prescott Brothers, Tracey Prescott and Lonesome Daddy, and Prescott Brown.

Singles

The Auctioneer 1966
Chew Tobacco Road 1966
Model "T" 1967

Albums

IRWIN PRESCOTT SINGS 1965
IRWIN PRESCOTT SINGS 1967
LET'S HAVE A PARTY WITH IRWIN PRESCOTT 1968
IRWIN PRESCOTT & FRIENDS n.d.
THE BEST OF IRWIN PRESCOTT n.d.

Orval Prophet

Born and raised in the village of Edwards, Ontario, Orval Prophet received his first guitar at age eleven. From 1944 to 1953 he was a regular performer on CFRA's *Fiddler's Fling.* During this time, he went to Nashville to record his first single on Decca Records, *I'm Going Back To Birmingham*, which was released on March 8, 1951. Later that same year his second single, *Judgement Day Express,* came out. In 1958 he recorded *Mademoiselle* under the name of Johnny Six, which was one of his most requested songs.

In 1966 he recorded the hit single, *The Travelling Snowman*, which was a tribute to Hank Snow. A year later, he signed a contract with Caledon Records. His debut single for the label was *Human Nature* in 1967.

Sidelined by major heart surgery in 1970, he recorded one of his biggest hits, *Mile After Mile*, in the fall of 1971. Prophet continued to record through the early 1980s. His last public performance was at The Hitching Post in Ottawa on New Year's Eve, 1983. He died on January 4, 1984.

Singles

I'm Going Back To Birmingham 1951
Judgement Day Express (DECCA) 1951
Mademoiselle (as JOHNNY SIX) SIX) 1958
Run Run Run 1962
The Traveling Snowman 1966

Human Nature 1967
Blue Side Of The Street 1968
Country Fair 1969
Headin' Down The Line 1972
Mile After Mile 1972
Judgement Day Express (COLUMBIA) 1972/73
Champlain & St. Lawrence Line 1973
Badger Bodine 1974
Eastbound Highway 1974
My Kind Of Woman 1975
Lisa Mae 1976
Leroy Can't Go Home 1977
Where Have All The Cowboys Gone 1978
Ol' Amos 1978
Sorry And The Hobo 1979
I've Seen Some Things 1979
The Mighty Tractor Pull 1979
The Canadian Ploughboy 1980
True Blue 1981
A Little League In Heaven 1981

Albums
FOREIGN LOVE AFFAIR 1958
PROPHITEERING 1959
THE TRAVELIN' KIND 1963
MILE AFTER MILE 1971
MY KIND OF WOMAN 1976
TRUE BLUE 1981
THE CANADIAN PLOUGHBOY 1981
THE TRAVELLING SNOWMAN 1995

Ronnie Prophet

Born in Hawkesbury, Ontario and raised on a farm in Calumet, Quebec, Ronnie Prophet wanted to be an entertainer ever since grade school. As a teenager he appeared as a guest on *The Happy Wanderers Show* on radio station CFRA in Ottawa. He teamed up with Dougie Trineer as a duo, but Ronnie left after a few months to pursue a solo career. In the 1960s he was busy on the club circuit in Fort Lauderdale, Florida, Nashville, Tennessee, and The Bahamas.

Back in Canada in the early 1970s, he hosted two shows on CTV—*Grand Ole Country* and *The Ronnie Prophet Show.* His career as a recording artist began in 1973 with the hit *San Diego*. Other hits followed such as *Sanctuary* (1975), *Shine On* (1976), and *Phantom of the Opry* (1980). In addition to his own recordings, he teamed up with Glory-Anne Carriere for some duets, whom he later married in 1986. (See GLORY-ANNE CARRIERE) During the mid-1980s, Ronnie started his own record label, Prophet Records. His son, Tony Prophet, is also a country singer.

As Ronnie Prophet:

Singles
San Diego 1973
Sanctuary 1975
Shine On 1975/76
It's Enough 1976
Big, Big World 1976
Phone Call From Allyson 1977
It Ain't Easy Lovin' Me 1977
Everybody Needs A Love Song 1979

Phantom Of The Opry 1979/80
Every Story In The Book 1981
The Ex-Superstar's Waltz 1982
I Need A Lover 1983
Sundown 1983
Smooth Operator 1983
I'm Gonna Love Him Out Of You 1983/84
Stealer Of Hearts 1986
For The Children 1986
Don't Take Her To Heart 1986/87
No Holiday In L.A. 1987
For The Children 1987
If You're Up For Love 1987/88
Fire In The Feeling 1988
Breakin' Up Ain't Hard To Do 1988
Trying To Outrun Your Memory 1989
Touch Of Class 1990
You've Got Me Right Where I Want Me 1990
The Feeling Of Love 1991
I Won't Be There 1991
Prophet Of Love 1992
I'm Your Old New Love 1992
The Real Thing 1993

Albums

THE PHANTOM 1981
I NEED A LOVER 1982
I'M GONNA LOVE HIM OUT OF YOU 1983
SATURDAY EVENING POST 1984
SURE THING (& GLORY-ANNE CARRIERE) 1987
PROPHET OF LOVE 1991

As Ronnie Prophet & Glory-Anne Carriere

Storybook Children 1982/83
If This Is Love 1984
I'm Glad We're Bad At Something 1985
I'll Be There 1986
Lucky In Love 1987
Two Hearts 1989

Tony Prophet

Tony Prophet was born in Montreal, Quebec and raised in Nashville and Florida. The son of Ronnie Prophet, he grew up playing country music on a classical guitar, and listened to Southern rock. He had two big hits in 1981 with *Kentucky Gold* and *Kentucky Serenade*. His idols were Waylon Jennings and Larry Gatlin.

Singles

Kentucky Gold 1981
Kentucky Serenade 1981/82
Horses Scare The Hell Out Of Me 1982/83
Okie Dokie O.K. City Blues 1983

MYRNA LORRIE

JOYCE SEAMONE

SOUTH MOUNTAIN

FARMER'S DAUGHTER

JIM WITTER
RON McMUNN
GEORGE PASHER
THE YORK COUNTY BOYS

JACK BAILEY
ORVAL PROPHET
VIC MULLEN
SONS OF THE SADDLE

RHODES & MARSHALL

BUD ROBERTS

STRAIGHT CLEAN & SIMPLE

JUNE EIKHARD
KEVIN SIMPSON
THE STOLTZ BROTHERS

SHANIA TWAIN

RON McLEOD AND THE LINCOLN COUNTY BOYS

TOM WILSON & HIS WESTERN ALL-STARS

Q

Quartette

Cindy Church
Caitlin Hanford
Colleen Peterson
Sylvia Tyson

Four female voices joined together in 1993 to form one of the most electrifying groups in Canadian country music history. Organized by Colleen Peterson who talked to Sylvia Tyson about doing a show together, they asked Cindy Church and Caitlin Hanford if they wanted to join them. The result was pure magic. They made their first public performance at Harbourfront in Toronto, Ontario in the summer of 1993. After they appeared on CBC radio's *Morningside* with host Peter Gzowski, there was an unprecedented demand for the their album, which had not been recorded yet. When it came out in 1994, it was a critical and commercial success. (See CINDY CHURCH, CHRIS WHITELY & CAITLIN HANFORD, COLLEEN PETERSON, SYLVIA TYSON)

Singles
Red Hot Blues 1994
King Of The Cowboys 1994
Unabashedley Blue 1995
O Canada 1995
It Never Rains On Me 1995
No Place Like Home 1995/96

CD
QUARTETTE 1994
WORK OF THE HEART 1995

R

Diana Rae

Diana Rae Stocks was born in Sherbrooke, Quebec and raised in Montreal. At an early age she entertained her parents' house guests by singing TV commercials. Not until she graduated from high school did she become interested in country music.

Bluegrass legend Bob Fuller was credited for starting Rae's musical career at the famous Blue Angel Club in Montreal, one of the few places that showcased English talent. She moved to Washington, D.C. in the mid-1970s to hone her craft as a songwriter and singer.

In 1980 she moved to Nashville and, four years later, she recorded her debut single on MCA/Curb, *Only Love Can Break A Heart*, a remake of Gene Pitney's 1962 pop hit. The B side was the same song sung in French.

Singles *Only Love Can Break A Heart* 1984

Diane Raeside

For Diane Raeside, a native of Scarborough, Ontario, music has always been a part of her life. As a youngster she and her two sisters gathered at their cousin John's knees while he played his guitar in the living room. Sunday afternoons were filled with song and laughter.

She began singing at age five and her first professional engagement was at an Italian wedding when she was eighteen. Her debut single, *Turning Into Strangers,* was released in 1989. Three years later, her debut cassette album, CRAZY INFATUATION, came out.

Singles

Turning Into Strangers 1989
Half A Heart 1989
I'll Cry About That Tomorrow 1989
Run For Your Money 1990
Love Is Where The Good Times Are 1990
Take Me In Your Arms Tonight 1990/91
I Don't Need You 1991
Just Another Day 1991
Crazy Infatuation 1991/92
List Of Broken Hearts 1992
Singing Songs Of Love 1992
Last Date 1992
Some Rivers Run Dry 1993
Slow Dance 1993
This Time Of Year 1994
I'm Stranger 1995/96
Since You Went Away 1995

Cassette CRAZY INFATUATION 1992

The Rainvilles

DOT RAINVILLE (*vocals*) MORRIS RAINVILLE (*vocals*)

The husband and wife team of Dot and Morris Rainville were born and raised in Sudbury, Ontario. They started their musical career in 1955, and seven years later they moved to St. Catharines, Ontario. In 1967 they recorded their first single on the Red Leaf label, *I Got What I Wanted.* By the early 1970s the Rainvilles had retired from the music business so they could raise their two daughters.

In mid-1989 Morris decided to record again, this time on his own RareRabit label. His debut single was *Good Ole Country Blues.* His second single, *Hum A Song In Your Soul,* came out in 1990.

Singles *I Got What I Wanted* 1967
Fortunate Son 1970
Wrote A Song 1970/71
When We Tried 1971
Polar Bear Express 1972

Albums THE RAINVILLES 1971
POLAR BEAR EXPRESS 1973

As Morris Rainville:

Singles *Good Old Country Blues* 1989
Always Hum A Song In Your Soul 1989/90
Born In The Country 1990/91
His Own Free Will 1991
Would'A Been Here Much Sooner 1991
Dealers & Heartaches 1992
The Mississauga Man 1993
Waiting Too Long 1993/94
Tell Me Where You've Been 1994
You Have To Go Back 1995

CD THE MISSISSAUGA MAN 1993

Keray Regan

Keray Regan was born Oscar Melvin Frederickson on November 23, 1923 in Pouce Coupe, British Columbia. When he entered the music business he chose the name "Keray Regan." While recovering from an illness at age eleven, he learned to play and sing with the ukelele. He took up the guitar later. When the family moved to Vancouver, he worked on the fishing boats. In his spare time he played the accordion and wrote songs. Two that he wrote were *Cobweb On Your Picture* and *My Home By The Fraser.* During this time he became ill with bronchitis. While he was in hospital, Keray's sister Veta took *My Home By The Fraser* to Bill Ray at CKNW in New Westminster. The independent recording went to number one on the local chart. Aragon Records later released and it became a big seller in 1949.

During the 1950s, Regan met Lucille Starr (nee Savoie) and he introduced her to his brother Bob. They became The Canadian Sweethearts. Keray later recorded and toured with Vic Siebert and The Sons of the Saddle.

Being on the road took its toll and Keray returned to his farm. In December 1960 he wrote *Poor, Poor Farmer,* which was released on the RCA Victor in 1961. In the early 1970s he recorded an album with Evan Kemp and The Trail Riders.

Failing health in the 1980s forced Keray to retire. He completed the independent cassette, ALASKA HIGHWAY, in honor of its 50th anniversary in 1992.

Singles

Peace River Waltz 1949
My Home By The Fraser 1949
A Mother's Love 1949
If The Moon Would Shine 1949
Peace River Waltz 1949
Picking Flowers 1950
My Dream and I (with VIC SIEBERT) 1950
I Can't Wait Forever For You 1950
Ola From Norway 1951
Christmas Card From Heaven 1951
I Don't Care If You Go A Little Further (with PETRIE SISTERS) 1951
Flying Saucers 1952
When You Say I Love You 1957
Poor Poor Farmer 1961

Albums

KERAY REGAN SINGS 1958
THE GREAT LORD'S PRAYER (with THE HACKEY BROTHERS) 1959
PEACE RIVER RANGERS-FERN, BOB & KERAY REGAN 1959
THE POPLAR TREE n.d.

Buddy Reynolds

Born in Vancouver, British Columbia on November 9, 1927, Ivan A. (Buddy) Reynolds first sang before an audience when he was nine years old. At twelve he combined his homework from school with songwriting and took a few piano lessons. At age eighteen he had his own radio show on CJIB in Vernon.

In 1947 he sang about the Okanagan Valley in a song called *Blue Okanagan*, and it was an instant hit. A friend at CJIB urged Buddy to make a commercial recording, so he went to Aragon Records who agreed to release it. He later signed a four-year contract and went on a cross country tour in 1951.

During the mid-to-late 1950s he took a hiatus from the music business to spend more time with his family. He worked as a railroad man and bus driver before his love of country music drew him back to the recording business. It was his wife Rosemarie who insisted he sign a contract with Zero Records in 1959. Under the name of Brad Reynolds, he recorded two singles, *Pretty Polly* and *Buy Me One Of Those.*

He died in 1984.

As Buddy Reynolds:

Singles

Blue Okanagan 1948
Make-Believe Castle 1951
Spruce Bug 1951
I Want To Be Your Valentine 1951
Rocky Mountain Rhythm 1951
An Angel In Disguise 1952
Ogo Pogo 1952
Roly Poly Heart 1953
Tundra 1953
Southbound 1953

Albums

BUDDY REYNOLDS SINGS SPRUCE BUG AND OTHER HITS 1958

As Brad Reynolds:

Singles

Pretty Polly 1959
Buy Me One Of Those 1959

Donn Reynolds

Donn Reynolds was born in Winnipeg, Manitoba. At age ten he received his first guitar and won his first amateur contest when he was thirteen. He later turned professional and became known as "The Yodeling Ranger." During World War II he served in the Royal Canadian Air Force. After the war he went to Australia, where he recorded a few songs on the Columbia Gramophone label, including *Salt Bush Sue*, *Stockman's Lullaby*, *Let Me Die With My Boots On*, *Just Saddle And Ride*, and *The Ring My Mother Wore.*

In 1949 he moved to Cumberland, Maryland. There he owned his own record store that specialized in country and spiritual music. He won the title of World's Champion Yodeler at the United States Yodeling Championships in September, 1956. That same year he recorded two singles for MGM, *Bella Belinda* and *Rose Of Old Pawnee.*

Back in Canada, Donn became known as "The Canadian Yodeling Cowboy." He toured New Zealand, Australia, Tasmania, and Great Britain. During the 1950s he acted in several movies, including the 3D film *Arena* with Robert Horton and Gig Young.

In the early 1960s he hosted CTV's *Cross Canada Barn Dance* in Winnipeg, and in 1965 he recorded his first of two albums for Arc Records, THE BLUE CANADIAN ROCKIES. The other, released in 1968, was SPRINGTIME IN THE ROCKIES.

On June 26, 1990 he broke the record of yodeling five tones (three falsettos) in 0.93 seconds atop the CN Tower in Toronto, Ontario. His feat is listed in the Guinness Book of World Records.

Singles

Blue Mountain Waltz 1951
Bella Belinda 1956
Rose Of Old Pawnee 1957
She Taught Me How To Yodel 1965
Lorelei 1965
Shut The Door 1968
Texas Yodel 1973
No One Will Ever Know n.d.

Albums

SPRINGTIME IN THE ROCKIES 1965
BLUE CANADIAN ROCKIES 1968
SONGS OF THE WEST 1974
KING OF THE YODELERS n.d.

Rhodes & Marshall

LISA-MARIE MARSHALL
ANDRE RHODES

Growing up in their native New Zealand, the sister duo of Andrea Rhodes and Lisa-Marie Marshall began singing at an early age. By their teens they had honed their musical talents and were members of the band, The Haka Billys. Rhodes went on to win several New Zealand country music awards such as Top Female Vocalist, Best Instrumentalist (for *Wabash Cannonball*), and Entertainer Of The Year in 1985 and 1987.

In 1988 Rhodes married a Canadian exchange student and emigrated to Canada. While waiting for her citizenship papers, she worked as a periodontal assistant. Based in Langley, British Columbia, Rhodes and Marshall signed a recording contract with Tomcat Records. Their debut album, TOO YOUNG FOR ELVIS, was released in 1994. *Rockin' Me Blue* was the first single.

Singles
Rockin' Me Blue 1994
Too Young For Elvis 1994
Cool New Country 1995
Brand New Me 1995

CD
TOO YOUNG FOR ELVIS 1994

The Rhythm Pals

MIKE FERBEY (*tenor, stand up bass*)
JACK JENSEN (*lead singer, acoustic guitar*)
MARC WALD (*baritone, accordion*)

The history of The Rhythm Pals goes back to the early 1940s when Marc Wald and Mike Ferbey had toured Western Canada with Sleepy and Swede (Leslie Frost and Nels Nelson) and The Tumbleweeds from Saskatchewan.

In 1946 disc jockey Bill Rae at CKNW, New Westminster, British Columbia introduced Marc and Mike to Jack Jensen, a colleague at the station. Bill suggested the three of them form a trio, but could not come up with a name. He gave his listeners a chance to win a prize if they could come up with one. A lady in Burnaby suggested The Rhythm Pals. They patterned their singing style after The Sons Of The Pioneers and made their radio debut on CKNW's *Bill Rae's Roundup*. Two years later, they were one of the first Canadian acts to appear on U.S. television on *The Spade Cooley Show* at the Santa Monica Ballroom.

The Rhythm Pals moved to Toronto in 1958, where they appeared on *The Tommy Hunter Radio Show* for the next seven years. Their theme song was *Blue Shadows On The Trail*, which they had recorded on Aragon Records in 1954. Mike, Marc, and Jack followed Tommy Hunter to CBC TV in 1965, where they stayed for eleven years.

Marc retired in 1987. Two new members joined the group and they became known as Mike, Jack, Dan, and Toller.

Singles
My Chapel In The Pines 1952
When Alberta's Sun Shines On The Rockies 1952
Lead Me Gently Home 1952
Saskatoon 1952
Roly Poly Heart (with BUDDY REYNOLDS) 1952
Two Hearts Forever 1953
I Keep Telling Myself (with JULIETTE) 1953

I Caught The Bride's Bouquet (with JULIETTE) 1953
I Shouldn't Cry 1953
Dreamy Okanagan Moon 1953
Your Love Is Mine 1953
Blue Shadows On The Trail 1954
Mountain By The Sea 1954
You Don't Have To Say Words To Pray 1963
I've Had My Knocks Out Of Life 1964
Iron Town 1965/66
This They Say Is Me 1966
The Mess I'm In 1970
Loved Me Enough To Change 1972
The Sound That Makes Me Blue 1973
Let My Memory Take Me Home 1974

Albums

THE RHYTHM PALS — MIKE, MARC & JACK SINGING HYMNS AND WESTERN BALLADS 1958
THE RHYTHM PALS (ARC) 1961
THE RHYTHM PALS (CTL 5020) 1963
THE RHYTHM PALS (CTL 5039) 1963
CANADIAN TOWN & COUNTRY SONGS 1967
TENNESSEE BIRDWALK 1970
HOME COUNTRY 1971
JUST FOR YOU 1973
COUNTRY CANADA n.d.
SINGING HYMNS AND WESTERN BALLADS n.d.
THANK GOD WE'VE GOT MUSIC n.d.
BEST OF/30 GOLDEN HITS n.d.
GET TOGETHER n.d.

Hank Rivers

Hank Rivers was born Henry LaRiviere in Hawkesbury, Ontario on January 23, 1917. Growing up he listened to Jimmie Rodgers, and had a great fascination for trains. At a very early age Hank moved with his parents to Ottawa, Ontario. His recording career began in 1939 when he signed a contract with RCA. One of his early hits was *Hooray For Camp Borden* (1939).

During World War II he enlisted in the army as an entertainer and became known as "The Singing Soldier." He added words to Ward Allen's fiddle hit *Maple Sugar,* which Hank renamed *Maple Sugar Sweetheart.*

In 1948 he became the featured vocalist on the *The Western Five*, a show broadcast over the CBC Dominion Radio Network.

On September 21, 1984 he was inducted into the Ottawa Valley Country Music Hall of Fame.

Singles

Hooray For Camp Borden 1939
Confederation Train 1967
Sister Mary 1967
Shoes Keep On Walkin' 1968
Christmas In The Maritimes 1968

Album

HANK LA RIVIERE AND THE COUNTRY KINGS 1958
HANK'S CENTENNIAL TRAVELS 1967
SOMETHING OLD, SOMETHING NEW 1968
BALLAD OF RODGER YOUNG n.d.
SONGS BY n.d.
A SALUTE TO GALLANT MEN n.d.

Bud Roberts

Born in Albert County near Moncton, New Brunswick on July 6, 1935, Bud Roberts first became interested in country music when he heard Wilf Carter on a phonograph. By the time he was eleven years old, Bud was writing his own songs.

When he was nineteen he left home to work the fields of northern Quebec. In 1957 he moved to Toronto, where he worked at a service station. Hotel manager Jack Starr hired Bud to sing at *The Horseshoe Tavern* in Toronto. He played there for eleven months.

In 1964 he filled Massey Hall for a concert and had eight encores. By 1967 Bud had recorded his first single, *The Alcan Run,* on Apex Records. Four years later, he signed with Boot Records. He also made two albums, THE ALCAN RUN and THIS IS BUD ROBERTS.

Singles

The Alcan Run 1967
The Working Man 1967/68
I've Got The Bottle 1971/72
Gonna Take A Little Bit Longer 1972
Sure Gonna Live Till I Die 1972
Don't Hold Your Breath 1973
While I'm Gone 1973
Benny The Bum 1972

Albums

THE ALCAN RUN 1967
THIS IS BUD ROBERTS 1971

The Romaniuk Family

ANNE ROMANIUK (*vocals, guitar*)
ELSIE ROMANIUK (*vocals, guitar*)
ED ROMANIUK (*vocals, guitar, autoharp*)

Growing up in Alberta, The Romaniuk Family were influenced by the legendary Carter Family. Anne (who was born in Chipman) first took up the guitar in 1938. Both her sister Elsie and brother Ed (both born in Foothills) learned from Anne. Evenings at home were spent by the radio, where they listened to Mother Maybelle and the rest of the Carters. Ed eventually learned her style of picking. He and Elsie sang as a duo for many years until Anne made it a trio in 1965.

On stage they sang mostly Carter Family songs with a few of their own. Their first self-titled album on the ACME label came out in 1959. Other albums followed until their breakup in 1981 due to the sudden death of Anne.

Albums

THE ROMANIUK FAMILY (ACME) 1959
THE ROMANIUK FAMILY (ARREX) 1965
COUNTRY CARTER STYLE 1967
SONGS WE LOVE TO SING 1967
THE ROMANIUK FAMILY (LEI) 1975
COUNTRY ECHOES 1980

Roll 'n' Thunder

(see the DEBENHAM BROTHERS)

Wayne Rostad

Ottawa born singer/songwriter Wayne Rostad has been part of the Ottawa Valley music scene for over thirty years, and a willing participant in various fund-raising events. He wrote his first song, *Just Friends*, in 1964.

He first worked in a lumber camp, and was a ranch hand and a cook before he became a radio personality on CJET in Smith Falls, Ontario. After a short stint as a TV anchorman on CKWS Kingston, he returned to his first love, country music.

In 1980 he recorded his first album, WRITER OF SONGS, featuring the singles *Willie Boy* and *Rideau Street Queen*. He has gained popularity as a TV host on such shows as *Out Your Way*, *Country Report*, and *On The Road*, all on the CBC network.

Singles

November Rain 1972
Burnett Road 1974/75
Baby, Lady, Poet And Writer Of Songs 1978
Willie Boy 1979
Rideau Street Queen 1980
King Of Fools 1981
Summer Rose 1983
Again 1983/84
Shebenacadie Tinsmith Man 1992

Albums

WRITER OF SONGS 1980
AGAIN 1983
STORYTELLER 1991

Bob Rowan

A native of Minto, New Brunswick, Bob Rowan learned the guitar at an early age. After leaving school he worked underground in the Minto mines, drove a truck for the Avon Coal Company, and spent four years as a bellhop at the Admiral Beattie Hotel in St. John.

In 1955 he had a regular Saturday night radio show on CFNB Frederiction with Earl Mitten. The following spring, Bob competed in a talent contest and won a Jumbo Gibson guitar. He went to Toronto in 1957, where he worked at various jobs by day while honing his talents as a musician by night.

His first album on Arc Records, JOHNNY CASH SONG HITS SUNG BY BOB ROWAN, was released in the summer of 1960. He then formed his first group, The Versatones, and recorded another album, JOHNNY CASH HITS, on Trans Canada Records. A third album called ROWAN COUNTRY (1972) contained the hit single, *One More Favor.*

Singles

One More Favor 1972

Albums

JOHNNY CASH SONG HITS SUNG BY BOB ROWAN 1960
ROWAN COUNTRY 1972
JOHNNY CASH HITS

Ruth Ann

(See under ANN)

Terilynn Ryan

Born and raised on the outskirts of Calgary, Alberta, Terilynn Ryan and her sister used to enter every talent show possible. With the addition of a third member, they became known as the Bow Valley Belles. Terilynn later studied piano, light opera, and drama before she concentrated on a music career in 1975. That same year she joined the group Hair Trigger Cowboys but left to perform as a solo act.

She later moved to Vancouver, where she recorded her debut single, *One Hour Away*. Her other hits include *No Time For Lovin'* (1986) and *Everytime* (1987).

Singles

One Hour Away 1983
Lovers And Love 1984
Everytime 1988
Close To Home 1990
The End Of The Dirt Road 1991
We Better Get Lovin' 1992
Downside Up 1992

S

Ron Scott

Ron Scott was born to a working class family in Amherst, Nova Scotia in 1926. His first exposure to music was from his mother's fiddle playing; an uncle and two brothers played guitar and sang. At age seven, he learned to play the guitar. He later picked up the fiddle, but his favorite instrument was the mandolin.

In 1943 he hitch-hiked across Canada with singer and guitarist Hank Harkness. They played on radio station CFCN in Calgary as the Prairie Serenaders. During the summer of 1946, he joined Harold King, "the Cobequid Mountain Boy," and together they worked small halls.

By 1950 Ron had formed his own band called Riders of the Southern Trails (later shortened to "The Riders"). Although they were a country band, they also played bluegrass, a style of music that was hard to sell in Canada. They toured with two famous bluegrass musicians, Wilma Lee and Stoney Cooper.

While in Montreal in 1954, Ron formed another group, the Cinch Brothers, who played on CFCF's *Hometown Jamboree*. Two years later, they broke up and Ron pursued a solo career.

In 1957 he recorded *When The Bees Are In Their Hive* on Spartan Records. It was Canada's first bluegrass single. Scott did not release an album until 1994, the independent release, NOVA SCOTIA CALLING.

Singles *When The Bees Are In Their Hive* 1957

Cassette NOVA SCOTIA CALLING 1994

Joyce Seamone

Ever since she was a little girl growing up in her hometown of Maplewood,Nova Scotia, Joyce Seamone has enjoyed music. Her main influences were the dances and shows that featured olde time country music. She loved to watch *The Don Messer Show* and *Singalong Jubilee* on television. After she moved to Ontario, she sang in a local band in Woodstock, which led to a recording contract with Marathon Records. Her debut single was *Testing 1-2-3.* Other hits followed but none equalled the success of her first. In 1994 she recorded the album THE OTHER SIDE OF ME on Gemini Records.

Singles

Testing 1-2-3 1972
Make Me Honest 1972
Stand By For An Announcement 1973
I Can See It In His Eyes 1976
My Head Is Spinning Round And Round 1976
There's More Love Where That Came From 1978
You're The Rock 1978
You Are The Only One For Me 1992
Two-Step Saturday Night 1994

Albums TESTING 1-2-3 1972
MERRY CHRISTMAS FROM JOYCE SEAMONE 1972
STAND BY FOR A SPECIAL ANNOUNCEMENT 1973
I CAN SEE IT IN HIS EYES 1976

CD THE OTHER SIDE OF ME 1994

Terry Sheridan

A native of Campbellford, Ontario, Terry Sheridan started singing as a youngster in the local junior choir. In high school he played and sang in a rock group. By the early 1980s he was lead singer for the group Pax. He later formed his own band, Axis. During this time he shifted from rock to a combination of traditional and contemporary country.

In 1985 he recorded his first hit, *She Gave Me A Memory,* under the name of T.J. Sheridan. After several more singles, he released his debut album, IF I HAD WINGS, in 1992 on his own independent Shadow Records label.

Singles
Love Strikes Again 1987/88
The Winning Hand 1988
I Better Go Now 1988/89
Never Missing You (CELEBRITY) 1989
I Can't Cross A New Bridge (CELEBRITY) 1989
Another Morning After 1989/90
Spend My Love On You 1990
Love's Last Stand 1991
I'm Doin' Fine 1991
Havin' A Lonely Time 1991
I Wanna Fly 1992
If I Had Wings 1992
One More Quarter 1993
A Long Way From Lonely 1993
What We Know 1994

Albums IF I HAD WINGS 1992

Shotgun

JAMES ANTHONY (*guitar*)
PETER SMITH (*saxophone*)
BRIAN TWAITES (*bass*)
RUSTY WALKER (*steel guitar*)
FRANK WOODCOCK (*drums*)
STEVE WOOLHEAD (*keyboards*)

This Oshawa based sextet has worked with various recording artists, and in 1983 they recorded the instrumental *Shotgun*. They followed it with several other hits, such as *Love Bandit* and *On Comin' Heartache.* Their debut album, TURNING POINT, came out in 1985.

Singles
Shotgun 1983
Love Bandit 1983/84
Fool In The Palm Of Your Hands 1984
On Comin' Heartache 1986
Early Morning After Midnight Lover 1985/86
We Chose To Play 1987

Album TURNING POINT 1985

Vic Siebert & The Sons of the Saddle

JOHN ALLEN (*steel guitar, vocals*) VIC SIEBERT (*rhythm guitar, vocals*) GENE SIEBERT (*accordion, vocals*) ROY WARHURST (*fiddle, mandolin*) LENNIE SIEBERT (*bass fiddle, vocals*)

Vic Siebert started The Sons of the Saddle in 1948 with brothers Gene and Lennie, John Allen, and Roy Warhurst in Calgary, Alberta. The Siebert brothers were all born in Alberta: Vic in Medicine Hat, Gene in Burdett, and Lennie in Redcliffe.

In 1956 they moved to Winnipeg where they hosted a weekly TV show called *Saddle Songs* and a radio show. Sister Lorraine Siebert and Connie Holt joined the group for both shows as The Mello Maids.

By 1960 they had moved to Toronto and toured with the cast of CBC's *Country Hoedown.* Vic Siebert and The Sons of the Saddle broke up in 1972. Lennie Siebert died in 1987.

As Vic Siebert & The Sons of the Saddle:

Singles *Orange Blossom Special* 1953

Albums SONS OF THE SADDLE VOL. 1 1958
THE STAMPEDER ALBUM n.d.
SONS OF THE SADDLE VOL. 2 1959

As Vic Siebert:

Singles *Just A Rollin' Stone* 1947
Settle Up, Or Settle Down 1948
My Dream And I (with KERAY REGAN) 1951

As Gene Siebert:

Singles *Prairie Chicken Polka* 1947
Aragon Polka 1951
Stein Waltz 1953

As Lennie Siebert & The Chuck Wagon Gang:

Singles *Songs Of The Wild* 1953
Female On The Loose 1957

Kevin Simpson

Born and raised in Kingston, Ontario, Kevin Simpson's strength as a musician is his songwriting ability. He began entertaining in local clubs in thelate 1970s and often sang other country artists' material.

Not until he met Rich Dodson of the rock group The Stampeders did Simpson begin to write seriously. In 1985 and 1986 Kevin produced two of his own TV shows entitled Simpson & Friends. During this time he recorded songs on his independent label, Ebony Records. His first of several hits was *Without You* in 1984.

Singles
Without You 1984
You Are My Woman 1985
Let's Not Be Strangers 1985
High On Emotion 1986
Magnum, P.I. 1986
Porsche 930s 1993
Good Looking You 1993

Albums
KEVIN SIMPSON 1993
YOUNG LOVE 1994

The Singing Post Family

DEBBIE POST (*washboard, tambourine, spoons*)
JOANNE POST (bass)
KEN POST (drums, guitar)
NORM POST (rhythm guitar)

Based in Rednersville, Ontario, The Singing Post Family started in 1966. The following year, they played at various talent shows in honor of Canada's Centennial. During the twelve years they toured Canada, they made eight albums together. When they disbanded in 1978, Debbie and Norm went on to successful solo careers, and Ken became the drummer for Prescott Brown. In 1992, Norm recorded the independent cassette *Finally Got Around To Me.*

Singles
He Loves Me When He's Got The Time 1976
Plant The Seeds 1976

Albums
THE SINGING POST FAMILY 1968
THE FAMILY BIBLE 1970
ONE SONG AWAY 1971
MY PRINCE EDWARD COUNTY HOME 1972
ITS A LOVELY LOVELY WORLD 1972
COUNTRY MUSIC 1973
CHRISTMAS TIME IN THE COUNTRY 1973
PLANT THE SEEDS 1976

Ray St. Germain

Ray St. Germain was born and raised in Winnipeg, Manitoba. At sixteen years of age he was hired by American legendary singer Hal Lone Pine,who wanted Ray because he could imitate Elvis Presley and leap around like Bill Haley.

In 1959 he entered and won the CBC-TV National Talent Caravan that led to hosting duties on his first TV series, *Like Young.* Other TV series followed, such as *Music Hop Hootenanny*, *Time For Livin'*, *Two For The Road, My Kind of Country,* and *Ray St. Germain Country.*

He started writing his own songs in the early 1960s. The Native Council of Canada in Ottawa honored Ray in November 1980 for his achievement and contributions. He is a Metis.

Singles
Thank You For Loving Me 1979
Please Don't Hurt Me 1979
Anyway You Want Me 1980
No More On The Outside 1984
Show Me The Way 1984
My Special Angel 1985
Anyway You Want Me (the old Elvis hit) 1989

Whiskey Train 1989
Is There Any Love 1992

Albums
RAY ST. GERMAIN 1968
EVERYBODY HAS TO FALL IN LOVE 1970
RAY ST. GERMAIN LIVE! n.d.
WITH THE HAMES SISTERS n.d.

Cassette
YOU CAN COUNT ON ME 1992

Alberta Slim

Born Eric C. Edwards, Alberta Slim, was raised on a ranch in Lloydminster, Alberta. He learned to sing and yodel by listening to the radio. When he was a young boy he rode a pinto pony named Kitten, which he trained to perform tricks at country gatherings.

He began his singing and songwriting career in the early 1930s. In 1937 he sang on an amateur radio show on CKCK in Regina, Saskatchewan. It was the beginning of a career in radio on CFQC Saskatoon, CKRM Regina and CKNW New Westminster.

Alberta Slim started recording in 1945. Some of his best known songs are *When It's Apple Blossom Time In Annapolis Valley, My Nova Scotia Home*, *Beautiful British Columbia*, and *Sitting On A Hilltop.* In the early 1990s he was living in Surrey, British Columbia.

Singles
When I Take My Last Ride 1950
I'm Lonesome For Mommy Tonight 1950
Red River Waltz 1950
New Canadian Polka 1950
My Nova Scotia Home 1952
Evelina Waltz 1952
Laughing Horse (with EVAN KEMP) 1953
Brother, You're Not Dead (with EVAN KEMP) 1953
Canada Song 1973

Albums
ALBERTA SLIM SINGS . . . FEATURING CLOVER LANE AND THE BAR X RANCH BOYS 1963
CANADA, MY HOMELAND 1967
WHEN IT'S APPLE BLOSSOM TIME n.d.
WITH HIS BAR X RANCH ROYS n.d.
WITH THE BAR & COWBOYS n.d.
PEACE OF MIND n.d.
GOLDEN MEMORIES (set of 3) n.d.
GOLDEN MEMORIES (single disc reissue) n.d.

Smilin' Johnnie & Eleanor Dahl

Smilin' Johnnie was born John Lucky on September 2, 1924 in Wroxton, Saskatchewan. While growing up on the family farm he taught himself to play the guitar. At Brandon Country School he played in the local dance orchestra called The Night Swingsters, and he also had his own radio show on CJGX, Yorkton, Saskatchewan every Saturday night.

In June 1946 he met a group of boys called the Sunset Five. A year later, they became known as The Prairie Pals, a name given to them by Jack Goodman, one of the announcers at CJGX. They later changed their name to Smilin' Johnnie and His Prairie Pals. During the peak years in the late 1940s they became popular in Western Canada,

Ontario, North Dakota, and Montana.

By 1961 Smilin' Johnny had met Eleanor Dahl, who toured with her father George. He asked her to join him, and together they became the new Smilin' Johnnie Show. They also had their own radio show on CJNB in North Battleford, Saskatchewan.

In 1963 they recorded their debut album, TREASURED COUNTRY FAVORITES. Cattle Records in Germany released THE BEST OF CANADA'S SMILIN' JOHNNY in 1976.

Albums

TREASURED COUNTRY FAVORITES 1963
SALUTE TO CANADA'S NORTHLAND 1964
SMILIN' JOHNNY SHOW IN ACTION 1964
HAPPY MUSICAL MOMENTS 1965
ROLLING ALONG 1968
INSTRUMENTALLY YOURS 1969
25 YEARS 1972
WATCHIN' OUR COUNTRY DIE 1974
BEST OF CANADA'S SMILIN' JOHNNY 1976

Hank Smith

Hank Smith was born Heinz Schmidt in Bavaria, Germany. His music career started in the late 1940s when he entertained British, Canadian, and American troops with his German country music band. He then moved with his family to Montreal, Quebec. In 1957 he decided to settle in Edmonton, Alberta, where he formed the group, The Rock-A-Tunes. The first single, *Danny Girl,* was a big hit in 1958. When the rest of the group left for the United States, Hank joined The Rodgers Brothers.

In 1963 he recorded his first country album, DARK SKIES, for London Records. Three years later, he signed with Decca, where he earned the title of "Canada's King Of Bluegrass." By 1970 he had organized another group called Wild Rose Country, and was recording for Quality Records.

For the past twenty-five years he has promoted Canadian music abroad in such countries as Australia, Switzerland, Germany, and Austria. Hank was the founding president of Academy of Country Music Entertainment (ACME) in 1976, which later became known as the Canadian Country Music Association (CCMA). In September 1994 he was inducted into the Canadian Country Music Hall of Honor.

Singles

Sharing The Good Life 1970
Morgen 1970
Sweet Dreams Of Yesterday 1970
The Final Hour 1971
Where Do We Go From Here 1971
Together Again 1972
Take Me Home 1972
But Tomorrow There's Another Day 1973
Everybody's Going To The Country 1975
If You Don't Laugh, I Promise I Won't Cry 1975/76
Give Me A Country Song 1977
Twenty-Five Years 1977
Baby Sittin' With The Blues 1978

Albums

DARK SKIES 1963
BOARD BLUE GRASS EXPRESS 1963
HANK SMITH AND THE RODGERS BROTHERS 1964
THE COUNTRY MUSICIAN 1964
COUNTRY MUSIC BLUE GRASS STYLE 1965
BLUE GRASS MUSIC'S HERE TO STAY 1965
TEN GOLDEN YEARS OF COUNTRY (with RODGERS BROS.) 1967
HANK "THE DRIFTER" SMITH 1968
THE NEW COUNTRY SOUNDS OF HANK SMITH 1970
HANK SMITH COUNTRY 1971
COUNTRY MY WAY 1971
HANK SMITH AND WILD ROSE COUNTRY 1972
HANK SMITH 1974
JUST PLAIN COUNTRY 1980
INTERNATIONAL LIVE 1985

R. Harlan Smith

Robert Harlan Smith was born in Central Butte, Saskatchewan. His musical career started in 1961 when he joined the group Two Flats And A Sharp with Bob Couture and Casey Forward. They later changed their name, first to The Bob Smith and Casey Forward Quartet and then to Bob Smith and The Common People.

His debut single was *Mary In The Morning* in 1967 on the Sound '67 label under the name of Bob Smith. He began recording as R. Harlan Smith in 1971. In the 1970s he also started his own record company, Royalty Records. The stable of artists on it included Chris Nielsen, Laura Vinson, Joyce Smith, and Gary Fjellgaard.

After a short hiatus from the music business in the early 1980s, Smith returned to Royalty Records to oversee the label and discover new Canadian talent.

Singles

Mary In The Morning (BOB SMITH & THE COMMON PEOPLE) 1967
Cold Day In October 1971/72
Loving You Losing You 1972
Ding-A-Ling Debbie 1972
More Than I Should Ask 1972
I've Been Through This Before 1973
I Remember Love Softly 1974
I Remember Love 1974
Momma Brown 1974
The Days Are Never Long Enough 1974
Song For Shelley 1975
Life & Love & You 1975
Mama's Voice 1975/76
Rusty Come Back 1976
Universal Soldier 1976
Son Of A Country Man 1976/77
Here Comes Yesterday 1977
Hold On To My Heart (& CHRIS NIELSEN) 1978
Daddy And A Man 1978
Stolen Moments (& CHRIS NIELSEN) 1979
Ding-A-Ling Debbie (re-release) 1979
Half Of What You've Been Meant To Me 1979
We Got The Magic 1979/80
To Be (& CHRIS NIELSEN) 1980
You've Got It All Wrong (& CHRIS NIELSEN) 1980
After The Fire Goes Out 1981
Friendly Persuasion (& CHRIS NIELSEN) 1981
Tears & Goodbyes 1981/82

Walk Beside Me 1982
Easy Feeling Dream (& Chris Nielsen) 1982
To Say Goodbye 1984
Just A Matter Of Time 1984
The Feel Of Comin' Down 1985
Too Much Of A Lady 1985
The Farmer 1986
Forever (& Chris Nielsen) 1986
There's Just One Light 1986/87
Believe Again 1987
Old Love Affair 1987
Fallin' In Love Kind Of Feeling 1988
Two Steppin' Around 1989
One More Time 1989
Wrong Seems So Right (& Chris Nielsen) 1989/90
Hurtin' Back To Me 1990
Yesterdays 1991
To Where The Cheatin' Starts 1992
The Greatest Game (*The Football Song*) 1993
Silver Buckles 1993/94
My Old Hometown 1994

Albums
BOB SMITH SINGS 1970
UPTOWN COUNTRY 1972
I REMEMBER LOVE 1973
SONG FOR SHELLEY 1975
SON OF A COUNTRY MAN 1975
BEST OF 1976
HERE COMES YESTERDAY 1977
WE'VE GOT THE MAGIC 1978
STOLEN MOMENTS (& Chris Nielsen) 1979

Reg Smith

Reg Smith was born in Stewiacke, Nova Scotia on August 30, 1924. Whenhe was nine years old, he started singing with his own band. During World War II he played drums in one of the army marching bands. After the war he worked in his father's electrical shop while playing in shows on weekends.

In 1944 he signed a contract with RCA, although his first record, *Leave My Woman Alone,* was not released until ten years later. On his recordings he was accompanied by his band, The Melody Four.

Cattle Records in Germany released the tribute album REG SMITH, STAR OF THE HOMETOWN JAMBOREE in 1986. He is Hank Snow's cousin.

Singles
Leave My Woman Alone 1954
Land of Evangeline n.d.
Pass Around The Sunshine n.d.
Sky Blue And Flower Pink n.d.
Loved and Lost n.d.
Don't Take Away My Chance (of Lovin' You) n.d.
Atlantic Lullaby n.d.
The Broken Ring n.d.

Albums
REG SMITH, STAR OF THE HOMETOWN JAMOREE 1986

Hank Snow

Clarence Eugene (Hank) Snow was born in Brooklyn, Nova Scotia on May 9, 1914. He had a rough childhood and at the age of twelve left home for an adventure at sea. In the late 1920s he heard country music on the radio aboard a schooner. Snow would entertain the crew with his mouth organ. By the early 1930s he had finished his sea voyages and moved in with his sister Nina. He also bought himself a new guitar, a T.E. Eaton Special, for $12.95.

His dream of singing on the radio and making records came from his idol, Jimmie Rodgers, "The Singing Brakeman." In 1933 Hank auditioned and won his own fifteen minute program on radio station CHNS in Halifax. At first he called himself "The Cowboy Blue Yodeler," and then, "Hank, The Yodeling Ranger."

Cecil Landry, chief engineer and chief announcer at CHNS, suggested that Hank write to RCA Victor in Montreal for an audition. On October 10, 1936 Hank recorded two songs in a church on Lenoir Street, *Prisoned Cowboy* and *Lonesome Blue Yodel.* On November 6, 1937 he recorded eight songs at the RCA Victor Studio in Montreal, one of which was called *The Blue Velvet Band.* He toured Nova Scotia, Cape Breton, Prince Edward Island, and Eastern Quebec.

During the summer of 1944 while playing at a theater in Amherst, Nova Scotia, he became known as "The Singing Ranger." By the end of the 1940s his records were selling well and he had become a major star in Canada.

The hit *I'm Movin' On* in 1950 was the one that made him a household name in the United States. Between 1950 and 1970 he had over fifty international hits.

In 1979 Hank was inducted into the Canadian Academy of Recording Arts and Sciences Hall Of Fame. Ten years later, he was elected into the Canadian Country Music Hall Of Fame.

Singles

Lonesome Blue Yodel 1936
Blue Velvet Band 1937
My Little Swiss Maiden 1938
The Hobo's Last Ride 1938
My San Antonio Mama 1938
The Texas Cowboy 1939
Yodeling Back To You 1939
Bluer Than Blue 1939
On The Mississippi Shore 1941
Under Hawaiian Skies 1941
You Didn't Have To Tell Me 1941
Broken Wedding Ring 1941
I'll Tell The World That I Love You 1942
The Alphabet Song 1942
Let's Pretend 1942
Broken Dreams 1942
When That Someone You Love, Doesn't Love You 1943
When It's Over, I'll Be Coming Back To You 1943
Mother Is Praying For You 1943
Old Moon Of Kentucky 1943
When My Blue Moon Turns To Gold Again 1943
Just Across The Bridge Of Gold 1943
Goodnight Little Buckaroo 1943
Rose of the Rio 1943
There's A Pony That's Lonely Tonight 1943
Soldier's Last Letter 1945
Your Little Band Of Gold 1945
Just Waiting For You 1945
Dry Those Tears Little Girl And Don't Cry 1945
Darling I'll Always Love You 1945
My Kalua Sweetheart 1945
In Memory Of You Old Pal 1945

I'll Not Forget My Mother's Prayer 1945
How She Could Yodel 1945
My Sweet Texas Bluebonnet Queen 1946
On That Old Hawaiian Shore 1946
Brand On My Heart 1946
Linda Lou 1946
The Drunkard's Son 1946
Down Where The Dark Waters Flow 1946
Withìn' This Broken Heart Of Mine 1948
My Filipino Rose 1948
Little Buddy 1948
Wasted Love 1948
Somewhere Along Life's Highway 1948
Journey My Baby Back Home 1948
My Filipino Rose 1949
The Night I Stole Sammy Morgan's Gin 1949
Marriage Vow 1949/50
I'm Movin' On 1950
I Wonder Where You Are Tonight 1950
Only A Rose From My Mother's Grave 1950
The Golden Rocket 1950/51
Rhumba Boogie 1951
Bluebird Island 1951
I Cried But My Tears Were Too Late 1951
Down The Trail Of Achin' Hearts 1951
Unwanted Sign Upon Your Heart 1951
Music Makin'Mama From Memphis 1951/52
Gold Rush Is Over 1952
Lady's Man 1952
Married By The Bible, Divorced By The Law 1952
I Went To Your Wedding 1952
Gal Who Invented Kissing/ Fool Such As I 1952/53
Honeymoon On A Rocket Ship 1953
Zeb Turney's Gal 1953
There Wasn't An Organ At Our Wedding 1953
Spanish Fire Ball 1953
For Now and Always 1953
When Mexican Joe Met Jole Blon 1953
I Don't Hurt Anymore 1954
That Crazy Mambo Thing 1954
Next Voice You Hear 1954
Let Me Go, Lover 1954/55
Yellow Roses/Would You Mind 1955
Cryin' Prayin' Waintin' Hopin' 1955
Mainliner/Born To Be Happy 1955
These Hands 1955
Conscience, I'm Guilty 1956
Stolen Moments 1956/57
Squid Jiggin' Around 1957
Tangled Mind/My Arms Are A House 1957
Whispering Rain 1958
Big Wheels 1958
I Wish I Was The Moon 1958
Love's Call From The Mountain 1958
A Woman Captured Me 1959
Doggone That Train 1959
Chasin' A Rainbow 1959
The Last Ride 1959
Rockin' Rollin' Ocean 1960
Miller's Cave 1960
Beggar To A King 1961
The Restless One 1961
You Take The Future 1962
I've Been Everywhere 1962
The Man Who Robbed The Bank At Sante Fe 1963
Ninety-Miles An Hour (Down A Dead End) 1963
Breakfast With The Blues 1964

I Stepped Over The Line 1964
The Wishing Well 1965
The Queen Of Draw Poker Town 1965
I've Cried A Mile 1965/66
The Count Down 1966
Hula Love 1966/67
Down At The Pawn Shop 1967
Learnin' A New Way Of Life 1967
Who Will Answer 1968
I Just Wanted To Know 1968
The Late And Great Love (Of My Heart) 1968
Name Of The Game Was Love 1968/69
Rome Wasn't Built In A Day 1969
That's When The Hurtin' Sets In 1969
Vanishing Breed 1970
Come The Morning 1970/71
The Seashores Of Old Mexico 1971/72
Governor's Hand 1972
North To Chicago 1973
Hello Love 1974
That's You And Me 1974
Easy To Love 1974/75
Merry-Go-Round Of Love 1975
The Mysterious Lady Of St. Martinique 1979
Hasn't It Been Good Together (with KELLY FOXTON) 1980

Albums

HANK SNOW SINGS FAMOUS RAILROADING SONGS 1951
HANK SNOW SINGS 1952
HANK SNOW SALUTES JIMMIE RODGERS 1953
HANK SNOW'S COUNTRY GUITAR 1954 (re-released in 1957)
OLD DOC BROWN & OTHER NARRATIONS 1955
COUNTRY AND WESTERN JAMBOREE 1957
HANK SNOW SINGS SACRED SONGS 1958
COUNTRY CLASSICS 1958
JUST KEEP A MOVIN' 1958
JAMBOREEE 1958
WHEN TRAGEDY STRUCK 1959
THE SINGING RANGER 1960
HANK SNOW SINGS JIMMIE RODGERS SONGS 1960
BIG COUNTRY HITS (SONGS I HADN'T RECORDED TIL NOW) 1961
HANK SNOW'S SOUVENIRS 1961
SINGS WITH THE CARTERS 1962
THE ONE AND ONLY HANK SNOW 1962
HANK SNOW & ANITA CARTER — TOGETHER AGAIN 1962
RAILROAD MAN 1963
I'VE BEEN EVERYWHERE 1963
MORE HANK SNOW SOUVENIRS 1964
OLD & GREAT SONGS BY HANK SNOW 1964
HANK SNOW & CHET AKINS — REMINISCING
THE HANK SNOW FOUR SQUARE ALBUM 1964
SONGS OF TRAGEDY 1964
GLORYLAND MARCH 1965
THE HANK SNOW COUNTRY SPECIAL — HIGHLIGHTER ALBUM 1965
YOUR FAVORITE COUNTRY HITS 1965
"THE HIGHEST BIDDER" & OTHER FAVORITES 1965
GOSPEL TRAIN 1966
HEARTBREAK TRAIL 1966
GUITAR STYLINGS OF HANK SNOW 1966

THIS IS MY STORY (2 RECORD SET) 1966
TRAVELIN' BLUES 1966
BEST OF HANK SNOW 1966
THE SOUTHERN CANNONBALL 1967
THE SINGING RANGER 1967
THE LAST RIDE 1967
OLD & GREAT SONGS (CAMDEN) 1967
MY EARLY COUNTRY FAVORITES 1967
CHRISTMAS WITH HANK SNOW 1967
MY NOVA SCOTIA HOME 1967
THE SPANISH FIREBALL 1967
SNOW IN HAWAII 1967
SOMEWHERE ALONG LIFE'S HIGHWAY 1968
LONELY AND HEARTSICK 1968
HITS, HITS & MORE HITS 1968
TALES OF THE YUKON 1968
"MY NOVA SCOTIA HOME" AND OTHER EARLY HANK SNOW FAVORITES 1968
HITS COVERED BY HANK SNOW 1969
SNOW IN ALL SEASONS 1969
I WENT TO YOUR WEDDING 1969
CURE FOR THE BLUES 1970
HANK SNOW & CHET ATKINS — SPECIAL REQUEST 1970
HANK SINGS IN MEMORY OF JIMMIE RODGERS 1970
MEMORIES ARE MADE OF THIS 1970
AWARD WINNERS 1971
WRECK OF THE OLD '97 (2 RECORD SET) 1971
TRACKS & TRAINS 1971
THE LEGEND OF OLD DOC BROWN 1972
LONESOME WHISTLE 1972
LIVE FROM EVANGEL TEMPLE 1972
THE JIMMIE RODGERS STORY 1972
HANK SNOW SINGS REISSUE) 1973
WHEN MY BLUE MOON TURNS TO GOLD AGAIN (2 RECORD SET) 1973
SNOWBIRD 1973
I'M MOVIN' ON 1974
THAT' YOU & ME 1974
THE HANK SNOW COLLECTION 1974
HELLO LOVE 1974
HELLO LOVE 1974
NOW IS THE HOUR (FOR ME TO SING TO MY FRIENDS IN NEW ZEALAND) 1974
YOU'RE EASY TO LOVE 1975
HANK SNOW & JIMMIE RODGERS 1975
THE HANK SNOW ALBUM 1976
THE HANK SNOW ALBUM 1976
COUNTRY CLUB — HITS OF HANK SNOW 1976
HANK SNOW SINGS GRAND OLE OPRY FAVORITES 1976
THE JIMMIE RODGERS STORY (WITH ALBERT FULLAM) 1977
COUNTRY CLUB — HITS OF HANK SNOW — VOL. 2 1977
NO. 104 STILL MOVIN' ON 1977
LIVING LEGEND (2 RECORD SET) 1978
INSTRUMENTALLY YOURS 1979
MYSTERIOUS LADY 1979
HANK SNOW & KELLY FOXTON — LOVINGLY YOURS 1980
HANK SNOW & KELLY FOXTON — WINSOME, LOSE SOME 1981
BY REQUEST 1981
I'M MOVIN' ON (2 RECORD SET) 1982
WILLIE NELSON AND HANK SNOW 1985

CDs

HANK SNOW — THE SINGING RANGER 1988
HANK SNOW — THE SINGING RANGER VOL. 2 1990
HANK SNOW — THE THESAURUS TRANSCRIPTION 1991
HANK SNOW — THE SINGING RANGER VOL. 3 1992
HANK SNOW — THE YODELING RANGER 1993
HANK SNOW — THE SINGING RANGER VOL. 4 1994

Mary Lou Sonmor

Saskatchewan's Mary Lou Sonmor began playing the piano at an early age. Born in Kindersley and raised in Loverna, she took up the guitar when herbabysitter left her guitar behind. Mary began to write her own songs and develop her own singing style. She moved to Edmonton, where she hoped her dream of the spotlight would come true.

Her hard work and perserverance finally paid off in 1984 when Royalty Records released her debut single, *Don't Start The Fire*. In 1987 The Mercey Brothers were impressed enough to sign her to their label, MBS Records. *That Look In Your Eye* was her first single.

Sonmor's songs have been recorded by Laura Vinson (*Just A Hurtin' Place*), R. Harlan Smith (*Just A Matter Of Time*), and Chris Nielsen (*Gators*).

Singles

Don't Start The Fire 1984
That Look In Your Eye 1987
Cheaters 1988
Only Strangers 1989
He Could Waltz 1990/91

South Mountain

JUDY HOTTE (*drums*); Replaced by BILLY CARRUTHERS (1990-94), CHRIS LINGARD (1994-)
TODD NOLAN (*lead vocals*); Replaced by DAN WASHBURN (1992-)
LAURIE-LAPORTE PITTICO (*guitar, vocals*)
STEVE PITTICO (*lead guitar, vocals*)
DON REED (*fiddle, mandolin*)

This quintet derived its name from South Mountain, Ontario, where founding members Steve and Laurie Pittico currently reside. Formed in 1989 they made their stage show debut at Carlisle Country Campout Festival in Carlisle, Ontario. Their first single, *Light Years Away,* came from the cassette album NEW TRADITION on the Burco label. In 1990 Judy Hotte, the group's original drummer, left. She was replaced by Billy Carruthers. Chris Linguard replaced him in 1994.

Steve Pittico is an accomplished guitarist who has been in The Prescott Brothers Band, Terry Carisse's backup band Tracks, and The Bobby Lalonde Band. In 1993 and 1994 he was honored by the D.C.M.A. with the International Instrumentalist Award. His wife Laurie worked as a backup singer for various artists in the Ottawa Valley.

Don Reed has won several fiddling championships in Canada and has played on albums by Dwight Yoakam and Buck Owens.

In 1992 Todd Nolan left and was replaced by Dan Washburn as lead singer. He had been a solo artist with five singles to his credit.

The group signed to Stony Plain Records in 1994. Their debut single, *Where There's A Will,* was also the name of their first album. (See DAN WASHBURN)

Singles

Light Years Away 1989
I Got The Blues 1989/90
That's The Truth 1990
Dixiefied 1990
Ridin' High, Ridin' Free 1991
Where Does The Good Times Go 1992
Tears Won't Dry In The Rain 1992
Diggin' Up Dirt 1993
Where There's A Will 1994/95
Radioland 1995
Truly Madly 1995/96

Cassettes/CDs

PICKIN' PARTNERS (cassette) 1990
SOUTH MOUNTAIN LIVE (cassette) 1990
DIXIEFIED 1991
SOUTH MOUNTAIN & FRIENDS 1992
WHERE THERE'S A WILL 1995

Lucille Starr

(see THE CANADIAN SWEETHEARTS)

Stevedore Steve

From St. John, New Brunswick, Steve Foote wrote songs about the real working man. He had worked at various jobs across Canada until he was eighteen, and began writing and singing songs as a hobby when he was twenty-one.

In 1970 he recorded his first single, *Newfie Screech,* on Dominion Records. A year later he signed with Boot Records and had several hits, including *Hard Workin' Men* and *I'm A Truckdriver.*

Singles

Newfie Screech 1970
Hard Workin' Men 1971
I'm A Truckdriver 1971
Minto Miners 1972
Lester The Lobster 1972
Steel Wheels On The Rails 1972
Snowflakes Are Falling 1972/73
Truly Madly 1995/96

Albums/CDs

HARD WORKIN' MEN 1971
I'VE LIVED 1972
NEW BRUNSWICK SPIRIT VOLUME ONE 1995

The Stoker Brothers

RICK COLWELL (*drums*); Replaced by SEAN MARRIOTT
Paul Kneller (*keyboards, bass*); Replaced by GORD FRANKLIN
D.J. (DON) MCDONALD (*vocals, rhythm guitar*)
MICKEY MCDONALD (*lead vocals, lead guitar, fiddle, banjo*)

Mickey and D.J. McDonald formed The Stoker Brothers in Brantford, Ontario in 1979. The group's name refers to the firemen on the railroad who started up the boilers. The two brothers began performing on stage with their mother Ila, who was a country singer. In their teens the family moved to Saskatchewan, where they played in The Family Band. They moved back to Ontario in 1974.

The first single by The Stoker Brothers was *Hey Country Singer* in 1984.

Singles

Hey Country Singer 1984
One Man's Loss 1984
Would You Like To Fool Around 1985
She Saves Her Love For Me 1985/86
You Can't Hide From Love 1986
I've Got You 1986/87
Listen To My Heart 1987
Fiddlin' My Time Away 1987
Highway To Heaven 1987/88
The Drive-In Show 1988
Could You Love A Working Man 1989
Ain't Nothing New 1989/90
Dance A Little Closer 1990
Love On The Run 1991
Singin' Cheating Songs 1992
Wild One 1992
Coup De Ville 1993

Album

THE WILD ONE 1989

The Stoltz Brothers

BILLY STOLTZ (*vocals, rhythm & lead guitar*)
EDDY STOLTZ (*vocals, steel guitar*)
JOHNNY STOLTZ (*vocals, guitar*)
PAUL STOLTZ (*vocals, bass*)

The Stoltz Brothers were one of Canada's early "brother" acts, along with the Siebert brothers in The Sons of the Saddle and The Mercey Brothers.

Billy, Eddy, Johnny, and Paul started in Calgary in the mid-1950s where they played at the Calgary Stampede. In 1956-57 they moved to Montreal and performed regularly at the Monterey Candlelight Room, which was the city's number one entertainment venue at that time. They later became famous at the Flame Cafe in Minneapolis, Minnesota and the 1000 Acres Resort in New York State.

On stage they were known for their variety and large repertoire that featured classic western songs. They sang in a style similar to the Sons of the Pioneers as each brother supported the other in vocal harmony.

The Stoltz Brothers stopped performing in 1966. Each of them went on to join other bands. Billy had a successful solo career, beginning in the late 1960s. Today, Paul, who is the oldest brother, is retired and lives in British Columbia. Eddy is back recording after a long hiatus, Billy plays part-time in Alberta, and Johnny, the youngest brother, is a full-time musician in New Brunswick.

As The Stoltz Brothers:

BIG WHEEL PRESENTS CANADIAN TALENT ON STAGE
(with GUIDO D'AMICO & TED WATERMAN) n.d.

As Billy Stoltz:

Singles

Blue Is The Color 1967
Walkin' With The Blues 1967
Queenston Heights 1968
Pub With No Beer 1968
Machine Gun Molly 1969
Dirty Old Slush 1970
Darlin' When Are You Comin' Back 1971
My Foolish Love 1971
Love Has Come To Stay 1972
Come On Back 1972
I Couldn't Sign My Name 1972

Albums

BILLY STOLTZ SINGS 1967
BY REQUEST 1969
GOLDEN GREATS OF BILLY STOLTZ 1970
A CANADIAN COUNTRY SONG BY THE SOFT VOICE OF BILLY STOLTZ 1971
BILL STOLTZ 1972
COME ON BACK 1973
MY PERSONAL FAVORITES n.d.
14 ALL TIME COUNTRY GREATS n.d.

Stoneridge

WAYNE CARDINAL (*rhythm guitar*)
WAYNE FAULCONER (*lead vocals*)
MICHAEL MCFARLANE (*drums*)
JOHNNY MYERS (*bass*)

Formed in the late 1970s in Thunder Bay, Ontario, Stoneridge first experienced success in 1981 with their debut single, *Sweet Satin-Eyed Lady*. Each member of the group gained experience in other bands: Wayne Faulconer in Jarvis Street Revue, Johnny Myers in The Myers Brothers Band, Wayne Cardinal in The Bells and Ocean, and Michael McFarlane in Nite Life.

Managed by Don Grashey, Stoneridge recorded on the Golden Eagle label. Their self-titled debut album came out in 1982.

As Wayne Faulconer & Stoneridge:

Singles

Sweet Satin-Eyed Lady 1980/81
Hay Seeds 1981

As Stoneridge:

Dreams Of Mexico 1982
You Live In One World Too Many 1982
Bad Habit Of Mine 1983
A Country Tune 1984

Album

STONERIDGE 1982

Straight, Clean & Simple

CHARLIE EDWARDS (*drums, background vocals*)
TED LLOYD (*bass guitar*)
ROY JORAWSKY (*rhythm guitar, vocals*)
LARRY LEE VANNATTA (*guitar, mandolin, banjo, harmonica*)
MARINA VANNATTA (*keyboards*)

From the rural town of Hussar, Alberta, Straight, Clean and Simple started in 1985. They played at various social events and rodeo dances throughout Southern Alberta. In 1988 they recorded their first single, *Life of a Trucker,* on the Comstock label. Their debut album, SECOND TO NONE, came out the following year.

Singles

Life Of A Trucker 1988
Really Hard To Say 1989
Don't Worry 'Bout Me 1990
Every Goodbye Means Hello 1990
Hillbilly Cowboy 1990/91
Put The Blame On Me 1991
What You Get Is What You See 1992
Misty Blue 1992
Country Junkie 1993
Pickin' Lonely Guitar Blues 1993
Raised On Country 1994
Hillbilly Jane 1994
Life After Thirty 1995
Til The River Runs Dry 1995

Albums/CDs

SECOND TO NONE 1989
DEAD HORSE LAKE 1995
IRON LADY 1991

Terry Sumsion

Born and raised in Burford, Ontario, Terry Sumsion first sang gospel in neighborhood churches when he was twelve years old. At twenty-one he formed his first country band, Stagecoach. In 1981 he recorded his first single, *Our Lovin' Place.*

During the next ten years he appeared on *The Tommy Hunter Show, Family Brown Country,* CTV's *Live It Up*, *The Andy Winter Show* in Halifax, and *Nashville Now* on The Nashville Network.

In 1983 his debut album, OUR LOVIN' PLACE, came out, and his second album, MIDNIGHT INVITATION, in 1984.

Singles

Our Lovin' Place 1981
Crazy Love Games 1982
Brand New Love Affair 1983
Born Again 1983
One More Time 1983
Midnight Invitation 1984
That's When You Know It's Over 1984/85
The Loneliest Star In Texas 1985
Lovin' The Night Away 1985/86
Too Bad We're Only Friends 1986
Out Of Hand Out Of Control 1986
When You Leave n.d.
That Way 1987
There Go I 1987
So Hard To Forget 1987/88
Don't Let The Morning Come 1988
I Only Have One Heart 1988
This Old Flame 1989
Only One Heart 1989
Love On The Run 1991
Wake Me Up I'm Dreamin' 1992
Ride The Storm 1992
Jinglin' Spurs 1993
Climbin' The Ladder 1995
I Saw Mommy Kissing Santa Claus 1995

Albums/CDs

OUR LOVIN' PLACE 1983
MIDNIGHT INVITATION 1984
RIDE THE STORM 1992
WHITE CHRISTMAS 1995

Julien Tailly

Born on December 10, 1926 in Sorel, Quebec, Julien Tailly was the leader and pioneer of French country music in Quebec. He was also the original French country crooner, and the first French-Canadian country singer. Willie Lamothe, who came along in 1946, took guitar lessons from Tailly.

Between 1944 and 1955, Julien made fifteen 78 RPM recordings. His music has been recorded by French singers Marcel Martel, the late Paul Brunnel, and chanteuse Julie Daraiche.

At the Chamber of Commerce building in his hometown, there is a window display in honor of Tailly. His son Pierre put together a special collection of his songs in 1995 as a remembrance.

Singles

Pourquoi Ris-Tu?
L'Amour revient
Esperance d'un enfant
Chambrette d'amour
Jardin des fleurs
Pour Ta fete
A.H. les femmes
Flots argentis
L'argent est interessant
Douze belles fleurs
Quand on est un cowboy
Je vous aime, je vous adore
La femme que j'aime
Cowboy joyeux
L'amour travaille tout l'temps

Gordie Tapp

Born in London, Ontario in 1924, Gordie Tapp's career as an actor-writer-singer began in his early teens. In 1942 he joined the army, where he was performer and emcee on *The Canadian Army Show*. After his discharge he joined the *Main Street Jamboree* on CHML in Hamilton, Ontario. His character on the program was Gaylord.

By the early 1950s he went to CBC Radio and then CBC television, where he emceed *Country Hoedown* from 1956 to 1965. He also introduced his comic character Cousin Clem who remains a favorite to this day. From 1969 to 1992 he was a regular on the comedy-variety series, *Hee Haw*.

Although he made only a few recordings he was, first and foremost, an entertainer who has taken Canadian and American performers around the world wherever Canadian Forces and diplomatic personnel were stationed.

Singles

My Home Town 1959
Many Others 1972
I'm Doin' Fine 1983
Cousin Clem — Johnny Gunn n.d

Album

BOTH SIDES OF LIFE n.d.

David Thompson

David Thompson was born in Kapuskasing, Ontario and grew up in Detroit and Thunder Bay, Ontario. He developed his baritone voice while a member of the high-school choir. When he was twenty years old, he returned to his birthplace, where he joined a group called The Richard Gordon Trio. They soon broke up and David went to work at a paper mill by day, and played in a local band on weekends.

In 1975 he visited Thunder Bay's DGM Sound Studios and met Chuck Williams who became his manager. On the road, David was accompanied by his own backup group called Thunder Road. Three years later, he recorded his first single, *Right To The End,* on the Citation label.

Singles

Right To The End 1978
Midnight Cowboy 1978
Rachel I'm Just Not That Strong 1978/79
Losers Bar And Grill 1979
My Broken Old Heart 1980
Caught By Your Call 1981
I Never Figured On This 1981/82
You Never Really Loved Me 1982
Giving Up Easy 1982
What's He Doing At The Door 1983
Nothing Left To Say, But Goodbye 1983
Still Falling In Love With You 1984
Why Do You Love To Torture Me 1984
You Can't Lose (*What You Never Had*) 1985
My World Ain't Turning Yet 1985
The Man Behind The Song 1986

Album

A SKETCH IN THE COUNTRY 1980 (re-released in 1982)

Tim Thorney

A native of Winnipeg, Manitoba, Tim Thorney began his career in the mid-1970s when he worked with such Canadian rock stars as Burton Cummings and Lisa Dal Bello.

In 1979 Tim moved to Toronto, where he worked with various acts and different musical styles. During the 1980s he met MUCHMUSIC veejay Erica Ehm and they became a songwriting team. They wrote all the songs on three debut albums: Joel Feeney's self-titled debut (1991), Cassandra Vasik's WILDFLOWERS (1991), and Don Neilson's BASED ON A TRUE STORY (1992).

Thorney recorded his own songs in 1993 on the album SOME OTHER TIME.

Singles

Missing Person 1993
Fortunate Home 1993
Faraway Story 1993
Chains (with CASSANDRA VASIK) 1994
All The Things I Do 1994
Sing 1995

CD

SOME OTHER TIME 1993

Graham Townsend

Graham Townsend was born in Toronto, Ontario and raised in Buckingham, Quebec. By the time he was six years old, he was playing thefiddle. At nine he was an accomplished fiddler who entered his first contest at the Canadian National Exhibition in Toronto. He entered in the thirty and over class, which he won three years in a row.

In 1953 he entered the North American Fiddling Contest in Shelburne, Ontario and came in third. He finally won it in 1963. The Canadian Armed Forces and the Canadian Broadcasting Corporation (CBC) hired him to tour Germany, France, and Italy to entertain the Canadian and American troops.

He joined the group The Happy Wanderers in 1966 with Papa Joe Brown, Ron Sparling, Vince Lebeau, and Curly Kenny. During Canada's Centennial year (1967), Townsend met the famous step-dancers Don Gilchrist and Gilles Roy. They performed together at Expo 67 and played for Her Majesty Queen Elizabeth II on July 1.

Townsend continued to make guest appearances on TV and radio. His wife Eleanor began to make a name for herself as a fiddler, and came in second at the fiddling championships in Shelburne in 1975.

Throughout the 1980s and 1990s, Graham has been in demand as a performer.

Single *Ice On The Road* 1966

Albums

FIDDLING TO FORTUNE 1958
FAMOUS CANADIAN FIDDLERS — VOL. 1 GRAHAM TOWNSEND 1960
FIDDLIN' FAVORITES 1963
INTERNATIONAL FIDDLING CHAMPION 1963 1964
CHAMPIONSHIP FIDDLE FAVORITES 1964
THE INIMITABLE 1965
SALUTES CANADA'S PRIME MINISTERS 1966
GRAHAM TOWNSEND AND HIS FIDDLE 1967
NORTH AMERICA'S FIDDLING CHAMP 1967
SALUTES CANADA'S PRIME MINISTERS 1867–1967 1967
FAVORITES OF WARD ALLEN 1967
HIS COUNTRY FIDDLE 1968
HARVEST HOME 1968
ON TOUR 1968
SWING YOUR PARTNER 1968
BY THE FIRESIDE 1969
I LIKE DON MESSER 1969
OLD TIME FIDDLE FAVORITES 1969
WORLD CHAMPION FOLK FIDDLER 1970
SALUTES CANADA'S CENTENNIAL 1971
ON TOUR WITH GRAHAM TOWNSEND 1971
SWING YOUR PARTNER 1971
WORLD CHAMPION FIDDLER 1971
MR. COUNTRY FIDDLE 1973
CLASSICS OF IRISH, SCOTTISH AND FRENCH CANADIAN FIDDLING 1976
THE GREAT CANADIAN FIDDLE 1977
LIVE AT BARRE, VERMONT 1981
FIDDLING THROUGH THE YEARS' CHAMPIONSHIP STYLE 1984
100 FIDDLE HITS — 35TH ANNIVERSARY ALBUM 1990

Tracey Prescott & Lonesome Daddy

(See FAMILY BROWN)

Dougie Trineer

Born in Calumet, Quebec on January 19, 1940, Dougal (Dougie) Trineer began playing the piano at square dances when he was eight years old. Bythe time he was thirteen he had picked up the guitar and mastered the Chet Atkins-Merle Travis finger style.

In 1956 he went to Burlington, Vermont, where he appeared on American television with Duke and the Swingbillies. The following year he moved back to Montreal, and worked on the club circuit with Ronnie Prophet as a duo. When Ronnie left to pursue a solo career, Dougie formed his first group called The Hackamores with the late Paul Menard.

Dougie moved to New England in 1959 and worked with the late Dick Curless. By the early 1960s he had returned to The Hackamores and also became A&R (Artist & Repertoire) Manager and musical director for George Taylor at Rodeo Records.

From 1961 to 1976 Dougie had either written, played, or produced over thirty thousand songs. In the 1990s he is still active as a producer/performer in his home studio in Quebec.

Singles

Don't Speak To Me Of Loneliness 1967
Two Shades Of Blue 1968
I Wonder If I'll Ever Smile Again 1969

Albums

LONESOME 1963
LITTLE GREY CHURCH ON THE HILL 1968
24 COUNTRY GUITAR SELECTIONS 1970
GOLDEN GREATS 1970
GOLDEN COUNTRY HITS OF BUCK OWENS & ROGER MILLER (& THE HACKAMORES) 1965
GOLDEN COUNTRY HITS VOL. 2 (& THE HACKAMORES) 1966
SONGS OF MEN AT WAR 1966
STRAIGHT FROM THE HEART (& THE HACKAMORES) 1967
LIVE AT THE CYCLE RANCH (THE HACKAMORES) n.d.
BY REQUEST n.d.
SOLO n.d.
THE COUNTRY MUSIC SOLUTION VOL. II n.d.
COUNTRY DUETS (with ROXANNE) n.d.
TO NASHVILLE AND BACK n.d.

Shania Twain

Born in Windsor, Ontario, and raised in Timmins, Ontario by an Ojibway father and a Canadian mother, Shania (which is pronounced shu-NYE-uh, an Ojibway name that means I'm On My Way) was ten years old when her mother brought her to local clubs and restaurants to sing. After high school, Shania left home to pursue music full-time.

When she was twenty-one years old, her parents were killed in a car accident, and she had to look after her younger brothers and sister. To make ends meet she worked as the headline vocalist at the Deerhurst Resort in Huntsville, Ontario. Mary Bailey later became her manager when she decided on a career in country music.

Shania's self-titled debut album on Polygram Records came out in 1993. Two years later, her second, THE WOMAN IN ME, was released. It contained the smash hits, *Whose Bed Have Your Boots Been Under*, and *Any Man Of Mine*. The latter became her first number one hit on the *Billboard* Country Singles Chart in 1995. She became the third Canadian country artist in forty-five years to have a number one hit single in the U.S. (The other two are Hank Snow and Anne Murray.)

Singles

Dance With The One Who Brought You 1993
What Made You Say That 1993
You Lay A Whole Lot Of Love On Me 1993
Whose Bed Have Your Boots Been Under? 1994/95
Any Man Of Mine 1995
The Woman In Me 1995
I'm Outta Here 1995/96

CDs

SHANIA TWAIN 1993
THE WOMAN IN ME 1995

Ian Tyson

Ian Dawson Tyson was born on September 25, 1933 in Victoria, British Columbia. He started playing the guitar in 1956 while in hospital because of a broken leg he sustained during a rodeo event in Cremona, British Columbia. Despite his interest in music, he had already enrolled in the Vancouver School of Art. When he graduated in 1958, he headed for Toronto, where folk music was becoming the 'in' thing. His first job was at the First Floor, a jazz club operated by actor and singer Don Francks. Francks and Tyson performed there as a duo.

In 1959 Ian met Sylvia Fricker from Chatham, Ontario, and they ended up working together. Two years later, they were invited to play at the first Mariposa Folk Festival. Their big break came later that same year at the Newport Folk Festival. Ian later wrote *Four Strong Winds*, the song most identified with Ian & Sylvia. (For more information on his early career, see *The Encyclopedia of Canadian Rock, Pop & Folk Music.)*

After Ian & Sylvia broke up as an act in 1974, Ian returned to Alberta to forge a new beginning. In 1977 he fronted a band called

Northwest Rebellion that played around Calgary and Saskatchewan. A year later, he recorded the album ONE JUMP AHEAD OF THE DEVIL on Boot Records.

By the early 1980s he began to write about the cowboy. His album, OLD CORRALS AND SAGEBRUSH was a critical success for him, marking the return of cowboy music to the charts.

Singles

Love Can Bless The Soul Of Anyone 1973
If She Just Lets Me 1973/74
Great Canadian Tour 1974
She's My Greatest Blessing 1974/75
Goodness Of Shirley 1975
One Too Many 1976
Turning 30 1977
Beverley 1977/78
Half A Mile Of Hell 1978/79
Lone Star & Coors 1979
The Moon Dancer 1980/81
Ol' Alberta Moon 1981/82
Old Corrals And Sagebrush 1983
Oklahoma Hills 1984
Navajo Rug 1987
Cowboy Pride 1987
The Gift 1987/88
So Hard To Forget 1988
Fifty Years Ago 1988
Adelita Rose 1989
Irving Berlin Is 100 Years Old Today 1989
Cowboys Don't Cry 1989
Casey Tibbs 1990
Since The Rain 1990
I Outgrew The Wagon 1990
Springtime In Alberta 1991
Black Nights 1991
Magpie 1992
Lights Of Laramie 1992
You're Not Alone Anymore 1992
Jaquima To Freno 1993
Non-Pro Song 1993
Alcohol In The Bloodstream 1994
Eighteen Inches Of Rain 1994
Heartaches Are Stealin' 1994
Horsethief Moon 1995

Albums/CDs

OL' EON 1975
ONE JUMP AHEAD OF THE DEVIL 1978
OLD CORRALS AND SAGEBRUSH 1983
IAN TYSON 1984
COWBOYOGRAPHY 1986
I OUTGREW THE WAGON 1989
AND STOOD THERE AMAZED 1991
EIGHTEEN INCHES OF RAIN 1994

Sylvia Tyson

Sylvia Fricker was born in Chatham, Ontario on September 19, 1940. In themid-1950s she played the Toronto club circuit, where she met her future husband, Ian Tyson, at the First Floor. Two years later they became a duo, and in 1964 they were married. They split up as an act ten years later. (For more information on her early career, see *The Encyclopedia of Canadian Rock, Pop & Folk Music.)*

From 1974 to 1980 Sylvia hosted the CBC radio program *Touch The Earth.* She then went on to host CBC-TV's *Heartland* in 1980 and *Country In My Soul* (1981-83), and was a scriptwriter and researcher on *Video Hits* with Samantha Taylor, also on CBC-TV.

In 1975 her debut solo album, WOMAN'S WORLD, was released by Capitol Records. Her second Capitol album, COLD WIND FROM THE

NORTH, came out in 1976. She formed her own SALT label and released two albums, SATIN ON STONE and SUGAR FOR SUGAR, SALT FOR SALT.

During the summer of 1993 she and Cindy Church, Caitlin Hanford, and Colleen Peterson performed together as Quartette. (See QUARTETTE)

Singles

Sleep On My Shoulder 1975
Good Old Song 1976
Love Is A Fire 1979
Up In Smoke 1985
Denim Blue Eyes 1987
Too Short A Ride 1987
Pepere's Mill (& LUCILLE STARR) 1989
You Were On My Mind 1989/90
Slow Moving Heart 1990
Rhythm Of The Road 1990
Thrown To The Wolves (& TOM RUSSELL) 1991
The Sound Of One Heart Breaking 1993

Albums

WOMAN'S WORLD 1975
COLD WIND FROM THE NORTH 1976
SATIN ON STONE 1978
SUGAR FOR SUGAR, SALT FOR SALT 1979
BIG SPOTLIGHT 1986
YOU WERE ON MY MIND 1989
GYPSY CADILLAC 1992

V

Cassandra Vasik

Born Cassandra Leigh in Blenheim, a farming community in Southwestern Ontario, she began singing in her early teens, and by age sixteen she had herown country/rock band. After moving to Toronto she was a regular on *The Tommy Hunter Show* in the mid-1980s.

She then joined an all female alternative music band called Little Egypt, and supplied background vocals on recordings by rock singers Art Bergman and Chris Tait.

In 1991 Sony Music Canada signed her to a record deal. Her debutalbum, WILDFLOWERS, was a critical success and one of the most talked about albums of the year. Two years later came her second, FEELS LIKE HOME. The first single, *Fortune Smiled On Me,* featured Russell deCarle, lead singer of PRAIRIE OYSTER.

Singles

It Comes Back To You 1991/92
Which Face Should I Put On Tonight 1992
The Black Book 1992
Wildflowers 1992
Those Stars 1992
Sadly Mistaken 1993
Fortune Smiled On Me (with RUSSELL DECARLE) 1993
Roll Like A Wheel 1993
Almost Like You Cared 1993/94
Stand Your Ground 1994

CDs

WILDFLOWERS 1991
FEELS LIKE HOME 1993

Laura Vinson

Born and raised in Jasper, Alberta, Laura Vinson grew up on a cattle ranch. Her mother was of French and Cree descent, while her father of English and Cherokee. Laura began writing poetry when she was eight years old. She worked for her father in the Tonquin Valley to earn enough money to buy her first guitar, and was fourteen when she wrote her first song, *Chinook Winds.*

While attending the University of Alberta in Edmonton, she worked as a lounge act and later with a fellow student named Bob Ruzicka, who went on to become a famous songwriter and children's dentist in Victoria, British Columbia.

With bassist Harry Lent and musician-vocalist Frank Walls, Laura formed the trio Red Wyng. They added two new members in 1976, Jim Hathaway on drums and Wayne Saunders on guitar. Stewart MacDougall of The Great Western Orchestra fame was a member from 1980-1984.

Signed to Royalty Records, Vinson's debut album, FIRST FLIGHT, came out in 1978. *The Sun Always Shines* was the first single.

Singles

The Sun Always Shines 1978
Mes Amis O Canada 1979
Sweet Mountain Music 1980
High Fashion Queen 1980
Rocky Mountain Skyline 1980
Hootch, Heartache & Hallelujah 1981
Crazy Heart 1981
Waitin' For The Weekend 1982
Can't Cry Forever 1983

Branded My Heart 1983
Back To The Rockies 1983
Adios Mexico 1984
More Heat Than Light 1984
Alberta Crude 1985
Goodbye 1985
Long Distance Love Affair (& CAM MOLLOY) 1986
Momma's Voice 1986
Blondes (& CHRIS NIELSEN) 1986
Many Moons Ago 1986
Don't Wait (& DENNIS CHARNEY) 1987
Two Sides To Every Story (& CHRIS NIELSEN and R. HARLAN SMITH) 1987
The Last Cowboy's Ride 1988
In My Dreams 1989
Indian Summer 1989
Gun Shy (& DAVE MARTINEAU) 1989/90
The Spirit Sings 1990
True Meaning Of Christmas 1990
Rode Hard 1992
One Of The Lucky Ones 1992/93
Roots That Go Deep 1995
Let It Go 1995/96
Voices On The Wind 1995

Albums

FIRST FLIGHT 1978
HOOTCH, HEARTACHE & HALLELUJAH 1981
ADIOS MEXICO 1984
MANY MOONS AGO 1986
BABY (with DAVE MARTINEAU) 1991
RISE LIKE A PHOENIX (LAURA VINSON & FREE SPIRIT) 1992
VOICES ON THE WIND 1995

W

JEAN CARIGNAN (*fiddle*)
BILL CORMIER (*fiddle*)
Francis Cormier (*fiddle*)
LAURY CORMIER (*fiddle*)
BILL MARTIN (*fiddle*)
TED STEVEN (*fiddle*)
JOHNNY BENTLEY (*fiddle*)
JOHNNY BURT (*piano*)
"DOC" BOYD (*banjo*)
TONY MONT (*guitar*)
CECIL MC EACHERN (*bass*)
GEORGE WADE (*leader*)

George Wade & His Cornhuskers

Led by George Wade, the Toronto based Cornhuskers performed at dances in Ontario and Quebec from the mid-1920s to the 1940s. They began broadcasting on CFRB, Toronto in 1928, and in 1933 they were the firstgroup of their kind to perform on the CRBC, the forerunner of the CBC. That same year they made several recordings on RCA Victor's Black label.

George Wade died on January 23, 1975. Jean Carignan (a.k.a. Ti-Jean) had a successful career with his own dance band until 1954, and continued to be in demand as a performer through to the early 1980s. He died in Delson, near Montreal on February 16, 1988.

Singles

My Darling Nellie/Rock Valley 1933
Fireman's Reel/The Mason's Apron 1933
The Devil's Dream/Soldier's Joy 1933
Opera Reel/Arkansaw Traveller 1933
Mountain High/The Chisholm Trail 1933
Cowboy's Reel/Uncle Jim 1933
Five Mile Chase/Medley of Reels 1933
Acrobat Reel/Waltz Quadrille 1933
Haste To The Wedding/Lord Saltoun's Reel 1933
Cullen House/Old Time Reel Medley 1933
Father O'Flynn/Little Brown Jug 1933
McDonald's Reel/Buffalo Girl 1933

Michael T. Wall

Born in Stephenville, Newfoundland, Michael T. Wall moved to Toronto in 1961. It took three years before Toronto audiences caught on to his music. By the late 1960s he appeared at the Grand Ole Opry in Nashville. Of all the recordings he made, one of his best known is *The Singing Newfoundlander* (1974).

The Royal Canadian Legion in Pickering, Ontario commemorated Wall's silver anniversary as a performer and promoter of Canadian country music in 1988.

Singles

If You Want It (Baby) I Got It 1970
What Am I Going To Do With You 1970
The Singing Newfoundlander 1974
Shake My Hand, I'm From Newfoundland 1975
Santa Claus Is A Newfie 1981
Daddy's Girl/The Ocean Ranger Disaster 1983

Albums

CHASER FOR THE BLUES 1972
THE SINGING NEWFOUNDLANDER 1974
MICHAEL T. WALL 1975
MORE OF CANADA'S SINGING NEWFOUNDLANDER, MICHAEL T. WALL 1975
KING OF THE NEWFIES 1979
WELCOME TO NEWFOUNDLAND 1981

Jerry Warren

Jerry Warren was born James R. Jordan in Stayner, Ontario. While living in Western Canada he started his professional career in country music. In 1969 he was signed to Capitol Records. One of his early hits was *You Ain't Changed A Bit From Baltimore*. After touring across Canada he moved to Niagara Falls, Ontario. Warren was also a prolific songwriter. Some of his songs were recorded by Mike Graham, Honey West, and Diane Leigh. During the mid-1980s, Jerry Warren attempted to make a comeback. He died of a heart attack on January 28, 1991.

Singles

You Ain't Changed A Bit From Baltimore (CAPITOL) 1970
The Meanest Man (CAPITOL) 1970
This Lovin' Feelin' (UA) 1974
Big Red Jimmy (UA) 1975
One Way Ticket To A Lady 1975/76
Fire In My Heart 1987/88

I'll Never Write Another (UA) 1975

Albums

LOUISIANA BLUE BOY 1973
FROM THE FALLS TO THE COAST 1974

Dan Washburn

Born and raised in Cobourg, Ontario, Dan Washburn learned to play theacoustic guitar at age nine, and at ten he wrote his first song. Before he graduated from public school, he was playing in his father's country band. In high school he listened to rock. After graduation he formed a duo with a friend Steve O'Connor, and later was in the Peterborough band Loose Change.

By 1989 Dan had recorded his first song, *Fiddle On The Mantle*, which was a tribute to his late grandfather. Other hits followed until late 1992 when he replaced Todd Nolan as lead vocalist in the group South Mountain. (See SOUTH MOUNTAIN)

Singles

Fiddle On The Mantle 1990
You Make It Easy 1990
Let Him Go 1990
Forever Never Ends 1991
The Kind Of Man I Am 1991/92

Sneezy Waters

Born Peter Hodgson in Ottawa, Ontario, he first billed himself as "The Great Sneezy Waters" in the mid-1960s. As a teenager he was influenced bythe Carter Family, Jimmie Rodgers, and Hank Williams. On stage he was accompanied by the group called His Excellent Band.

In the 1960s he was also a member of The Children, and later performed in the duo A Rosewood Daydream with Susan Jains.

By the early 1970s he was a solo act and had performed throughout Europe and Asia, including the Canadian Pavilion at Expo 70 in Osaka, Japan. He later made an indelible impression as Hank Williams in the stage and movie versions of *The Show He Never Gave*, the concert Williams might have given had he not died on New Year's Eve, 1952. Sneezy's most famous for the song *(You've Got) Sawdust On The Floor Of Your Heart*, which was written by Sneezy's older brother Murky.

Albums

(YOU'VE GOT) SAWDUST ON THE FLOOR OF YOUR HEART 1978
SNEEZY WATERS SINGS HANK WILLIAMS 1981

Paul Weber

Born and raised in Kitchener, Ontario, Paul Weber grew up in a musical family. In the family band he played flat top guitar and sang. In 1974 he left to play bass with Joe Firth. For the next seven years he toured across Canada and either backed up or performed with such stars as The Kendalls, Don Gibson, and Dallas Harms.

Weber decided to pursue a solo career in 1981, and organized his own backup group, Top Hand. That same year his debut album, TWO BITS OF HURTIN', came out on Boot Records. The title track and *Where Beauty Lives In Memory* are among his biggest hits.

Singles

Two Bits Worth Of Hurtin' 1981
Holdin' On To You 1982
Under The Influence (While Getting) 1982
Where Beauty Lives In Memory 1983
Two Bits Worth Of Hurtin' 1983
I Can't Say No 1984
One More Shot At Your Love 1984
Change Of Heart 1984
She's No Lady 1985
I Could Love You By Heart 1985
Whiskey Tears 1986
Time To Turn The Page 1987
A Little Bit Older And A Lot Wiser 1990
She'll Never Know 1990/91
No One Can Hurt Me Any Better Than You 1991
Growing Pains 1991
First Second Thoughts 1992
All Messed Up (No Place To Go) 1993
The Fall (In Fallin' In Love) 1994

Albums

TWO BITS WORTH OF HURTIN' 1981
WHISKEY TEARS 1984
OLDER AND WISER 1991

The Western Sweethearts

BESSIE BRUNETTE (*lead guitar, vocals*)
LORRIE GALE (*rhythm guitar, vocals*)
MYRTLE GIFFORD (*bass, vocals*)
PATTI JO (*drums*)

Under the leadership of Myrtle Gifford, The Western Sweethearts from Toronto, Ontario began as a trio in 1953 comprised of Gifford, Bessie Brunette, and Nema Hawkes. They opened at the Nanza Bar in Toronto. Hawkes was later replaced by Shirley Mae Carr of Toronto.

By the early 1960s Carr had left. The addition of Lorrie Gale (a.k.a. Lorraine Gallant) and Patti Jo (a.k.a. Patricia Hennessey) made the group a quartet. In addition to being with the group, Bessie and Myrtle also entertained as a duo.

In 1965 their name changed to The Rhythm Sweethearts. That same year Arc Records released their only album, which had previously been issued in 1964 as THE WESTERN SWEETHEARTS.

The group broke up in 1972.

Albums THE WESTERN SWEETHEARTS 1964; THE RHYTHM SWEEHEARTS 1965

Billy Whelan

For forty-five years, Billy Whelan was one of Nova Scotia's biggest country stars. When he was fifteen he received his first guitar and it wasn't long before he was making personal appearances. He served in the Armed Forces during World War II, and returned to his music career when the war was over. His big break came when John Fisher and John Crosby featured him on CBC Radio. By 1957 he had his own coast-to-coast show.

In 1949 he signed with Hart-Van Records in LaGrange, Illinois. He later recorded for Banff/Rodeo Records.

Billy was a prolific songwriter, the creator of over seventy-five songs. In the mid-1950s he performed with his own group, The Western Serenaders. By the early 1960s he only appeared occasionally in public. From 1962 to 1972 he was a guide with the Department of Lands and Forests. He spent his final years in Bedford, Nova Scotia, where he committed suicide in December 1987.

Singles

At The End Of A Long Lonely Day 1956
I Dreamed Of An Old Love Affair 1956
The Letter Edged In Black 1956
Anytime 1956
Have I Told You Lately That I Love You 1956
Your Cheatin' Heart 1956
Bouquet Of Roses 1956
Just A Closer Walk With Thee 1956
Rockin' Alone In An Old Rockin' Chair 1956
Let The Lower Lights Be Burning n.d.
Near The Cross n.d.
I Love Old New Brunswick n.d.

Album

NEAR THE CROSS 1964
CANADIAN COUNTRY SOUVENIRS OF THE 1950S 1987
COUNTRY MEMORIES n.d

Whiskey Jack

DUNCAN FREMLIN (*banjo*)
JOHN HOFFMAN (*fiddle, mandolin*)
BOB MCNIVEN (*electric & acoustic guitars, vocals*)
GREG STREET (*stand-up bass*); Replaced by CAMERON MACLENNAN
CRAIG BIGNELL (*drums, vocals*)

Toronto based Whiskey Jack formed in 1979 and became one of the best bluegrass groups in North America. In addition to bluegrass, they also played country, pop, swing, and jazz numbers. When they performed, their act was complemented by John Hoffman's humor and hilarious stage antics. Their debut album UPTOWN was released in 1979.

Singles
One In A Million 1985
Fiddlin' Man 1985/86

Albums
UPTOWN 1979
ONE MORE TIME 1982
WHISKEY JACK 1985

Chris Whitely & Caitlin Hanford

Both Chris Whiteley and Caitlin Hanford were born in Kansas. Chris was raised in Toronto, where he began his professional career with the folk/blues group, The Original Sloth Band. Caitlin lived in Seattle,Washington before she moved to Montreal, where she worked with singer/songwriter Linda Morrison.

The two met while working the Montreal coffeehouse circuit and it wasn't long before they became a singing team. Their debut album, LOVIN' IN ADVANCE, in 1981 contained eight songs written by Whitely.

They enjoyed several hits throughout the 1980s. In 1994 Hanford joined Sylvia Tyson, Colleen Peterson, and Cindy Church to form the country supergroup, Quartette. Whitely pursued his interest in jazz.

Singles
Take Your Time And Do It Right 1981
Milwaukee Here I Come 1981
Settin' Sun 1981/82
Tomorrow's Not What It Used To Be 1982/83
Wanted Poster 1983/84
That Piece Of Your Heart 1984
Honky Tonk High-Rise 1984/85

Albums
LOVIN' IN ADVANCE 1981
CHRIS WHITELY & CAITLIN HANFORD 1984

As Caitlin Hanford:

Single
Tear This Old Heart Down 1992/93

Darlene Wiebe

Born on March 27, 1965 in Gouldtown, Saskatchewan, Darlene Wiebe started performing at age twelve. Managed by CKRM Regina's Fred King, she recorded for Sunshine Records. Her debut single was called *Heartbreaking Melodies.* The flip side, a remake of Dusty Springfield's *Silver Threads and Golden Needless*, was a bigger hit.

On stage she was accompanied by her own band, Country Roads, which was comprised of Darlene's cousins Ron, Myron, and Dwayne Wiebe and her brother Barry.

Singles

Heartbreaking Melodies 1981
As Long As We Love Like This 1982
Silver Threads And Golden Needles 1982
Just Another Woman In Love 1983
Somewhere Between I Love You 1983

Brent Williams

A native of Hassett, Nova Scotia, Brent Williams was born on March 25, 1940. By the time he was nine years old he was playing guitar and singing. His main influences were the country stars he heard on the Grand Ole Opry and from Wheeling, West Virginia. He was performing before audiences in his mid-teens and was an accomplished fiddle player.

From 1958-1960 he joined Vic Mullen's Birch Mountain Boys bluegrass band. During the winter of 1961 Brent signed a recording contract with Rodeo Records. His first single was *Oh So Lonely.*

Known as "Canada's Charley Pride" because he was black, Williams was a much sought after guest on some of the early country TV shows and was a regular on a show that originated in Sherbrooke, Quebec.

Singles

Oh So Lonely 1961
Back Home In Georgia 1972
It Rained The Day After 1972/73
Till I Can't Take It Anymore 1973
I Wish You Were With Me Tonight 1978
Soft Shoulders & Dangerous Curves 1980

Albums

BRENT & HARRY — COUNTRY SPECIAL 1964
MORE COUNTRY WITH BRENT & HARRY 1965
ON THE GO 1970
EVERYBODY'S BEAUTIFUL 1971
IN YOU I BELIEVE 1972
I WISH YOU WERE HERE WITH ME TONIGHT 1978
NORTHERN REFLECTIONS — LIVE n.d
I THINK I'LL MAKE IT n.d.

A. Frank Willis

Born into a musical family in Dover, Newfoundland, A. Frank Willis shared a love for the button accordion and violin. At age eleven he joined his brothers to form the Willis Brothers Quartet.

Frank left for Toronto to seek fame and fortune but ended up working in a factory. He returned home to rejoin his brothers, and later moved to Hare Bay where he concentrated on a solo career. One of his biggest hits was *Take Me As I Am*, which was co-written by Wayne Rostad, and became one of the longest charted records in the history of Newfoundland radio.

Singles

Take Me As I Am 1978
You And I (Underneath The Moon) 1984
Hello Mom And Dad (We're Coming Home For Xmas) 1984
I Lobster And Never Flounder (with PETER F. QUINLAN) 1985
Too Long In The Rain 1985/86
Dust On The Pillow 1987
Rockin' On The Rock 1990
Forever Don't Last Too Long 1991

Album

GETTING MYSELF TOGETHER 1979

Tom Wilson & His Western All-Stars

EDGAR "EDDIE ROY" BEAUDOIN (*steel guitar*)
BRIAN BRAMHALL (*bass*); Replaced by CLAIR WALLACE
GILBERT WILSON (*lead guitar, banjo*)
TOM WILSON (*rhythm guitar, vocals*)
JOHNNIE WOODS (*fiddle*)

The history of Tom Wilson and his Western All-Stars began in 1958 when they played at various social events and dances in their hometown of Brockville, Ontario, and the Thousand Islands. The original group consisted of brothers Tom and Gilbert Wilson, Brian Bramhall, "Eddie Roy" Beaudoin, and Johnnie Woods. They were both a bluegrass and country group.

Their popularity extended to radio. On May 1, 1965 they had their own weekly show on CFJR in Brockville that lasted until the early 1970s. They also recorded their first album for Rodeo Records in 1965, IT'S COUNTRY, IT'S BLUEGRASS. Their next album in 1966, TOM WILSON AND HIS WESTERN ALL STARS, contained the first of four singles, *The St. Lawrence River's My Home.*

In 1982 Tom Wilson had started another group, the bluegrass band Tom Wilson and Border Bluegrass. They recorded an album of bluegrass and gospel called ELECTRIC RADIO in 1988. Wilson continued to play country and western with his Western All Stars.

During the last fifteen years they have lost two of their members. Johnnie Woods died in 1984, and Edgar Beaudoin in the early 1980s.

Singles

The St. Lawrence River's My Home 1966
Hillbilly Hotel 1968
The St. Lawrence River's My Home (re-released) 1986
Electric Radio 1988

Albums

IT'S COUNTRY, IT'S BLUEGRASS 1965
TOM WILSON & HIS WESTERN ALL-STARS 1966
TOM WILSON, GOLDEN STEREO 1968
BLUE MOUNTAIN BLUES 1986
ELECTRIC RADIO 1988
SOUVENIR 1990
GETTYSBURG 1992

Jim Witter

Born in Hamilton, Ontario on November 2, 1964, Jim Witter learned to play the piano from his mother and the guitar from his older brother Rob. When he was seven years old, Jim learned his first song, *Yesterday,* by The Beatles. At fourteen, he wrote his first song, *Maybe Someday You'll Be Mine.*

He has been performing as a solo artist since 1983 and was a featured vocalist and pianist with the Hamilton Philharmonic. In 1993 his self-titled debut album was released. The first single was *Everything And More.*

Singles

Everything And More 1993
Distant Drum 1993
Stolen Moments 1993/94
Sweet Sweet Poison 1994
Human Highway (with CASSANDRA VASIK) 1994
Chevy Coupe 1994/95

CD

JIM WITTER 1993

Michelle Wright

Born in Chatham, Ontario on July 1, 1961, Michelle Wright grew up in thesmall farming community of Merlin not far away. She was thirteen when she began playing the acoustic guitar. While in high school she joined her first band, The Marquis. After she graduated she toured and played clubs until she met Brian Ferriman of the Toronto-based Savannah Music Group, who became her manager. In 1988 his label Savannah Records released Michelle's album, DO RIGHT BY ME.

During the next two years her popularity in Canada grew. She also was invited to play at the music festival in Maxville, Ontario, where she was introduced to the songwriting team of Rick Giles and Steve Bogard. They were struck by her powerful voice and wanted her to go to Nashville to record some demos. Tim DuBois, senior Vice President and General Manager of Arista Records, flew to Toronto to see her at *The Diamond Club* in May 1989. She was immediately offered a record deal.

Her 1990 self-titled debut album on Arista/BMG drew critical raves, and her second, NOW & THEN, produced her first U.S. Top Ten hit, *Take It Like A Man.* The video for the song went to number one on both Country Music Television (CMT) and The Nashville Network (TNN).

On October 1, 1992 she performed on the Grand Ole Opry for the first time. Two years later, her third album, THE REASONS WHY, was released in Canada. She received The Academy of Country Music (ACM) award as Top New Female Vocalist (1992), the only Canadian performer to receive this honor.

Singles

I Want To Count On You 1986/87
New Fool At An Old Game 1987
The Rhythm Of Romance 1988
Do Right By Me 1988/89
I Wish I Were Only Lonely 1989
Rock Me Gently 1989
I Wish I Were Only Lonely 1989
I Don't Want To Wonder 1989/90
Woman's Intuition 1990
The Change 1993
One Good Man 1994
The Wall 1994/95
Safe In The Arms Of Love 1995

CDs

DO RIGHT BY ME 1988
MICHELLE WRIGHT 1990
NOW AND THEN 1992
THE REASONS WHY 1994

The York County Boys

BRIAN BARRON (*fiddle*)
MIKE CAMERON (*flat top guitar, vocals*)
ALFRED "DUSTY" LEGER (*bass*)
"BIG" JOHN MCMANAMAN (*lead vocals, banjo, guitar, fiddle*)
REX YETMAN (*mandolin, vocals*)

Formed in 1954 in Toronto, The York County Boys were Canada's first bluegrass group. They started out as a trio with "Big" John McManaman, Mike Cameron, and Rex Yetman. By 1956 they had become a quintet with the addition of Brian Barron and Alfred Leger. They also toured Nova Scotia and New Brunswick. In 1959 they recorded Canada's first bluegrass album, BLUE GRASS JAMBOREE, which Arc Records released a year later.

During the early 1960s, they performed at the Mariposa Folk Festival. They continued to perform until the 1970s. They have since reunited for special shows.

In 1990 they were honored, along with friend and colleague Ron Scott, with the first Pioneer Bluegrass Award from The Toronto Area Bluegrass Association (TABA).

Barron and McManaman launched solo careers in 1960 and 1961, respectively. They are the only members of the York County Boys who are still performing in the 1990s.

As The York County Boys:

Albums A BLUEGRASS LEGEND—THE YORK COUNTY BOYS 1983 (reissue of 1960 album)

BLUE GRASS JAMBOREE 1960

As Brian Barron:

Album OLD TYME FIDDLE JAMBOREE 1960

As Big John McManaman:

Albums FIVE STRING BANJO FESTIVAL 1961

BLUE GRASS HOOTENANNY 1963

Appendix A: *Noteworthy Artists*

The following recording artists released songs that reached the charts. Information on these acts is scant or sketchy. The author would be delighted to receive letters or news clippings telling their story for possible inclusion in another edition of this Encyclopedia.

Clint Curtiss

Singles

Stop The World 1969
Sweet Sweet Feeling 1969
Nobody's Foolin' Me 1970
There's No Price Tag
On The Doors In Newfoundland 1970
Better Be Good It's Christmas 1970
Maritimes Are Callin' To Me 1971
My Sweet Mama 1971
It's Only Lonely Me 1971
Driftin' Away From My Heart 1971
Smallwood's Lament 1972
Please Daddy Don't Go Away 1975
I've Gambled And There's No More To Lose 1990

Albums

SWEET SWEET FEELING 1969
NOBODY'S FOOLIN' ME 1970
CLINT CURTISS 1971
THE MARITIMES ARE CALLING TO ME 1971
ODE TO NEWFOUNDLAND 1971
I'M A NEWFIE NOW 1973
A BREED OF HIS OWN 1974
THE WAYWARD BOY 1975
I'VE GAMBLED AND THERE'S NO MORE TO LOSE 1988

Jim & Don Haggert

Singles

I'm Comin' Home 1972
Pictou County Jail 1973
He 1973/74
What Used To Be A River 1974
The Balladeer 1974
Follow Your Heart 1975
Early Morning Prayer 1975
One Day At A Time 1976
A Special Feeling 1976

Album

BALLADEERS 1975

Paul Hann

Singles

I Almost Fell In Her Eyes 1976
The Heart Of Saturday Night 1981

Albums A FINE, WHITE THREAD 1974
ANOTHER TUMBLEWEED 1976
PAUL HANN 1977
HIGH TEST 1980
HOMETOWN HERO 1981

Jack Hennig

Singles *Poppa Told Me* 1970
Thumb-Trippin' 1973
The Dreams Are Never Ended 1976
Craisy Daisy 1976
Big City Lights 1977
Candy & Brandy 1977
George The Hermit 1978
Mindy 1978
Last Summer's Love 1979
Caught In The Middle 1980

Album JACK HENNIG SINGS 1974

Debbie Lori Kaye

Singles *Picking Up My Hat* 1965
Ride Ride Ride 1967/68
Come On Home 1968
Baby's Come Home 1969

Roy Maccaull

Singles *Time* 1969
And That's All On My Mind 1969
In The Morning 1972
When The Sun Goes Down 1972
Shores Of P.E.I. 1973
Ballad Of The Hotel Waitress 1974
Thrills Of Winter 1975
House That Love Built 1976

Albums COUNTRY BOY 1968
THIS MIGHTY & WICKED LAND 1968
COUNTRY MANDOLIN (with EDDIE POIRIER) 1969
ROY MACCAULL 1970
COUNTRY ROADS 1971
DRIFTIN' LIKE THE WIND 1973
BALLAD OF A HOTEL WAITRESS 1974

Artie Maclaren

Singles *Skip, Hop & Wobble* 1965
Lost Love 1965/66
Down Home Country Songs 1976
Jacob 1977
The Picker 1978
Daddy's Soul Guitar 1978

Where Would John Baptize Jesus 1978/79
Grandpa 1979
Everything Is Warm In Texas 1980
The November Sky 1983

Albums WEBB PIERCE SONGBOOK 1965
DOWN HOME COUNTRY 1976
SONGS OF LOVE AND LIFE 1978
THE ENTERTAINER 1979

Harry Rusk

Singles *My Northern Memories* 1967/68
My Rose Of Mexico 1968/69
Pineville County Jail 1969
Little Rosa 1970
A Big Man 1970
Diggin' For Gold 1970
The Redman And The Train 1972
Cinderella Girl 1973
Pretty Mary 1976
The Crystal Waltz 1977
Remember I'll Always Love You 1978

Albums HARRY RUSK 1965
THE COUNTRY FAVORITES OF HARRY RUSK 1966
CANADIAN COUNTRY HITS WITH HARRY RUSK 1970
HAWAIIAN SOUVENIRS 1976
FROM THE TRAP-LINE TO NASHVILLE'S
GRAND OLE OPRY 1978

Scotty Stevenson

Singles *Dandelion Wine* 1968
Love Is What Happiness Is 1968
Can't Go Back To Winnipeg 1969
Keep Canada Strong 1971
My Daddy's Blackland Farm 1972

Honey West

Singles *The Moods Of My Man* 1971
Country Soul 1972
His Colored Television 1972
Hold It Up To The Sun 1972/73
The Locket 1973
I'm A Person Too 1976

Albums MEET HONEY WEST 1969
A TOUCH OF HONEY 1969
SWEET DREAMS 1970
THE MOODS OF MY MAN 1971
COUNTRY SOUL 1972
GETTING TOGETHER (with JOE FIRTH) 1972
SILVER BELLS 1972
IN THE SHADOW OF THE PAST 1973

The following country artists and groups have also made a significant contribution to Canadian country music. Any information on these would be gratefully received by the author for inclusion in a future edition of the Encyclopedia.

The Altones
Gurney Anderson
Bev Barker
Marlene Beaudry
Dave Boyer
Robbie Brass & Red Wine
Coralie Buell
Bunkhouse Boys
Jessie Burns
Calhoun Twins
Cliff Carroll
The Chaparrals
Eddie Chwill
Terry Cousineau
Ivan Daines
Fern Dauth
The Drylanders
Jamie Donald
The Frontiersmen
Fustukian
Norma Gale
The Garrison Brothers
Russ Gurr
The Haggertys
Jack Hennig
Gord & Audie Henry
James Lee Hitchener
Wendy Jenkins
Dusty King
Joey Knight
Floyd Lloyd
Wayne Mack
Lee Marlow
Larry & Laura Mattson
Paul Menard
Pat Menard
Mark Middler
Cameron Molloy
Donna Moon
The Myers Brothers
Spade Nielsen
Jimmy Arthur Ordge
B.W. Pawley
Jimmy Phair
Showdown
Laurie Thain
Angus Walker
Roy Warhurst
Reg Watkins
Bryan Way
Ted Wesley
Carmen Westphal
John R. Winters

Appendix B: Canadian Country Music Association (CCMA) Awards (1982–1995)

1982 Entertainer of the Year . . . . . . Family Brown
Male Vocalist of the Year . . . . . . Terry Carisse
Female Vocalist of the Year . . . . . . Carroll Baker
Group of the Year . . . . . . Family Brown
Single of the Year . . . . . . *Some Never Stand A Chance* — Family Brown
Album of the Year . . . . . . *Raised On Country Music* — Family Brown
SOCAN Song of the Year . . . . . . *Some Never Stand A Chance* — Family Brown
Vista (*Rising Star Award*) . . . . . . Ruth Ann
Back Up Band of the Year . . . . . . Baker Street
Manager of the Year . . . . . . Ron Sparling
Country Club of the Year . . . . . . Golden Rail, Lafontaine Hotel, Ottawa, Ont.
Record Producer of the Year . . . . . . Jack Feeney
Country Music Person . . . . . . Ron Sparling

1983 Entertainer of the Year . . . . . . Family Brown
Male Vocalist of the Year . . . . . . Dick Damron
Female Vocalist of the Year . . . . . . Marie Bottrell
Group of the Year . . . . . . Family Brown
Single of the Year . . . . . . *Raised On Country Music* — Family Brown
Album of the Year . . . . . . RAISED ON COUNTRY MUSIC — Family Brown
SOCAN Song of the Year . . . . . . *Raised On Country Music* — Family Brown
Duo of the Year . . . . . . Donna & LeRoy Anderson
Vista (*Rising Star Award*) . . . . . . Kelita Haverland
Back Up Band of the Year . . . . . . Baker Street
Manager of the Year . . . . . . Ron Sparling
Country Club of the Year . . . . . . Urban Corral, Moncton, N.B.
Record Producer of the Year . . . . . . Dallas Harms
Country Music Person . . . . . . Gordon Burnett

1984 Entertainer of the Year . . . . . . Ronnie Prophet
Male Vocalist of the Year . . . . . . Terry Carisse
Female Vocalist of the Year . . . . . . Marie Bottrell
Group of the Year . . . . . . Family Brown

Single of the Year. . . . . . . *A Little Good News*
— Anne Murray
Album of the Year . . . . . . REPEAT AFTER ME
— Family Brown
SOCAN Song of the Year . . . . . . *Jesus It's Me Again*
— Dick Damron
Duo of the Year . . . . . . Glory Anne Carriere
& Ronnie Prophet
Vista (*Rising Star Award* . . . . . . Roni Sommers
Back Up Band of the Year . . . . . . Baker Street
Manager of the Year . . . . . . Ron Sparling
Country Club of the Year . . . . . . Urban Corral, Moncton, N.B.
Record Producer of the Year . . . . . . Dallas Harms / Mike Francis
Instrumentalist of the Year . . . . . . Bobby Lalonde
Hall of Honor Inductees . . . . . . Wilf Carter, Tommy Hunter,
William Harold Moon &
Orval Prophet

1985 Entertainer of the Year . . . . . . Dick Damron
Male Vocalist of the Year . . . . . . Terry Carisse
Female Vocalist of the Year . . . . . . Carroll Baker
Group of the Year . . . . . . The Mercey Brothers
Single of the Year . . . . . . Riding On The Wind
— Gary Fjellgaard
Album of the Year . . . . . . CLOSEST THING TO YOU
— Terry Carisse
SOCAN Song of the Year . . . . . . *Counting The I Love You's*
—Terry Carisse & Bruce Rawlins
Duo of the Year . . . . . . Anita Perras & Tim Taylor
Vista (*Rising Star Award*) . . . . . . Ginny Mitchell
Back Up Band of the Year . . . . . . Tracks
Manager of the Year . . . . . . Brian Ferriman
Country Club of the Year . . . . . . Cook County Saloon, Edmonton, Alta.
Record Producer of the Year . . . . . . Terry Carisse
Instrumentalist of the Year . . . . . . Steve Piticco
Hall of Honor Inductees . . . . . . Hank Snow & Don Messer

1986 Entertainer of the Year . . . . . . Family Brown
Male Vocalist of the Year . . . . . . Terry Carisse
Female Vocalist of the Year . . . . . . Anita Perras
Group of the Year . . . . . . Family Brown
Single of the Year . . . . . . *Now And Forever* (*You and Me*)
— Anne Murray
Album of the Year . . . . . . FEEL THE FIRE
— Family Brown

SOCAN Song of the Year . . . . . . *Now and Forever*
— David Foster/
Jim Vallance/Charles Goodrum
Duo of the Year . . . . . . Anita Perras & Tim Taylor
Vista (*Rising Star Award*). . . . . . . J.K. Gulley
Back Up Band of the Year . . . . . . The Bobby Lalonde Band
Manager of the Year . . . . . . Brian Ferriman
Country Club of the Year . . . . . . Urban Corral, Moncton, N.B.
Record Producer of the Year . . . . . . Mike Francis
Instrumentalist of the Year . . . . . . Bobby Lalonde
Hall of Honor Inductee . . . . . . Papa Joe Brown

1987 Entertainer of the Year . . . . . . k.d. lang
Male Vocalist of the Year . . . . . . Ian Tyson
Female Vocalist of the Year . . . . . . Anita Perras
Group of the Year . . . . . . Family Brown
Single of the Year . . . . . . *Navajo Rug* — Ian Tyson
Album of the Year . . . . . . COWBOYOGRAPHY — Ian Tyson
SOCAN Song of the Year . . . . . . *Heroes* — Gary Fjellgaard MBS
Duo of the Year . . . . . . Anita Perras & Tim Taylor
Vista (*Rising Star Award*) . . . . . . k.d. lang
Back Up Band of the Year . . . . . . The Bobby Lalonde Band
Manager of the Year . . . . . . Brian Ferriman
Country Club of the Year . . . . . . Rodeo Roadhouse, Kingston, Ont.
Record Producer of the Year . . . . . . Mike Francis
Instrumentalist of the Year . . . . . . Bobby Lalonde
Hall of Honor Inductee . . . . . . Lucille Starr

1988 Entertainer of the Year . . . . . . k.d. lang
Male Vocalist of the Year . . . . . . Ian Tyson
Female Vocalist of the Year . . . . . . k.d. lang
Group of the Year . . . . . . Family Brown
Single of the Year . . . . . . *One Smokey Rose* — Anita Perras
Album of the Year . . . . . . SHADOWLAND — k.d. lang
SOCAN Song of the Year . . . . . . *One Smokey Rose* — Tim Taylor
Duo of the Year . . . . . . Anita Perras & Tim Taylor
Vista (*Rising Star Award*) . . . . . . Blue Rodeo
Back Up Band of the Year . . . . . . The Reclines
Manager of the Year . . . . . . Brian Ferriman
Country Club of the Year . . . . . . Rodeo Roadhouse, Kingston, Ont.
Record Producer of the Year . . . . . . Randall Prescott
Instrumentalist of the Year . . . . . . Randall Prescott
Hall of Honor Inductee . . . . . . Jack Feeney

1989 Entertainer of the Year . . . . . . k.d. lang
Male Vocalist of the Year . . . . . . Gary Fjellgaard
Female Vocalist of the Year . . . . . . k.d. lang
Group of the Year . . . . . . Family Brown
Single of the Year . . . . . . *Town of Tears* — Family Brown
Album of the Year . . . . . . SHADOWLAND — k.d. lang
SOCAN Song of the Year . . . . . . *Town of Tears* — Barry Brown/Randall Prescott/Bruce Campbell
Duo of the Year . . . . . . Gary Fjellgaard & Linda Kidder
Vista (*Rising Star Award*) . . . . . . George Fox
Back Up Band of the Year . . . . . . The Reclines
Manager of the Year . . . . . . Leonard Rambeau
Country Club of the Year . . . . . . Rodeo Roadhouse, Kingston, Ont.
Record Producer of the Year . . . . . . Randall Prescott
Instrumentalist of the Year . . . . . . Dick Damron
Hall of Honor Inductees . . . . . . Ian Tyson & Don Grashey

1990 Bud Country Fans' Choice of
Entertainer of the Year . . . . . . k.d. lang
Male Vocalist of the Year . . . . . . George Fox
Female Vocalist of the Year . . . . . . Michelle Wright
Group of the Year . . . . . . Prairie Oyster
Single of the Year . . . . . . *Goodbye, So Long, Hello* — Prairie Oyster
Album of the Year . . . . . . ABSOLUTE TORCH AND TWANG — k.d. lang
SOCAN Song of the Year . . . . . . *Pioneers* — Barry Brown
Duo of the Year . . . . . . Gary Fjellgaard & Linda Kidder
Vista (*Rising Star Award*) . . . . . . Patricia Conroy
Back Up Band of the Year . . . . . . The Reclines
Manager of the Year . . . . . . Leonard Rambeau
Country Club of the Year . . . . . . Cook County Saloon, Edmonton, Alta.
Instrumentalist of the Year . . . . . . Steve Piticco
Record Producer of the Year . . . . . . Randall Prescott
Hall of Honor Inductees . . . . . . Gordie Tapp & Ron Sparling

1991 Bud Country Fans' Choice of
Entertainer of the Year . . . . . . Rita MacNeil
Male Vocalist of the Year . . . . . . George Fox
Female Vocalist of the Year . . . . . . Michelle Wright
Group of the Year . . . . . . Prairie Oyster
Single of the Year . . . . . . *New Kind of Love* — Michelle Wright

Album of the Year . . . . . . MICHELLE WRIGHT
— Michelle Wright
SOCAN Song of the Year . . . . . . *Lonely You, Lonely Me* — Joan Besen
Duo of the Year . . . . . . The Johner Brothers
Vista (*Rising Star Award*) . . . . . . South Mountain
Back Up Band of the Year . . . . . . The Michelle Wright Band
Manager of the Year . . . . . . Brian Ferriman
Country Club of the Year . . . . . . Cook County Saloon, Edmonton, Alta.
Instrumentalist of the Year . . . . . . Steve Piticco
Hall of Honor Inductees. . . . . . . The Rhythm Pals & Hugh Joseph

1992 Bud Country Fans' Choice of
Entertainer of the Year . . . . . . Rita MacNeil
Male Vocalist of the Year . . . . . . Ian Tyson
Female Vocalist of the Year . . . . . . Michelle Wright
Vocal Duo or Group of the Year . . . . . . Prairie Oyster
Single of the Year . . . . . . *Take It Like A Man* — Michelle Wright
Album of the Year . . . . . . EVERYBODY KNOWS — Prairie Oyster
SOCAN Song of the Year . . . . . . *Did You Fall In Love With Me* — Joan Besen
Vista (*Rising Star Award*) . . . . . . Cassandra Vasik
Back Up Band of the Year . . . . . . The Michelle Wright Band
Manager of the Year . . . . . . Brian Ferriman
Country Club of the Year . . . . . . Cook County Saloon, Edmonton, Alta.
Record Producer of the Year . . . . . . Randall Prescott
Hall of Honor Inductees . . . . . . Carroll Baker & Gordon Burnett

1993 Bud Country Fans' Choice of
Entertainer of the Year . . . . . . Michelle Wright
Male Vocalist of the Year . . . . . . George Fox
Female Vocalist of the Year . . . . . . Michelle Wright
Duo or Group of the Year . . . . . . The Rankin Family
Single of the Year . . . . . . He Would Be Sixteen — Michelle Wright
Album of the Year . . . . . . BAD DAY FOR TRAINS — Patricia Conroy
SOCAN Song of the Year . . . . . . Backroads — Charlie Major
Vista (*Rising Star Award*) . . . . . . The Rankin Family
Back Up Band of the Year . . . . . . The Michelle Wright Band
Manager of the Year . . . . . . Brian Ferriman
Country Club of the Year . . . . . . Cook County Saloon, Edmonton, Alta.
Record Producer of the Year . . . . . . Randall Prescott
Hall of Honor Inductees . . . . . . Bob Nolan & Frank Jones

1994 Bud Country Fans' Choice of
Entertainer of the Year . . . . . . Prairie Oyster
Male Vocalist of the Year . . . . . . Charlie Major
Female Vocalist of the Year . . . . . . Patricia Conroy
Duo or Group of the Year . . . . . . Prairie Oyster
SOCAN Song of the Year . . . . . . *I'm Gonna Drive You Out Of My Mind* — Charlie Major/Barry Brown
Single of the Year . . . . . . *I'm Gonna Drive You Out Of My Mind* — Charlie Major
Album of the Year . . . . . . THE OTHER SIDE — Charlie Major
Vista (*Rising Star Award*) . . . . . . Susan Aglukark
Back Up Band of the Year . . . . . . Coda The West
Manager of the Year . . . . . . Alan Kates
Country Club of the Year . . . . . . Cook County Saloon, Edmonton, Alta.
Hall of Honor Inductees . . . . . . Hank Smith & Dick Damron

1995 Bud Country Fans' Choice of
Entertainer of the Year . . . . . . Michelle Wright
Female Vocalist of the Year . . . . . . Shania Twain
Male Vocalist of the Year . . . . . . Charlie Major
Duo or Group of the Year . . . . . . Prairie Oyster
SOCAN Song of the Year . . . . . . *Whose Bed Have Your Boots Been Under* — Shania Twain/Robert John Lange
Single of the Year . . . . . . *Any Man of Mine* — Shania Twain
Album of the Year . . . . . . THE WOMAN IN ME — Shania Twain
Vista (*Rising Star Award*) . . . . . . Farmer's Daughter
Video of the Year . . . . . . *Any Man of Mine* — performed by Shania Twain
Manager of the Year . . . . . . Leonard Rambeau
Hall of Honor Inductees . . . . . . Gene MacLellan

Appendix C: Country Juno Award Winners 1964–1995

1964 Country Male Singer Of The Year . . . . . . Gary Buck
Country Female Singer Of The Year . . . . . . Pat Hervey

1965 Country Singer Of The Year (Male) . . . . . . Gary Buck
Country Singer Of The Year (Female) . . . . . . Diane Leigh
Most Promising Country Singer (Male) . . . . . . Angus Walker
Most Promising Country Singer (Female) . . . . . . Sharon Strong
Country Instrumental Vocal Group . . . . . . The Rhythm Pals
Country Instrumentalist Of The Year . . . . . . Roy Penney

1966 Country Singer Of The Year (Male) . . . . . . Gary Buck
Country Singer Of The Year (Female) . . . . . . Diane Leigh
Most Promising Country Singer (Male). . . . . . . Johnny Burke
Most Promising Country Singer (Female) . . . . . . Debbie Lori Kaye
Country Instrumental Vocal Group . . . . . . Mercey Brothers
Country Instrumentalist Of The Year . . . . . . Roy Penney

1967 Country Male Singer Of The Year . . . . . . Tommy Hunter
Country Female Singer Of The Year . . . . . . Diane Leigh
Most Promising Country Male Singer . . . . . . Odie Workman
Most Promising Country Female Singer . . . . . . Lynn Jones
Country Group Of The Year . . . . . . The Rhythm Pals

1968 Top Country Singer Male . . . . . . Tommy Hunter
Top Country Singer Female . . . . . . Diane Leigh
Top Country Instrumental Vocal Group . . . . . . The Rhythm Pals

1969 Top Country Singer Male . . . . . . Tommy Hunter
Top Country Singer Female . . . . . . Diane Leigh
Top Country Group . . . . . . Mercey Brothers

1970 Top Country Singer Male . . . . . . Stompin' Tom Connors
Top Country Singer Female . . . . . . Myrna Lorrie
Top Country Instrumental Vocal Group . . . . . . Mercey Brothers

1971 Male Country Singer Of The Year . . . . . . Stompin' Tom Connors
Female Country Singer Of The Year . . . . . . Myrna Lorrie
Country Group Of The Year . . . . . . Mercey Brothers

1972 Male Country Singer Of The Year . . . . . . Stompin' Tom Connors
Female Country Singer Of The Year . . . . . . Shirley Eikhard
Country Group Of The Year . . . . . . Mercey Brothers

1973 Country Vocalist (Male) . . . . . . Stompin' Tom Connors
Country Vocalist (Female) . . . . . . Shirley Eikhard
Country Group Of The Year . . . . . . Mercey Brothers

1974 Country Male Artist Of The Year . . . . . . Stompin' Tom Connors
Country Female Artist Of The Year . . . . . . Anne Murray
Country Group Of The Year . . . . . . Carlton Showband

1975 Country Male Artist Of The Year . . . . . . Murray McLauchlan
Country Female Artist Of The Year . . . . . . Anne Murray
Country Group Of The Year. . . . . . Mercey Brothers

1976 Country Male Artist . . . . . . Murray McLauchlan
Country Female Artist . . . . . . Carroll Baker
Country Group Of The Year . . . . . . The Good Brothers

1977 Country Male Vocalist Of The Year . . . . . . Ronnie Prophet
Country Female Vocalist Of The Year . . . . . . Carroll Baker
Country Group Of The Year . . . . . . The Good Brothers

1978 Country Male Vocalist Of The Year . . . . . . Ronnie Prophet
Country Female Vocalist Of The Year . . . . . . Carroll Baker
Country Group Of The Year . . . . . . The Good Brothers

1979 Country Male Vocalist Of The Year . . . . . . Murray McLauchlan
Country Female Vocalist Of The Year . . . . . . Anne Murray
Country Group or Duo Of The Year . . . . . . The Good Brothers

1980 Country Male Vocalist Of The Year . . . . . . Eddie Eastman
Country Female Vocalist Of The Year . . . . . . Anne Murray
Country Group or Duo of the Year . . . . . . The Good Brothers

1982 Country Male Vocalist Of The Year . . . . . . Ronnie Hawkins
Country Female Vocalist Of The Year . . . . . . Anne Murray
Country Group or Duo of the Year . . . . . . The Good Brothers

1982 Country Male Vocalist Of The Year . . . . . . Eddie Eastman
Country Female Vocalist Of The Year . . . . . . Anne Murray
Country Group or Duo of the Year . . . . . . The Good Brothers

1983-84 Country Male Vocalist of the Year . . . . . . Murray McLauchlan
Country Female Vocalist of the Year . . . . . . Anne Murray
Country Group or Duo of the Year . . . . . . The Good Brothers

1985 Country Male Vocalist of the Year . . . . . . Murray McLauchlan
Country Female Vocalist of the Year . . . . . . Anne Murray
Country Group or Duo of the Year . . . . . . Family Brown

1986 Country Male Vocalist of the Year . . . . . . Murray McLauchlan
Country Female Vocalist of the Year . . . . . . Anne Murray
Country Group or Duo of the Year . . . . . . Prairie Oyster

1987 Country Male Vocalist of the Year . . . . . . Ian Tyson
Country Female Vocalist of the Year . . . . . . k.d. lang
Country Group or Duo of the Year . . . . . . Prairie Oyster

1989 Country Male Vocalist of the Year . . . . . . Murray McLauchlan
Country Female Vocalist of the Year . . . . . . k.d. lang
Country Group or Duo of the Year . . . . . . Family Brown

1990 Country Male Vocalist of the Year . . . . . . George Fox
Country Female Vocalist of the Year . . . . . . k.d. lang
Country Group or Duo of the Year . . . . . . Family Brown

1991 Country Male Vocalist of the Year . . . . . . George Fox
Country Female Vocalist of the Year . . . . . . Rita MacNeil
Country Group or Duo of the Year . . . . . . Prairie Oyster

1992 Country Male Vocalist of the Year . . . . . . George Fox
Country Female Vocalist of the Year . . . . . . Cassandra Vasik
Country Group or Duo of the Year . . . . . . Prairie Oyster

1993 Country Male Vocalist of the Year . . . . . . Gary Fjellgaard
Country Female Vocalist of the Year . . . . . . Michelle Wright
Country Group or Duo of the Year . . . . . . Tracey Prescott & Lonesome Daddy

1994 Country Male Vocalist of the Year . . . . . . Charlie Major
Country Female Vocalist of the Year . . . . . . Cassandra Vasik
Country Group or Duo of the Year . . . . . . The Rankin Family

1995 Country Male Vocalist of the Year . . . . . . Charlie Major
Country Female Vocalist of the Year . . . . . . Michelle Wright
Country Group or Duo of the Year . . . . . . Prairie Oyster

Bibliography

"About our Steve (Stevedore Steve)." *World Of Country Music*, Vol. 1, No. 3 (December 1972), 27.

Austen, Doug. "Roy Payne: A Lonely Singer in the Big City." *Canadian Composer*, No. 84 (October 1973), 32-35.

Barr, Steven C. *The Almost Complete 78 RPM Record Dating Guide*. Huntington Beach: Yesterday Once Again, 1992.

Beattie, Mac. *This Ottawa Valley of Mine*. Arnprior: Beattie Music Inc., 1982.

Beyer, Susan. "The Beautiful Dream of Orval Prophet."*Country Music News*, Vol. 4, No. 11 (February 1984), 1.

Beyer, Susan. "David Thompson — The Waiting's the Hardest Part." *Country Music News*, Vol. 2, No. 10 (January 1982), 1, 2, 11.

Beyer, Susan. "The Discreet Charm and High Hopes of The C-Weed Band." *Capital Country News*, Vol. 2, No. 9 (December 1981), 1-3.

Beyer, Susan. "Harold MacIntyre And Area Code 705: A Quarter to High Noon." *Country Music News*, Vol. 3, No. 2 (May 1982), 1-3.

Beyer, Susan (with Leon Major). "Len Henry . . . In Good Company."*Capital Country News*, Vol. 2, No. 2 (May 1981), 1-2.

Beyer, Susan. "Update: Family Brown." *Country Music News*, Vol. 3, No. 4 (July 1982), 1-2.

Beyer, Susan. "What Makes Ronnie Run." *Capital Country News*, Vol. 2, No. 4 (July 1981), 1-3, 18.

"Bob 'Mr. Sunshine' King, One Of Canada's Country Greats of the 50s Passes On At Age 55." *Country Music News*, Vol. 9, No. 12 (February 1989).

Bourassa, Kevin. "Burton & Honeyman A Success, But Not Overnight." *Music Scene*, No. 302 (July/August 1978), 13.

Brown, Jim. "Patricia Conroy . . . This Time." *Country Music News*, Vol. 11, No. 9 (December 1990), 1, 10, 27.

"Burton and Honeyman — Two of A Kind." *RPM Magazine*, Vol. 26, No. 18 (January 29, 1977), 19.

Bye, Christine. "Shattered Dreams (Tommy Common)." *Toronto Star*, February 15, 1986.

Cameron, Frank. "Myrna Lorrie Rebounds to National TV Scene." *Music Scene*, No. 261 (September/October 1971), 8.

"Canada's Donn Reynolds Breaks World Record Atop CN Tower." *Country Music News*, Vol. 11, No. 5 (August 1990), 26.

"Canada's Own Echoes of the Carter Family." *Country Musical Trails Less Traveled*, (December-January 1990-91), 4-5.

" 'Canadian Sweetheart' Bob Regan, Dead At 59." *Country Music News*, Vol. 11, No. 5 (August 1990), 1.

Carolan, Trevor. "Peter Chipman — Working Hard To Move Ahead in the Tough M-O-R Music Field." *Canadian Composer*, No. 170 (April 1982), 32-35.

Charney, Dennis. "Greg Paul . . . Farkle & Sparkle." *Country Music News*, Vol. 15, No. 1 (April 1994), 1.

Charney, Dennis. "Laura Vinson . . . Rocky Mountain Lady." *Country Music News*, Vol. 7, No. 5 (July 1986), 1, 3.

Charney, Dennis. "Myrna Lorrie — More Than A Myth." *Country Music News*, Vol. 11, No. 2 (May 1990), 1,8.

Country Canada. Kelowna, B.C.: Canadian Chart Research, March 1994.

Covington, Vicki. "The Three Sides of R. Harlan Smith." *Country Music News*, Vol. 12, No. 10 (January 1992), 1,2.

"Debbie Bechamp Band — Francophone Singer Tours West." *Country Ramblings*, Vol. 1, No 2 (March 1983), 11.

Delaney, Larry. "Albert Hall . . . The Song Painter." *Country Music News*, Vol. 8, No. 11 (February 1988), 1-2.

Delaney, Larry. "Anita and Tim . . . Harmony in The Family." *Country Music News*, Vol. 8, No. 8 (November 1987), 1, 31.

Delaney, Larry. "Bach In The Swing of Things." *Country Music News*, Vol. 10, No. 11 (February 1990), 1-2.

Delaney, Larry. "Bobby Lalonde — Music Maestro Please." *Country Music News*, Vol. 10, No. 3 (May 1989), 1, 2.

Delaney, Larry. "The Butler Did It . . . The Colin Butler Story." *Country Music News*, Vol. 8, No. 9 (December 1987), 22.

Delaney, Larry. "Carroll Baker . . . A Star in Everyone's Eyes." *Country Music News*, Vol. 6, No. 11 (February 1986), 1-2.

Delaney, Larry. "Cathy Chambers." *Country Music News*, Vol. 4, No. 2 (May 1983), 1.

Delaney, Larry. "Charlie Major . . . In the Major Leagues." *Country Music News*, Vol. 14, No. 4 (July 1993), 1, 2.

Delaney, Larry. "Cindi Cain . . . Zeroing in on Success." *Country Music News*, Vol. 11, No. 4 (July 1990), 1, 7.

Delaney, Larry. "Chris Krienke Made Of 'Good Stuff.' " *Country Music News*, Vol. 8, No. 1 (April 1987), 1, 2.

Delaney, Larry. "Chris Whitely and Caitlin Hanford." *Capital Country News*, Vol. 2, No. 7 (October 1981).

Delaney, Larry. "Cindi Churko — Hotter Than Hot!!" *Country Music News*, Vol. 8, No. 1 (April 1987), 15.

Delaney, Larry. "Country Hearts." *Country Music News*, Vol. 14, No. 1 (April 1993), 1, 12.

Delaney, Larry. "Country Sketches — Linda Brown." *Capital Country News*, Vol. 2, No. 2 (May 1981), 11.

Delaney, Larry. "Curtis Grambo — Big News Back Home." *Country Music News*, Vol. 15, No. 1 (April 1994), 15.

Delaney, Larry. "Dyanne Halliday — How Sweet It Is." *Country Music News*, Vol. 12, No.2 (May 1991), 1-2.

Delaney, Larry. "The Double Eagle Band — "The Eagle Has Landed." *Country Music News*, Vol. 5, No. 2 (May 1984), 11.

Delaney, Larry. "Eddie Eastman — On The Winning Side." *Country Music News*, Vol. 6, No. 4 (July 1985), 1.

Delaney, Larry. "The Ellis Family Band — Easy To Love." *Country Music News*, Vol. 5, No.10 (January 1985), 1-2.

Delaney, Larry. "Errol Ranville: Flying High." *Country Music News*, Vol. 11, No. 6 (September 1990), 1, 10.

Delaney, Larry. ". . . Fortune Smiles On Cassandra Vasik." *Country Music News*, Vol. 14, No. 3 (June 1993), 1-2.

Delaney, Larry. "Gilles Godard . . . Have I Got News For You." *Country Music News*, Vol. 6, No. 9 (December 1985), 1, 2.

Delaney, Larry. "Glory-Anne Carriere . . . 'Changes.' " *Country Music News*, Vol. 7, No. 1 (April 1986), 1-2.

Delaney, Larry. "Graham Townsend — The Man With The Magic Bow." *Country Music News*, Vol. 10, No. 12 (March 1990), 1, 24.

Delaney, Larry. "Jack Scott & Carroll Baker — Country Duets." *Country Music News*, Vol. 8, No. 12 (March 1988), 1-2.

Delaney, Larry. "Jim Matt — The L.A. Sessions Go North." *Country Music News*, Vol. 16, No. 1 (April 1995), 1, 18.

Delaney, Larry. "The Johner Brothers . . . Country Boys!!" *Country Music News*, Vol. 13, No. 12 (March 1993), 1.

Delaney, Larry. "Johnny Comfort — On The Move." *Country Music News*, Vol. 5, No. 2 (May 1984), 2-3.

Delaney, Larry. "Lisa Brokop . . . Heading For The Top!!" *Country Music News*, Vol. 13, No. 1 (April 1992), 1-2.

Delaney, Larry. "The Many Sides Of Michael Dee Graham." *Country Music News*, Vol. 8, No. 2 (May 1987), 1-2.

Delaney, Larry. "Mark LaForme — Making Nashville Dreams Come True." *Country Music News*, Vol. 8, No. 2 (May 1987), 11.

Delaney, Larry. "Rae Palmer . . . Walkin' Her Way To Stardom." *Country Music News*, Vol. 5, No. 6 (September 1984), 10.

Delaney, Larry. "Ralph Carlson — 'Hooked on music' — Country music that is . . ." *Capital Country News*, Vol. 2, No. 3 (June 1981), 1-3.

Delaney, Larry. "Ray Griff — 'They Call Him Raymond.' " *Country Music News*, Vol. 7, No. 3 (June 1986), 1-2.

Delaney, Larry. "Terilynn — The Lady Let's Her Music Do The Talking." *Country Music News,* Vol. 8, No. 6 (September 1987), 11.

Delaney, Larry. "Terry Christenson . . . B-O-O-M !!" *Country Music News*, Vol. 7, No. 11 (February 1987), 1.

Delaney, Larry. "Terry Sheridan: Flyin' High." *Country Music News*, Vol. 13, No. 2 (May 1992), 1,7.

Delaney, Larry. "The Sun Is Rising on Brent McAthey." *Country Music News*, Vol. 15, No. 8 (November 1994), 1, 18.

Delaney, Larry. "Tim Taylor and Anita Perras in a Country Paradise." *Country Music News*, Vol. 5, No. 3 (June 1984), 1-2.

Delaney, Larry. "Tim Thorney . . . Country's Invisible Force!!" *Country Music News*, Vol. 15, No. 2 (May 1994), 6.

Delaney, Larry. "Twinkle Twinkle . . . Lucille Starr." *Country Music News*, Vol. 8, No. 10 (January 1988), 1, 25.

Delaney, Larry. "Wayne Rostad Out Your Way." *Country Music News*, Vol. 9, No. 3 (June, 1988), 1-2.

Delaney, Larry. "Scott King . . . 'An Eye' On The Charts." *Country Music News*, Vol. 12 No. 9 (December 1991), 24.

Doer, Faye. "The Saint . . . The 60's, The 70's, The 80's." *Country Music News*, Vol. 5, No. 4 (July 1984), 1.

"Don Messer Favorite Charlie Chamberlain Dies near Hometown." *The Daily Gleaner*, (July 17), 1972.

Encyclopaedia Of Music In Canada. Second Edition: Toronto, University of Toronto Press, 1992.

"Fiddling Star King Ganam Capped His Tunes With A Wink." *Toronto Star*, April 28, 1994

Flohil, Richard. "Terry Christenson — Singing His Way Into The Big City." *Canadian Composer*, No. 118 (February 1977), 20-23.

Foster, Don. "Hank Snow — A Legend In His Own Time." *Country Music News*, Vol. 5, No. 1 (April 1984), 1.

Foster, Don. "The Stu Davis Story." *Country Music News*, Vol. 10, No. 10 (January 1990), 1, 23.

"A. Frank Willis: Music — A Newfie Family Tradition." *Country Ramblings*, Vol. 1, No. 2 (March 1983), 28.

Frechette, Joey. "Shotgun: They Chose To Play." *Country Music News*, Vol. 8, No. 2 (May 1987), 16.

Fryer, Tim. "Michael T. Wall, Music Ambassador To Newfoundland." *Country Ramblings*, Vol. 1, No. 5 (June 1983), 4-5.

"Gerry Allard — Pitching His Way Into Country Music." *Country Ramblings*, Vol. 1, No. 2 (March 1983), 29.

"Gerry Allard — Breaking Out." *Country Music News*, Vol. 4, No. 4 (July 1983), 3-4.

Goddard, Peter. "Fallen Singing Star Tommy Common A Canadian Tragedy." *Toronto Star*, August 16, 1985.

"The Good Brothers: The 'Good' Guys Of Countrified Rock." *Country Ramblings*, Vol. 1, No. 5 (June 1983), 12.

Grigsby, Wayne. "Meet The Least-Known Television Star Of All." *Canadian Composer*, No. 66 (January 1972), 18-23, 46.

Hall, Ron. *The Chum Chart Book.* Etobicoke: Stardust Productions, 1990.

Harrington, Peter. "Darlene Wiebe — Another Singing Sensation From Saskatchewan." *Country Ramblings*, Vol. 1, No. 2 (March 1983), 4,5.

Harris, Reta. "Bob Rowan Country." *The World Of Country Music*, Vol. 2, No. 1 (February 1973), 30.

"Harvey Henry: The Pride Of Manitoba." *Country Ramblings*, Vol. 1, No. 1 (February 1983), 11.

Hunter, Tommy (with Liane Heller). *My Story.* Toronto: Methuen, 1985.

Ingham, George. "North Country — The Rainville Duo" *Country & Western News Roundup*, Vol. 1, No. 3 (November 1980), 7.

Ingram, Mathew. "The King of Make-Believe: Cochrane-born George Fox Is a Country-Singing Dream Come True. *Alberta (Western) Report*, Vol. 16, No. 37 (August 28, 1989), 38-39.

"Irwin Prescott & Company with Friends." *World Of Country Music*, Vol. 1, No. 3 (December 1972), 5.

Isenor, Fred. "Tex Cochrane — Early Star of Canadian Country Music." *Canadian Bluegrass Review*, (February/ March 1981), 6-7.

"Jerry Palmer: At Home in the Country." *Country Ramblings*, Vol. 1, No. 1 (February 1983), 23.

Jobin, Claude. "Willie Lamothe Marks 30 Years as a Performer." *Music Scene*, No. 285 (September/ October 1975), 2.

Joel Whitburn's Top Country & Western Records 1949-1971. Wisconsin: Record Research Inc., 1972.

"John Lindsay — Getting To Know You." *Country Music News*, Vol. 9, No. 13 (March 1989), 15.

Jones, Virginia. "Kelita — The Country Chameleon." *Country Music News*, Vol. 5, No. 6 (September 1984), 1.

"Kenny Hess — Singing & Writing The Hits." *Country Music News*, Vol. 15, No. 4 (July 1994), 24.

Linden, J.J. "Marie Bottrell — Destined For International Success." *RPM Weekly*, Vol. 33, No. 10 (May 31, 1980), 12-13.

McGibbon, Don. "A Minstrel in Cowboy Clothes." *The Vancouver Sun*, (April 5), 1952.

McGuirk, Henry. "Donna and Leroy . . . 'Destiny's Plan.' " *Country Music News*, Vol. 7, No. 5 (July 1986), 1, 2.

McGuirk, Henry. "Joe Firth — A Dream Comes True." *Country Music News*, Vol. 4, No. 12 (March 1984), 1, 2.

McGuirk, Henry. "Paul Weber . . . Country Music in His Soul." *Country Music News*, Vol. 5, No. 9 (December 1984), 1.

Marshman, Paul and Bill Oja. "The Stoker Bros . . . All In The Family." *Country Music News*, Vol. 7, No. 2 (May 1986), 1, 2.

"Mary-Lou Sonmor — In The Spotlight." *Country Music News*, Vol. 9, No. 3 (June 1988), 15.

Mason, Henry. "Diamond Jim Hopson — Enjoying the Best of Two Worlds." *Country Music News*, Vol. 10, No. 4 (July 1989), 24.

Mason, Henry. "Goin' Home with Hal Bruce." *Country Music News*, Vol. 12, No. 1 (April 1991), 1-2.

"Michael 'Dee' Graham Loses Fight To Cancer." *RPM*, Vol. 58, No. 7 (August 28, 1993), 8.

"Mister Country Music (Gary Buck)." *World Of Country Music*, Vol. 2, No. 2 (December 1972), 23.

Mulholland, Dave. "Carisse Will Experiment After Songs Are Commercial Success." *Music Scene*, No. 318 (March/April 1981), 8, 13.

Mulholland, Dave."Sneezy Waters' Album To Follow Success Of Stage Show." *Music Scene,* No. 300 (March/April 1978), 8

Murphy, Johnny. "Shelly-Lou Marie." *Capital Country News*, Vol. 2, No. 1 (April 1981), 8.

Musselman, Bill. "Bill Hersh . . . Where There's a Bill, There's a Way." *Country Music News*, Vol. 5, No. 5 (August 1984), 1-2.

Musselman, Bill. "Iris [Larratt]." *Country Music News*, Vol. 3, No. 3 (June 1982), 1-2.

Musselman, Bill. "Midnite Rodeo Band — From Out of the West." *Country Music News*, Vol. 5, No. 2 (May 1984), 1-2.

Pedneault, Helene. "Jerry and Jo'Anne Fight in Support of Pop-Country." *Music Scene,* No. 291 (September/October 1976), 6.

"Rena Gaile . . . Country Gold."*Country Music News*, Vol. 12, No. 1 (April 1991), 25.

Rogers, Doc. "Allen Erwin: The Calgary Kid (Part 1)." *Country Music News*, Vol. 9, No. 5 (August 1988), 24.

Rogers, Doc. "Allen Erwin: The Calgary Kid (Part 2)." *Country Music News*, Vol. 9, No. 6 (September 1988), 10-11.

"Ruth Ann — From An Apple Orchard To Stardom." *Country Ramblings*, Vol. 1, No. 2 (March 1983), 14-15.

Sellick, L.B. "Marg Loved To Sing." *Atlantic Advocate*, Vol. 68, No. 10 (June 1978), 28-30.

"Sharon Anderson — The Bottom Line . . . and Beyond!!" *Country Music News*, Vol. 12, No. 4 (July 1991).

St. Jean, Ron. "Sharon Lowness And The Teddy Bears." *World Of Country Music*, Vol. 1, No. 1 (September 1972), 3.

Snow, Hank (with Jack Owenbey and Bob Burris). *The Hank Snow Story*. Chicago: University of Illinois Press, 1994.

"Terry Sumsion — From The Wheel Of A Truck." *Country Ramblings*, Vol. 1, No. 5 (June 1983), 22.

Therien, Robert and Isabelle D'Amours. *Dictionnaire de la Musique Populaire au Quebec 1955-1992*. Quebec: Bibliotheque nationale du Quebec, 1992.

Titterington, Keith. "Poor, Poor Farmer — The Keray Regan Story." *Country Musical Trails Less Traveled*, (January/ February 1994), 4,5.

"Tommy Common Shot To Death." *Toronto Star*, (August 15), 1985.

Tompkins, John."Dick Damron Worked The Country Before Writing About It." *Music Scene*, No. 267 (September/October 1972), 6.

Tyson, Ian (with Colin Escott). *I Never Sold My Saddle*. Toronto: Douglas & MacIntyre, 1994.

Waxman, Ken. "Julie Lynn: Between Uptown Country and Pop for the People." *Canadian Composer*, No. 40 (November 1976), 24-26.

"Whiskey Jack — Uptown Bluegrass At Its Best." *Country Ramblings*, Vol. 1, No. 4 (May 1983), 28-29.

THE GOOD BROTHERS

THE MERCEY BROTHERS

SONS OF THE SADDLE

EVAN KEMP

JOHNNY BURKE

JOAN KENNEDY

CHARLIE MAJOR

THE RHYTHM PALS

EARL HEYWOOD